SCAPEGOAT FOR
MURDER

The Truth About the Killing
of Carl Bridgewater

First published 2016 by DB Publishing, an imprint of JMD Media Ltd,
Nottingham, United Kingdom.

ISBN 9781780914770

SCAPEGOAT FOR
MURDER

The Truth About the Killing
of Carl Bridgewater

Simon W. Golding
In discussion with Bert Spencer

PUBLISHING

*This book is dedicated to the memory of
Carl Bridgewater and his family.*

'You cannot hope to bribe or twist,
thank God! the British journalist.
But, seeing what the man will do
unbribed, there's no occasion to.'
Humbert Wolfe

Contents

Author's Note 10

Introduction 15

1. Horror at Yew Tree Farm 16

2. The Last Coincidence 44

3. A Gathering Storm 59

4. Connections and Investigations 75

5. The Piece of Card 104

6. A Cocktail for Murder 123

7. The Silent Defendant 138

8. An Inspector Calls 173

9. The Prison 'Confessions' 191

10. A Case to Answer 209

11. The Fight for Freedom 248

12. The Last Appeal! 276

13. Final Thoughts 296

14. The New Documentary 319

Epilogue 325

Acknowledgements 327

Author's Note

....

The echoes of the horrific killing of the 13-year-old paperboy in the Midlands rumble on despite the intervening decades. Three men and a youth; Patrick (Pat) Molloy, James (Jimmy) Robinson, Vincent and the young Michael Hickey (cousins), were convicted of the crime. Following a campaign bandwagon, spearheaded by the *Daily Mirror* journalist Paul Foot and Michael's mother, Ann Whelan, the case against the four was quashed by the Court of Appeal in February 1997. They ruled that the trial had been unfair, due to certain areas of evidence fabricated by police in order to persuade Molloy to make a confession.

However, the Appeal Judges noted that in the light of Vincent Hickey's confessions, and subsequent evidence, to being present at the farm where Carl Bridgewater was shot dead, stated, 'We consider that there remains evidence on which a reasonable jury properly directed could convict.'

Despite this, in the light of the judgment, the Crown Prosecution Service had decided it was not in the public interest to apply for a retrial involving Vincent Hickey or proceed with an outstanding armed robbery charge against him.

This I believe to be the correct decision as it was quite apparent the West Midlands Serious Crime Squad had serious flaws. There is no doubt that Pat Molloy was shown a false statement, together with a forged signature of Vincent Hickey, and this started the ball rolling – and made the conviction of all four men unsafe.

Following this ruling once again the attention turned violently towards Hubert (Bert) Spencer as the real perpetrator of this horrendous crime.

Bert Spencer served fourteen and a half years in prison for a different and later crime, the murder of his friend Hubert Wilkes. However, more than 20 years after his release, he is still being hounded over the Bridgewater murder, even though there is a total lack of evidence against him.

The ex-Ambulance Liaison Officer even had a cast iron alibi – but still the accusations come pouring in. Over the years people have slowly been brainwashed by the media and it has almost become folklore – similar to the well-worn saying, 'The Butler did it!' The mantra now, when anyone is discussing the Carl Bridgewater case, is that, 'The ambulance man did it!'

The passage of time has seen much of the anger and emotion, which years of misleading and false accusation engendered, drained from Bert Spencer. In the following pages Bert makes a rational and dispassionate appraisal of the allegations, which have been made against him and reconstructs, as far as he is able, the background detail of his own seemingly inexplicable crime. In so doing he has been able to add what may well be a decisive piece to the jigsaw to the mystery surrounding the terrible happening at Yew Tree Farm.

Bert Spencer tells his story, a tale with as many twists and turns as an Agatha Christie plot. It dismantles Paul Foot's bestseller, *Murder at the Farm*, and questions his often aggressive and exaggerated hypothesis – presented to the general public as fact. What prompts a well-known journalist, a member of a distinguished, if eccentric family, to conduct a somewhat questionable and exaggerated campaign against a helpless man?

By breaking a stubborn silence lasting well over three decades, Spencer answers the mystery of the killing of Hubert Wilkes and so negates any possibility of it having been the much-publicised 'copycat' killing syndrome beloved of the supporters of the Bridgewater Four or should we call them the anti-Spencer lobbyists.

*   *   *

Most of what you read came from Hubert Spencer, known as Bert, with some help from a prison pal, Mark Roman*. Bert originally started working on a manuscript, secretly, as it was totally against prison rules, in the spring of 1992, whilst at North Sea Camp. After years of living his life in maximum security prisons up and down the country, a slightly relaxed regime enabled Bert to pick up the pen, and try and hit back at the media, the Bridgewater Four followers and campaigners who had hounded him for many, many years.

The prison sits on the east coast not far from Boston, England. Bert, coming to the end of a very long stretch for murder was joined by a familiar face – his name was Mark Roman, an ex-soldier and mercenary who, incredibly, Bert had met before, in the mid 1960s. Bert Spencer ran a professional judo course and Mark would introduce his mercenary colleagues to tone up their self-defence skills, ready for whatever theatre of battle they would face next.

The incredible chance meeting at the Category D prison, with both men sharing a small hut, would produce a document that would blow the whole case surrounding the awful murder of the paperboy, Carl Bridgewater, wide open. Serious questions would be asked and previous evidence that was treated as cast iron, melted down to a tissue of lies and exaggerations.

This book follows the terrible hounding of Bert Spencer through the decades by award winning journalist Paul Foot, together with his sidekick Ann Whelan and the Bridgewater Four campaigners. The media had a feeding frenzy, fuelled by Foot's hard-hitting pieces in his column for the *Daily Mirror*. A best-selling book, *Murder at the Farm,* followed, together with documentaries and a hit movie, *Bad Company* – all pointed an accusing finger at Bert Spencer as the real murderer of young Carl Bridgewater. The rooftop protests of the three remaining Bridgewater prisoners (Pat Molloy died in prison on 12 June 1981), Michael Hickey, Vincent Hickey and Jimmy Robinson, fanned the flames by daubing various rooftop messages that Spencer was the real murderer. For months these protests lasted – and for years watched by the world press, with a defenceless Spencer locked away for his own conviction, unable to defend himself.

Scapegoat for Murder also casts doubt on Spencer's own conviction for the murder of his close friend, farm owner Hubert Wilkes and his long sentence of nearly 15 years.

I have added a lot of my own text to this manuscript. I was careful not to be carried away and let the facts speak for themselves. I have checked any information, wherever possible, and I have written an honest account of events as they happened or were told to me. I also included information and evidence – regardless of whether it placed Bert Spencer in a good or bad light. My loyalty is purely serving the truth and no individuals have been allowed to influence that.

At last the truth can come out surrounding these tragic cases of murder and serious questions are raised that should have been aired nearly 40 years ago.

Another huge boost to my book, helping to bring it to a national or even international audience, was when I was contacted by one of my heroes, top criminologist Professor David Wilson. The famous professor had heard about my manuscript, as too had ITN Productions and now *Scapegoat for Murder* was going to be a major Channel 4 documentary.

Simon W. Golding (August 2016)

*NOTE: * For security reasons Mark Roman is a pseudonym and some of his military and mercenary history has been altered to protect his identity.*

Introduction

....

Like most of the nation I was outraged and disgusted at the brutal murder of 13-year-old paperboy Carl Bridgewater in late September 1978. The crime scene was a farmhouse called Yew Tree Farm, near Stourbridge in Staffordshire.

The police launched a massive manhunt for the killer or killers. Detective Chief Superintendent Bob Stewart headed the inquiry and stated that the shocking murder of such a young boy seemed completely unnecessary.

During an early press conference he commented, 'Every police officer on this inquiry is appalled by the viciousness of this unmerciful killing.'

The police were under enormous pressure to find the man or men responsible. Often their overzealous actions crossed the line of criminal procedure. In the late 1970s the West Midlands Serious Crime Squad was a law unto itself, especially with the absence of Big Brother, in the shape of state-of-the-art recording and monitoring equipment, looking over their shoulder, observing and listening to every second of every interview. The squad was disbanded, after an investigation into allegations against some officers of 'incompetence and abuses of power', in 1989.

As the unsolved murder case reached a crescendo more and more sightings of people and vehicles came flooding in, as did a few possible suspects. Trawled in the net was Bert Spencer, a married man with a young family, working for the West Midlands Authority as an Ambulance Liaison Officer at Corbett Hospital, Stourbridge in the West Midlands.

Due to a few extraordinary coincidences, something that has figured heavily in Bert's life, everything was about to be turned upside down. Spencer was quite rightly questioned over the Carl Bridgewater case, but instead of his cast-iron alibi eliminating him from the police's enquiry – he was about to become a *scapegoat for murder*!

I.

Horror at Yew Tree Farm

....

Less than half a mile from where Bert Spencer first met Hubert Wilkes stands Yew Tree Farm. Separated from encroaching suburbia by a wide belt of rolling countryside, the farm could well be described as being isolated. The growing army of media people, seeking to create an evocative backdrop, have portrayed the rambling, old buildings as *eerie, remote* and even *haunted*. Eerie and haunted afterwards, maybe, but the legacy of Yew Tree Farm was not bequeathed until 19 September 1978, when 13-year-old paperboy, Carl Bridgewater, was brutally murdered.

The farm certainly carried an air of neglect and dereliction. The bare ribs of long disused outbuildings stood starkly exposed, the tiles lying where they had fallen, partially hidden by weeds and brambles. The gardens and apple orchard had long been left to fend for themselves. The cattle yard was a jungle of nettles and fireweed, the thick undergrowth strewn with rusting farm tools and the odd perished tractor tyre. Nearer to the dwelling, incongruously the hedges were neatly trimmed and the living area near the house cleanly kept.

The farmhouse is situated at the junction of the A449, which links Kidderminster and Wolverhampton, and Lawnswood Road, which sweeps down from the village of Wordsley. The house itself lies back some 30 yards from the flow of traffic and alongside a popular public footpath. Remote, was not a word you would associate with Yew Tree Farm.

In 1978 the arthritic residents were a 72-year-old retired farmer, Fred Jones, and his cousin, the equally elderly Mary Poole whose husband, Jack, had died the previous year. The surviving pair were both infirm and had limited mobility. They had the help of a regular cleaner, a trusted friend and neighbour, Mrs Gladys Jones (no relation to Fred), who lived at Yew

Tree Cottage, some 250 yards away on a rise in Lawnswood Road. The old couple had a restricted social life, much of which was enjoyed by them both standing at the back gate watching the world go by, waving to passing walkers and farm workers. Most necessities were delivered to the farm by local tradesmen. Even the hairdresser made a house call and the doctor, a near neighbour, often called in on a social-come-medical basis. Only occasionally did they leave the farmhouse when a friend took them out for a car ride.

Since Carl's violent death it has been suggested by the media, led by renowned *Daily Mirror* journalist Paul Foot that this very ordinary farmhouse, occupied by the arthritic couple and their small dog, had been the site of mysterious happenings and subject to close surveillance over a considerable period of time.

In fact, the 'mysterious' happenings were run of the mill occurrences and no good reason has ever been put forward which would provide a motive for such covert attention to be paid to the elderly residents, their property or their possessions. There were no local rumours of hidden hoards of gold sovereigns or a time-warp room cluttered with priceless antiques. Yew Tree was an ordinary old farmhouse, inhabited by pleasantly ordinary old people with little of unusual value.

The catalogue of so-called 'weird' happenings at the 'haunted' farmhouse, as Foot describes it in his best-selling book, *Murder at the Farm,* in the years prior to the tragedy were less than mysterious.

It began in 1974. Hubert Wilkes owned near-by Holloway House Farm and leased part of the Yew Tree estate, some of it to run sheep on. Wilkes' son, Anthony, was responsible for organising work on the land. Hubert Wilkes notified the local paper, the *Express & Star,* of his intention to shoot any dogs found on Yew Tree land that may worry sheep and interfere with lambing.

Despite receiving anonymous telephone calls threatening reprisal by arson if he were to carry out his threat, Hubert went ahead and shot two stray dogs and was subsequently pictured in the *Express & Star* displaying one of the carcases for the benefit of the camera.

A few nights later one of the already dilapidated farm outbuildings was set alight. The arsonist had misdirected his anger and had burned down Yew Tree property instead of anything belonging to the Wilkes family at Holloway House. The act of revenge was criminally irresponsible and potentially dangerous, but it was hardly mysterious.

Another bone the media would jump on, and much was made of it, was the series of nuisance telephone calls made to Yew Tree Farm, with the suggestion that there was a connection with the later robbery and murder of the young paperboy. The calls began in autumn of 1977 when Mary Poole's husband, Jack, was still alive. They occurred over a period of a few weeks, mostly in reasonably social hours. Nothing was ever said by the unknown caller. There was no 'heavy breathing' and the call was cut off as soon as the receiver was lifted. Jack Poole died in the December. There were no more calls for nine months. A few weeks before the murder of Carl Bridgewater the calls began again. While this type of telephonic intrusion is annoying and even disturbing for the elderly folk, it was still a common enough experience for many people, in those days, who were listed in the telephone directory.

For Fred Jones and Mary Poole, living as they did with no immediate neighbours and being in a state of some infirmity, it was, no doubt, a somewhat frightening experience – but not one that could be categorised as 'weird'. Nor did it merit the conclusions that were later drawn from the happenings.

Another incident that journalist Paul Foot would describe as 'curious' was the loss, theft or misplacement of a cash sum of seventy pounds from the farmhouse. Fred Jones had tucked the money away in a chest of drawers in his bedroom. It was four months later that he discovered that the cash was missing. Maybe it really had been stolen or perhaps Mr Jones had been the victim of an old man's failing memory and he had used or moved the money himself. Access to the farmhouse without the use of forced entry was limited to a very small circle and visitors were few. Mr Jones was convinced that the money had been taken a couple of weeks before, on the day when he and Mary made a rare trip to Birmingham. As usual, he had left the key to the back door on the window ledge of an outhouse, covered over with one of the fallen tiles from the decaying roof. It was so placed in order that their trusted neighbour, Mrs Gladys Jones, had access to the farmhouse to let the dog out for a run during their absence. When the old couple returned home Fred was sure that the key was not in its original position, although it was still beneath the slate. Mrs Jones was adamant that she had not been in the house and that she had not let the dog out. There were often small sums of money left around the farmhouse, but never had any gone missing. Mr Jones concluded that an outside agency had entered the farmhouse and removed his cash. At about the same time a small axe and a scythe had gone missing from the property.

Time and time again various journalists would describe these happenings with incredulous and outrageous prose. Certainly one of the worst culprits was Paul Foot. In his book, *Murder at the Farm*, he states, '...the farmhouse had, for some months, been the object of mysterious and macabre scrutiny by someone who knew it.' In this brief statement Mr Foot managed to incorporate some substantial assumptions. It might be thought that such reasoning required something more than a close scrutiny of the facts, perhaps a certain degree of mental callisthenics are in order to persuade his readership to a desired conclusion. One might be forgiven for thinking that such lengthy and covert surveillance could form part of the preparation for a sophisticated bullion robbery – but it hardly merited the potential haul to be obtained from a very ordinary farmhouse inhabited by old age pensioners. When the farmhouse was indeed robbed on that fateful night, despite every one of its rooms having been ransacked in the search for valuables, the police estimated the eventual stolen booty at a few hundred pounds. Certainly anyone who knew the farm would have been aware of the limited dividends available. Also anyone even mildly familiar with the farmhouse would have no need of long-term scrutiny in order to establish the limited and basic movement patterns of its occupants. There was a simple rule of thumb. Apart from times of the most inclement of weather, during daylight hours, if the back door of the farmhouse was open then the residents were at home; if the door was shut then they were away.

Fred Jones and Mary Poole were to be away on the 19 September 1978. It had all the makings of a halcyon day. The kind of perfect weather which, so the old country wives would say, would occur on only thirteen days a year. On those few days kingfishers would choose to mate on the wing. Early autumnal sunshine and only a zephyr breeze made it an ideal day for a special outing. For Fred and Mary it was also to be their lucky day – their large helping of good fortune being borne on an extremely ill wind.

The same day, for Bert Spencer, was a routine working one at his post as Ambulance Liaison Officer at Corbett Hospital, some three miles away. His workstation was a desk in an open plan office. The secretary, Mrs Barbara Riebold, sat behind the same counter at an adjoining desk where they were both in full view of other hospital staff and rows of patients.

For the elderly couple at Yew Tree Farm a guardian angel was to arrive in the form of a Methodist friend, Mrs Kit Parrot. At about 11.00 am the lady arrived in her car, drove Mary Poole into the village of Wordsley to collect her pension and, on returning to the farm for Fred, took the couple for a drive out to Wenlock Edge in Shropshire. What was to happen at Yew Tree Farm in their absence was beyond belief.

*   *   *

Carl Bridgewater was thirteen years old and had recently been taken on as a regular paperboy by Davis's newsagents in Wordsley. On this day he was a little later than usual owing to a previous dental appointment. Yew Tree Farm was his last call but two, but on this sunny September day the last two papers were never to be delivered.

A car full of workers from the Severn Trent Water Board passed Carl as he was remounting his cycle after making a delivery at a large house, known as White Friars. The time was 4.15 pm. One of the workers, teenager Richard Parkes, shouted a greeting to him. Carl waved back and set off downhill towards the farm. This was the best part of the run; he loved his bright yellow bicycle, and was one of the finest cyclists in his school class.

He turned in to the public footpath, which leads past the rear entrance to Yew Tree, rode the 30 yards to the driveway of the farm and probably lay down his cycle against the wicket gate in the hedge that divided the driveway from the farmyard. The door may have been open; it certainly was about twenty minutes earlier as Mrs Gladys Jones was to testify. Mrs Jones claimed she saw a vehicle parked in the drive at 4.00 pm, from the rear garden of her home, next to the farm, at Yew Tree Cottage. The back door to the farmhouse, she noticed, was shut – as it always was when Fred and Mary were out. The neighbour had then moved into the field for a better look, the door was now open, and it was still open when the car had gone. It was quite obvious that the vehicle Gladys had seen was connected to the murder.

Later the paper was found in the collection basket behind the letter-box. The exact truth of what happened next will now probably never be established with any certainty. Confession, retraction, accusation and speculation have made such evidence uncertain. But what did happen was vile, vicious and totally unnecessary.

While the detail of events following Carl's arrival at the farm are misty in the extreme the next known concrete fact is that there was another caller at the farm a few minutes before 5.30 pm. Dr Angus MacDonald, a Scottish chest physician at Wordsley hospital, had to pass Yew Tree Farm on his drive home. Often, out of concerned interest for the old couple, he would stop off to make an unscheduled call on Fred Jones and Mary Poole. On Tuesday, 19 September, the visit was to be filled with undreamed of shock and horror.

The doctor drove down the track, turned right into the farmyard, parked his car, and walked through the open wicket gate.

He commented sometime later, 'I don't know if you go for this sort of thing, but I felt as I walked up there that something was very strange about the place. It was something to do with the wind, I don't know.'

The back door of the farmhouse was slightly ajar, the Yale lock had been smashed and the red painted surface of the door was chipped and scratched. On the ground beneath the door lay a spade with traces of the same red paint on the blade. It must have been a heart-stopping moment of high apprehension for the doctor. The dog, Skip, was yapping around in the yard. From inside the farmhouse there was no sound. As far as Dr MacDonald knew, the elderly couple were inside, in distress, under duress, injured or worse. He braced himself, pushed open the door wide and stepped inside.

'The place was in chaos,' commented Angus. 'Crockery and ornaments had been swept off nearly every surface, and cupboard space ransacked.'

Then his eyes fell upon Carl slumped across the settee, in the middle of the room, with a gaping wound to his head, resting on a bolster. Copious amounts of blood covered the floor around the settee. He had been blasted at close range with a 12-bore shotgun. Still slung across his shoulder was his paper bag. The house had quite obviously been plundered. Stopping only to confirm that the young boy was dead, concerned also that a ruthless and maybe crazy gunman might still be lurking somewhere in the rambling, old buildings, the doctor raced from the scene to his home nearby and telephoned the police at the Kinver station. PC Michael Fallon took the call at exactly 5.30 pm and then hurriedly drove to Yew Tree Farm. He arrived at 5.37 pm, followed closely by the returning Dr MacDonald who immediately reaffirmed that the paperboy was dead.

PC Fallon quickly checked that the farmhouse was empty and requested assistance from the Kinver station. Two more police constables arrived and conducted a thorough search of the whole house. The place was in total disarray. Strangely, a ground floor window at the front of the building had been smashed and opened – in addition to the back door having been forced open with the spade. Fallon secured the back door and crept out through the open window and waited for senior officers to arrive at the murder scene. Officers would be despatched from near-by Wombourne and from police headquarters thirty miles away at Stafford. In Carl's short bicycle ride that afternoon he had crossed the boundary between the West Midlands, which was policed at the time by the second biggest force in England, into Staffordshire, whose police force is one of the smallest.

Detective Chief Superintendent Robert Stewart was soon at the farm to take charge of the investigation and was there to meet Fred Jones and Mary Poole when they returned from their outing at 7.30 pm. After a brief chat with senior detectives the elderly couple accepted accommodation at Dr MacDonald's house. But for Mrs Parrot's kindness, taking the couple out on the day, DCS Stewart may well have had a triple murder to investigate.

Around 9.00 pm a Home Office pathologist from Birmingham University, Dr Benjamin Davis, arrived at the farm and began to take samples from the body and the scene of the horrific crime. Sergeant Vincent Potts, an experienced scene-of-crime officer at Stafford police headquarters, began his search of the house and ordered photographs to be taken. At 10.00 pm the undertakers arrived to collect the boy's body and take it to the mortuary at Wordsley Hospital. There it was identified by Carl's grieving and distraught father, Brian Bridgewater, a Wordsley pipe fitter.

The following day, and chillingly ironic, the same paper Carl was delivering on the previous night, the *Express & Star*, screamed about the murderous event.

In it the paper quoted DCS Stewart as saying, 'I am satisfied that Carl disturbed or came across intruders forcing entry to the house. Why they felt obliged to shoot a lad who could do them no physical harm is beyond me.'

From the very beginning the reliable hunch was that Carl was murdered by a 'gang'. This was DCS Stewart's view from the very first day and was backed up by his scene-of-crime officer, Sergeant Potts, plus a team of over fifty officers. The conclusion was not a difficult one to arrive at, as every room in the farm had been scrutinised and ransacked. In some bedrooms the drawers had been completely removed, in some cases stacked, and others just left open. As well as ornaments and crockery, plants had been clumsily knocked over, and contents of boxes and even a sewing basket scattered on the floor. Every aspect of the whole murder case and burglary pointed to a routine and random case of a burglary, gone wrong, by a team of bungling thieves.

So began a massive police investigation, one unusually devoid of forensic clues, and an endlessly haunting tragedy for Carl's parents, Brian and Janet, and for his brother and sister, Jane and Philip. The murder, incredibly, was also to herald the start of many years of persecution for Ambulance Liaison Officer, Bert Spencer.

The names of the three men and the youth who were to be arrested, convicted and sentenced for the murder are now almost household property – the young Michael Hickey and his cousin, Vincent Hickey, Jimmy Robinson and Pat Molloy. After their arrest a tangled web was to be woven which the passing of years was to complicate rather than unravel.

It started when Vincent Hickey, then 25, was arrested for an armed robbery, in which he was the driver, at Chapel Farm, Romsley. The robbery was strikingly similar to that of Yew Tree Farm. A farmhouse occupied by elderly relatives. The police realised straightaway of a possible connection and one assumes so did Vincent Hickey. As we shall see later, it is strongly suspected that he simply wanted bail and was willing to say anything to secure it. It was at this point he introduced the Bridgewater murder, claiming he knew who was involved. After hours of cat and mouse games he finally gave the names; Michael Hickey, Jimmy Robinson and his mate, Pat Molloy. Not surprisingly, after such an admission regarding a case the whole Staffordshire Police squad was trying to solve, Hickey was not given bail.

I have spoken to Vincent Hickey at length about the case and his involvement in it. There is no doubt he is a man in torment. I believe Mr Hickey when he says he had nothing at all to do with the murder of Carl Bridgewater and he has never visited Yew Tree Farm. The successful appeal for the Bridgewater Four, in 1997, when Vincent had his conviction quashed, appears not to have lessened the demons that surround him. He still feels there is a question mark hanging over his innocence. In 2011 Hickey admitted to being in possession of small quantities of illegal substances, including heroin. Two years later, with a far more serious charge of intent to supply drugs, he was spared a jail sentence by a sympathetic Judge Richard Rundell, who chose instead to impose a two-year community order. Under the circumstances it represented extreme leniency. Certainly with a compassionate eye on Hickey's unjust time served for the Bridgewater murder, the judge commented, "If you fail to comply with the order you will be brought back and might be sentenced to prison – nobody wants to see that."

Oddly enough our contact finished as abruptly as it had started. Suddenly Vincent Hickey went quiet on me and my many efforts to try and contact him were ignored. It remains a mystery to me and is somewhat of a shame. It would have helped a great deal in peeling back some of the mist in those early days of alleged confessions and retractions – from the horse's mouth so to speak. After all Vincent was the catalyst in all this. He was the one that aimed the police in a very distinctive line of enquiry – bringing in, as he did, Jimmy Robinson, Pat Molloy and his cousin, Michael Hickey. He was the only one, out of the remaining Bridgewater Four, that spoke out publicly about the case.

Some of the offers to prove his innocence were confusing. Mr Hickey, who still lives in Birmingham, said he was willing to offer himself for DNA tests that would clear his name. However, there was no forensic evidence found at Yew Tree Farm to make any sort of a comparison.

Although he still stated in the *Birmingham Mail*, in 2012, to reporter Anuji Varma, "There is all this technology the police can use. I'm sure if they carried out new DNA tests the results would lead them to whoever really killed Carl."

In the same article, the tortured Hickey, continued, "I want to know who killed Carl and I will write letters to the police demanding they reopen this case. Even though I was cleared, I still want justice for Carl and his family. This has been gnawing away at me for 30 years. I went through a very traumatic time in prison, and am still suffering. I have always wanted this case to be reopened and now is the right time."

Probably what was a very familiar phrase made by the Staffordshire

Police, regarding Vincent's outburst, saying that they would review the case
if new evidence was to come to light.

Vincent Hickey's verbal confession regarding the Yew Tree Farm
murder certainly had an effect on Pat Molloy. At first, in what has been
described as pure revenge, Pat named the Hickey cousins, Robinson and
himself as having been at the farmhouse, when the paperboy was murdered.
Molloy, at different times, named first Robinson and then Michael Hickey
as having pulled the trigger. We now know, or are pretty certain, that a false
confession was beaten out of Molloy or at least the threat of bodily harm. He
was almost certainly shown a fake confession statement made by Vincent
Hickey, which also included Hickey's forged signature. Hickey never signed
a statement and on realising the grave situation he was in, albeit most of his
own making, he retracted his verbal confession and again echoed the fact
that he had done so purely to get bail.

There were several examples of so called 'confessions' made by Robinson and Michael Hickey, either during their time in police custody or when
on remand in various prisons. As we later see with Spencer during *Chapter
9 – The Prison 'Confessions'*, such admissions can rarely be relied upon.

Quite early on the Bridgewater Four, now convicted and protesting
their innocence, some of the early back-stabbing put aside for the good of
the cause, reunited and looked outside for a new target of accusation. Taking their lead from Michael Hickey's mother, Ann Whelan, and her leading
co-campaigner, Paul Foot, they directed all their energy and suspicion in
the direction of Bert Spencer, the Ambulance Liaison Officer. This they
did, together with the press, and have continued so to do for many, many
years, despite the fact that the most searching of police investigations have
resulted in their dismissal of any Spencer involvement in the killing of the
paperboy. Even today, after nearly four decades after the tragedy, articles
printed surrounding the paperboy's death, always include details about
Spencer being an early important suspect in the case.

In the immediate aftermath of the murder, surprisingly, little evidence
of any substance was found, despite the state of disorder that the robbers

had left and the resulting inch-by-inch police search. There was later to be significance in the unpublished fact that drawers in the ransacked bedroom had been neatly stacked, one on top of the other after being emptied – Molloy, unprompted, had described the scene perfectly. A button was found beside the smashed and open window, one of two entry points used to break into the farm, but it was never matched to any article of clothing. The murder weapon, a 12-bore shotgun, has never been found; nor was there a discharged cartridge case found at the scene. In the event of a shotgun killing, the empty cartridge casing is the only means of matching gun with ammunition – a fact most criminals are aware of. There is no solid, bulleted projectile to be forced down a rifled barrel leaving identifying marks scoured on the bullet surface; only the mark of the firing pin upon the cartridge, can link missile to weapon.

In the area around the farmhouse items from inside were found placed in a wide radius, in the cattle yard, in the driveway and in the orchard. There were no fingerprints found on these items, but some prints were found on the frame of the smashed front window. More importantly, it would have appeared, were a set of fingerprints found on the paperboy's bicycle. There was also damage to the front wheel spokes, which could have been made by a clumsy boot, one assumes by accident. The bike had ended up over a wall in the pigsty. Were these unidentified prints on the frame of the bicycle, labelled D and F, made by the killer? However, whatever initial interest was shown by these findings, discovered by Scene-of-Crime officer, DS Potts, the lead appeared to crumble and disappear. Expert evidence produced by police forensics, at the time, made the assumption that these prints were more than likely made by a child of Carl's age and not of an adult male. This later proved a very important and possible crucial oversight. It would later be challenged by Jim Nichol, acting on behalf of the Bridgewater Four, that the original opinion of DCI Martin, the officer in charge of the Fingerprint Bureau at the Midland Criminal Record Office, given on 27 March 1979, was misleading and possibly incorrect. It was a tough call for DCI Martin as he had little to work with – but his evidence would come back to haunt him later on at the Court of Appeal. Although the fingerprints on Carl's bike were thought that of a child, together with the window frame prints – none of these remotely matched those of anyone who had any connection with the farmhouse, nor of anyone whose fingerprints were already on record or were taken during the following police investigation.

Inside the farmhouse the safe had not been touched, nor had any attempt been made to remove it – facts which could explain the apparent reluctance of some of the killers to leave the murder scene, as witnessed by the later sightings of vehicles and men at the farm. Was there some council of war going on in that farmhouse – as men decided on the best course of action?

So, with virtually nothing to use as a start point, the scene was set for a long and painstaking investigation by the police, coloured only by the hope of a lucky breakthrough, perhaps through one of the expected flood of anonymous phone calls or the emergence of a surprise witness. However, when the breakthrough did come it was from no such source.

*   *   *

In the light of developments to come it is interesting to consider the major sightings that were reported in and around Yew Tree Farm on the day of the murder. In so doing it is difficult to understand Paul Foot's total obsession with the sighting of the Vauxhall Viva and his dismissal of the proliferation of sightings relating to estates, mostly Ford. Of course it could be that Foot knew Bert Spencer had a Vauxhall Viva and this fitted his own personal agenda.

There was naturally a plethora of sightings in this case. I think little, if any, would argue that this was a robbery gone wrong, as echoed by the detective heading the case, DCS Robert Stewart. Only when this crime escalated from a mundane burglary into a brutal and violent murder, were the criminal or criminals responsible placed under microscopic evaluation.

There were quite a few witness statements that the police did not

attach much importance to. Often the sightings were vague and contradictory. Some were more positive of the sighting, but unsure of when the incident occurred. The police quite rightly concentrated on statements from
witnesses who reported seeing something in and around Yew Tree Farm
between 12.30 pm and 5.00 pm on Tuesday, 19 September 1978.

It is vitally important to remember that some sightings were reported
and the occupants checked out and subsequently eliminated by the police.
Obviously we are only interested in vehicles and individuals not accounted
for. There could be a perfectly innocent reason why people did not come
forward. Maybe they were visitors to the area or had simply not seen the
request asking for help with the enquiry. Although it is worth remembering
this was a nationwide appeal on radio, television and in print.

Almost immediately the police enquiry team, which was 200 strong,
had their first lead. Within an hour of the discovery of the body, DC John
Crowe interviewed near neighbour and friend of the elderly occupants at
Yew Tree Farm, Gladys Jones (No. 12 – Log 4.00 pm). Mrs Jones, from her
garden at Yew Tree Cottage, looked directly down on the farm and its back
driveway.

She made a full statement on Sunday 24 September, in which she
stated, 'At about 4.00 pm that afternoon I was in the rear garden of my
home. I looked in the direction of Yew Tree Farm, and in the drive immediately in front of the front door I saw a vehicle parked. I could clearly see
it was a blue estate vehicle. It was facing towards my home, and I could see
that the tailgate was raised. I could not see anyone with the vehicle.' Later
in the statement Gladys reported, 'I decided to get an even better view to
see just who it was. I walked from my garden into the field where I had a
completely uninterrupted view of the farm and the vehicle. ... I would not
commit myself completely to the make, but I am more or less sure that it
was a Ford Cortina. It was most certainly a vehicle of the Cortina size. I
stood in the field for a good five minutes waiting to see who came to the
vehicle, but no one did.'

The good neighbourly actions of Mrs Jones did not end there, she also added, 'After about five minutes I collected my washing from the line and went into the house, where I remained until 4.30 pm. I then went out into the rear garden again and saw the estate vehicle had gone.'

However, from where she stood it is not possible to see a car parked to the right or left of the farm driveway. When she said that the estate had gone, she really meant that she could no longer see it. Other witnesses, Wendy Stagg and Geraldine Waldron, confirmed the presence of a blue vehicle on the farm track around 4.45 pm.

In a second statement taken by Detective Inspector Colin Wordley, Mrs Jones stated that when she first saw the car, the back door to the farmhouse was closed, as it only was when Fred and Mary were out. By the time she had moved into the field for a second, better look, the door was open, and it was still open when she returned to look some 25 minutes later, when she could no longer see the vehicle. One thing is for certain, clear beyond doubt, that the person or persons who had broken into Yew Tree Farm and murdered the paperboy, had driven the car Mrs Gladys Jones had seen.

Paul Foot often threw doubt on Mrs Jones' statement. In May 1983, nearly five years after the incident, he went, together with Ann Whelan, to Yew Tree Farm. They parked a blue Vauxhall Viva saloon with its back to the farm, and its boot up. They then walked to Mrs Jones' cottage and looked down at the car.

'It was quite clear to us that it was not possible for anybody of ordinary eyesight to tell the *make* of the car from that distance, and when we asked Mrs Jones she certainly could not do so on that occasion (italics author's emphasise).'

I think there are a few points of contention with this hypothesis. Firstly, Foot makes the distinction to the 'make' only. Gladys Jones is quite certain it was a Ford Cortina estate, which she could have been familiar with as it was a vehicle driven by the daughter-in-law of Fred Jones. The shape of a Vauxhall Viva could have been quite alien to her. It also depends on where they stood for this sighting, together with the weather conditions. Furthermore, this does not account for the time delay – this was five years later and an elderly person's eyesight can deteriorate quite significantly during this time lapse. One also has to take into account that Mrs Jones moved into the field to get a closer look. There are a few estimations of the exact distance from Yew Tree Cottage to Yew Tree Farm. This ranges from 220 to 300 yards. I think anyone who has been to a professional golf tournament and watched the pros drive off in excess of 300 yards – you can see the small white ball, just over 4cm in diameter, bouncing its way hopefully towards the flag.

Another point that Foot makes, regarding Mrs Jones' testimony, was that on first sighting the vehicle she had thought it belonged to a regular visitor, Mrs Julie Jones, daughter-in-law of Fred Jones, because she had a similar blue estate. Even claiming in her statement, '... I then saw that it was a lighter blue than Julie Jones' vehicle.' This appears pretty conclusive, as she was familiar down to the shade of blue. This does not take into account when Gladys Jones moved from her garden, into the field, where she had a closer and 'uninterrupted' view. One would assume someone who was familiar with estate cars would go in their favour. Alas, Paul Foot uses this against her, which he says is the most 'interesting part of the statement', comments, *'She had seen a blue Ford Cortina estate at the farm before* (Paul Foot's italics). This could have influenced her not just as to the make but also as to whether or not the car was an estate.'

In *Chapter 10 - A Case to Answer*, two witness statements are visited in more detail – Roger Edwards and Gladys Jones – as they offered pivotal evidence.

The exhaustive police hunt for the murderer was matched by the public's disgust and thirst to find the criminal or criminals responsible. The whole media machine united in a rare common goal to reach anyone who had the slightest suspicion of who might be responsible for such a terrible crime. From the start witnesses began to flood in.

A local mobile police unit was set up to take statements from anyone who might have information, together with a battery of personnel answering a special inquiry number. Hundreds of written questionnaires were handed out to the householders of Wordsley.

Mrs Janet Bridgewater, stricken with grief, was persuaded to make a public announcement for information surrounding the death of her son, Carl. She also asked the families of the murderers to give them up.

When looking at the list of sightings, timings given are approximate in some cases. The vast majority were sure the time given was a good estimation, certainly within a few minutes.

The scant amount of significant sightings, again after certain vehicles/ people were happily eliminated, in the face of the volume of traffic, which uses Lawnswood Road, is due to the narrowness of the footpath and the fact that the entrance is bounded by hedges on both sides. A vehicle parked in the driveway of the farm would be quite invisible from the road, as would a vehicle parked anywhere down the footpath at a distance beyond the bend in the path at about the 75 yard point.

The known facts and the central eyewitness accounts of activity in and around Yew Tree Farm combine to produce the following log of the day which started so pleasantly and which ended in grim horror:

Tuesday 19 September 1978

No.	Log time	Witness sightings qualified (timeline information in bold)
1.	11.30 am.	**Mrs Parrot takes Fred and Mary for a day's outing to Wenlock Edge. The farmhouse is empty apart from the dog, Skip.**
2.	12.30 pm.	Robert and Janet Light noticed a blue car reversing from the drive, it stopped, before driving off towards Wordsley. Mrs Light said the car was a light blue estate, with two Caucasians in the vehicle. Although her husband thought there was only one.

3.   1.30 pm.   Alfred Bishop noticed a vehicle, possibly
                  blue, turning into the driveway of Yew Tree
                  Farm. The witness claimed it was a small
                  to medium-sized model, possibly the size
                  of a Vauxhall Viva. He could not remember
                  if it was an estate or an ordinary car.

4.   2.40 pm.   Mrs Catherine Moyle spotted a blue Ford
                  Cortina estate parked on the A449 some 100
                  yards or more from the farm. She saw two
                  men walking away from the car, one wearing
                  a white shirt and tie, stocky build, about 40
                  years of age, the second man rather younger.

5.   2.50 pm.   Roger Edwards saw a pale blue Vauxhall Viva,
                  reasonably new, turning into the driveway. The
                  driver, male, about 55 years of age, dark, wavy,
                  greying hair, wearing dark blue uniform tunic
                  with one shoulder pip. No passengers seen.

6.   2.55 pm.   Joseph Hadley and his son, Peter, saw a
                  blue vehicle in the driveway. Neither could
                  say whether it was a saloon or estate.

7.   3.00 pm.   Nicholas Holden noticed two blue Ford estates.
                  One was parked in Lawnswood Road, the same
                  side and not very far from the farm. The other
                  was turning into the A449 from Prestwood Drive,
                  a bumpy lane, which runs down near to the
                  farm. The second estate was driven by a solidly
                  build man of about 35 years with light brown
                  hair. There was a male passenger with him.

8.   3.15 pm.   Leonard Bick spotted a man in the yard of Yew
                  Tree Farm, he said the outstanding feature was
                  that he had blond hair, the colour of corn.

9.   3.25 pm.   Mario Sabetta said he saw a parked car, it
                        may have been a Ford, in Lawnswood Road
                        about 100 yards away from the farm. Two
                        men came out from behind the car and one
                        was carrying a shotgun. They went and looked
                        over the hedge towards Yew Tree Farm. One
                        of the men was 27–28 years old, broad build,
                        with fair, shoulder length, wavy curly hair –
                        he was the one carrying the gun. The other
                        man was thirty-five to forty, slim, with dark
                        brown hair and long straight sideboards.

10.   3.30 pm.   Frank Cogsell saw a blue estate car
                        parked in the track up against the right
                        hand hedge. He thought the make was
                        an Avenger or Ford Escort estate.

11.   3.50 pm.   Mr Anthony Cross saw a blue car, not on the
                        track itself but in the open space between the
                        track and the farmhouse. He was sure the car
                        was an estate, either a Ford Cortina or Granada.

12.   4.00 pm.   Mrs Gladys Jones, from her home next to
                        the farm at Yew Tree Cottage, observed
                        a blue Ford Cortina estate car parked in
                        the gateway of the farm. She noticed the
                        tailgate was raised, but saw no driver.

13.   4.10 pm.   Mrs Dorothy Southall, a pedestrian, saw
                        a mid blue coloured van roof, possibly
                        a Transit or something smaller.

14.   4.15 pm.   Fred Edwards, who spotted Carl on his bike on
                        his way to Yew Tree, saw a light blue vehicle
                        parked nose-in to the driveway of the farm.

15.   4.15 pm.   Mrs Margaret Heary, who also spotted Carl
                        on his bike on his way to Yew Tree, saw a
                        vehicle parked in the driveway. The colour
                        was light or possibly blue, she was not able to
                        confirm whether it was a saloon or an estate,
                        with the impression it had a long roof.

16.   4.20 pm.   **Carl arrives at the farm to
                        deliver the newspaper.**

17.   4.30 pm.   David Foreman said he saw a dark blue
                        Ford Escort estate in Lawnswood Road
                        'that was creeping up to the junction'.
                        The driver he described as stocky, 45–50
                        years, round face, average length, straight
                        dark brown hair, parted on the left. Also
                        clean shaven and not wearing glasses.

18.   4.30 pm.   Mrs Barbara Walker noticed an orange
                        coloured mini, parked partly on the
                        footpath on the Wordsley side of the
                        driveway. The vehicle was unoccupied.

19.   4.45 pm.   Wendy Stagg spotted a blue estate car parked in
                        the farm track. Next to that was a plum-coloured
                        Allegro or Maxi. A man was seen standing in
                        the road talking to the driver of the estate.

20.   4.45 pm.   Edward Dickens noticed a medium-ranged car,
                        probably a 1,500 or 1,600cc. It was parked
                        diagonally across the drive, a short distance
                        from the road, facing towards the farmhouse.

21.   4.45 pm.   Mrs Geraldine Waldron spotted a medium to
                        dark blue car, parked in the track leading to
                        the farm. She could not remember if it was a
                        saloon or estate. Mrs Monica Ellison, travelling
                        with her niece, Geraldine, saw a tallish man
                        standing in the track, wearing lightish clothes.

22.   4.55 pm.   Brian Clarke saw a medium blue Austin/
                        Morris J4 van, parked at an angle in the
                        farm driveway. He said there was a heavily
                        built man with light, shoulder length
                        hair, standing next to the vehicle.

23.   5.00 pm.   Terence Phelps saw a blue car with two or three
                        men in it. He thought the vehicle was a Ford
                        Escort estate. The driver, wearing a shirt and
                        tie, was in his late forties with thick dark hair.

This is the tally of main vehicles/people sightings in and around Yew Tree
Farm up until 5.00 pm. Concentrating on the vehicles, as we must assume
studying the evidence, that the assailant or assailants travelled by car or
van or both – there were 22 sightings in all. These are broken down into
10 confirmed sightings of blue estate cars, five blue saloon cars (although
some eye-witnesses could not confirm they saw a saloon or estate), two blue
vans and five other cars. This latter number of five cars – three could not
be sure of the colour and one witness claimed to see an orange mini, the
other a plum coloured Allegro or Maxi. Vehicle makes also differed, although
nearly half the 22 sightings were blue Fords, with most of that number being
estates.

Without doubt the eyewitness statement (No. 5 - 2.50 pm) by company director, Roger Edwards, caused Bert Spencer the most trouble. It
was an important focus for Paul Foot and the Bridgewater campaigners. It
would also lead the police to Spencer's door. Initial interest was stirred by
Edwards' statement saying he saw a 'pale blue Vauxhall Viva' turning into

the driveway of Yew Tree Farm at around 2.50 pm. Spencer owned such a car, so this fitted neatly into their scenario of events surrounding Carl's death. He also claimed that the driver, who he had quite a clear view of, was age around 55, his hair dark, but greying and somewhat wavy. His most damning statement for Spencer, under the circumstances, surrounded the driver's attire, 'he was wearing a dark blue uniform with a single pip on the epaulette of his jacket'. It may appear a small matter but Bert's dark blue uniform contained two pips – although much would be made of this discrepancy by the Bridgewater campaigners.

There was, however, another sighting at 1.30 pm by Alfred Bishop, although he stressed that he was not sure it was a Vauxhall Viva, and certainly did not remember anything about the car's occupant or occupants.

Even from a cursory glance at the list of sightings it is obvious that such a course of action is in defiance of elementary logic. So much so that it is difficult to discount a considerable element of cynical deliberation in the programme of anti-Spencer propaganda, which was hinged around it.

There was, however, an obvious line of enquiry the police failed to exploit at the time of the murder. Unlike criminals, who can often move about at will, Spencer held down an important job at the hospital and his movements were documented. At both Corbett Hospital and Ambulance Control at Warley were official movement records. These documented any movement, between hospitals, of the liaison officers, of which Spencer was one of them. All travel expenses were claimed by the officers and these record sheets were of importance to monitor these payments and keep track of personnel.

In 1980, shortly after the murder of Hubert Wilkes by Spencer, interest returned to the Bridgewater case and police re-investigated previous suspect, Hubert Spencer. The first thing they found was that the Corbett Hospital A3 movement sheets, that covered the murder date of the paperboy, were missing. More alarmingly, the movement record book was missing from the secured office at Warley. The facts surrounding the missing records are discussed later in the book in more detail.

Three weeks after Bert Spencer's arrest, early in January, 1980, spurred by the apparent coincidences linking the farmhouse murders, police officers went to Corbett Hospital for the purpose of checking the past movement records in the ambulance liaison section. They found that most of the sheets relating to 1978, up to and beyond the date of Carl's murder, were missing. This equated to nearly 10 months of missing records from January 12 to late October '78. There were also nine days missing from 1977 and 13 days missing from 1979.

These records were handwritten notes made by Bert Spencer on a day-to-day basis. They were written on large A3 size loose sheets, detailing the movement of patients in and out of Corbett Hospital. Informally made out, they were purely a visual aid for the liaison officer – at the time, Bert himself. There was no requirement for the sheets to be filed, stored, or passed on to any other department – unless there had been some notable happening on a particular day, in which case the day's report sheet would be sent to Ambulance Control at Warley.

The Mario Sabetta sighting (No. 9 – 3.25 pm) has constantly been slated by Paul Foot and his followers. Every area of his testimony seemed ripe for attack by Foot and the Bridgewater campaigners.

It was 3.25 pm on the day of the murder of Carl Bridgewater when Mr Mario Sabetta, restaurant manager of the nearby Summerhill House Hotel, made his significant sighting of a vehicle and two men in Lawnswood Road, only 100 yards or so from Yew Tree Farm. Lawnswood Road is fairly narrow and a parked car amounts to an obstruction. Mr Sabetta slowed down to pass what he was sure was a Ford vehicle, possibly an estate.

His description of the two men who crossed from the Ford to the other side of the road, the side on which Gladys Jones' cottage and the Yew Tree Farm are located, was much more definite. The police regarded Mario's statement as important to the investigation, as far as the identification of two of Carl's killers was concerned.

Coincidentally, I have personally known and respected Mario Sabetta for a number of years. Not only was I a previous near neighbour, and know his son well, Gilio, but I also frequented the Parlors Hall Hotel, in Bridgnorth, where he runs the restaurant.

What has not been made clear, only coming to light in the mid-nineties, was just how important Mario Sabetta's account was in favour of Bert Spencer.

Mr Sabetta had seen both of these men two weeks earlier, in early September, 1978, on a bridge over the river Stour, about 300 yards from the farm. Now, the same two men, one carrying a shotgun, crossed the road and gazed over the hedge at Yew Tree land. Directly ahead of them was a large, mown field, scattered with bundles of hay. To their left was the garden of Gladys Jones' cottage, but to their right was the wide gateway leading from the field to the footpath, which runs past the rear of Yew Tree Farm. Only ten minutes or so before, a man had been seen in the yard of Yew Tree Farm, a man with corn-coloured hair. It would seem to be a reasonable conjecture that the two men were looking towards the farm gate or an all-clear signal before driving their Ford down to the farm.

For Bert Spencer it is irrelevant that Mr Sabetta was unable to positively pick out Jimmy Robinson on the subsequent identity parade, although he managed to do that later in court. In fairness to Robinson the Sabetta sighting, if he was accurate in estimating the time at 3.25 pm, is probably too early. The evidence suggests that some, if not all, of the Bridgewater Four were in Birmingham pubs, 20 miles away, at around 3.20 pm.

What matters to Bert Spencer is that he himself was known to Mr Sabetta. Bert had applied to him for a part time job in his restaurant only three weeks before. Certainly Mr Sabetta would have recognized him instantly had he seen him in the area on the day of the murder. Bert had spent some considerable time in Mr Sabetta's company when he had been interviewed by him and shown around the hotel premises.

Again no one came forward to be eliminated from the police enquiry. If Sabetta is correct it would suggest that the men spotted in and around Yew Tree Farm were up to no good on the day of the murder.

There is some puzzlement about the last sighting offered by Terence

Phelps (No. 23 – 5.00 pm), which appears to confirm there were two or maybe three men in the vehicle, facing outwards from Yew Tree drive. Phelps confirmed he saw a blue Ford Escort estate and described the driver; wearing a shirt and tie and in his late forties with thick dark hair. The police marked the eyewitness evidence as highly important.

On 27 September, eight days after the murder, Chief Superintendent Stewart took the decision to publish an Identikit picture of the driver of the car Phelps had seen – he could not help regards the passenger or passengers. The witness had spent hours with the Identikit officers and the picture was published with a flourish in all the papers the following morning. Some papers screamed, enthusiastically, 'FACE OF A KILLER!' *(Express & Star)* and 'IS THIS THE FACE OF CARL'S KILLER?' *(Birmingham Evening Mail)*.

Surely this was not the reluctance, of what was probably the murderous gang, to leave the crime scene due to the fact that they were still virtually empty-handed? Was it at all possible that the gang had little interest in traceable antiques and the killers had come for cash only?

Again at the farm was a large, old-fashioned safe; too heavy to load into most non-commercial vehicles, too obvious to transport and too difficult to open in-situ. Were the occupants of the blue Ford Escort estate awaiting the return of the residents of the farm – monitoring their return from the relative safety of their vehicle and poised to abort the robbery with a quick getaway if the old people had any accompanying opposition with them? It would have certainly been no problem to obtain the safe key from the elderly and arthritic couple.

With regards to vehicles mentioned, either by Vincent Hickey or Pat Molloy – how much can be relied upon from the alleged admissions is unsure. They admitted to making early confessions for various reasons as documented. One has to wonder, during those early admissions, why the police would wish to fabricate evidence. I assume the police wished to find out honestly how any team or individual arrived at the scene. As we can see there were many sightings, although a theme was emerging.

With regard to vehicles catalogued in the so-called 'confessions',

Vincent stated there were two cars on the job, one which was a sky-blue Cortina estate. Although during various interviews the colour would change to dark blue. He also mentioned a blue van with a white roof. There had been a van at Redditch impounded with stolen goods.

'You said the van found at Redditch was blue,' said DC Millington. 'We've been told it was grey.'

Hickey replied, 'It *was* grey.'

The murder vehicle had changed colour!

During Molloy's interview, DC Perkins, asked about the transport to Yew Tree Farm.

'There was a blue Cortina estate van Jimmy borrowed from someone at the Dog and Partridge. It had a white top,' explained the Irishman. 'I went with Vinny Hickey – he drove. Mickey, his relation, came with us. I sat in the back.'

He was asked how Jimmy Robinson reached the farm.

'Jimmy drove the van. We parked them away from the farm and walked down to the farm.'

At a later interview, after the Irishman had signed the statement, DCI Watson asked again about the car he was in.

'A Ford Cortina Estate, I think, I'm certain it was one with a folding seat ...'

During this latter interview the van, which he said Robinson had borrowed for the job, was no longer an 'estate van', when Molloy commented, 'It was a transit van, dark blue or black. I think it had a white top, but I'm hazy about that.'

Another important point was where Molloy allegedly said they parked the car, he claimed was driven by Vincent, and the van, in which he said Jimmy Robinson was at the wheel.

DCI Richard Wood, asked, '... Can you remember where you left the car, for instance?'

'Yes, I think we parked it on some sort of roadway and walked to the house,' explained Molloy.

'How far did you walk?' questioned Wood.

'I would think about 100 yards,' answered the Irishman.

'Where was the van?'

'I did not see it but Jimmy must have parked it somewhere near because he was walking just behind us,' responded Molloy.

Strangely, this conversation between DCI Wood and Molloy took place after they had diverted down the track and parked by the outhouses at Yew Tree Farm. Pat Molloy appeared to have no knowledge of the area or the farm, which he had claimed to have robbed just three months earlier, and which a violent murder had taken place.

It was an odd point that Molloy and Vincent both allegedly talked of arriving at the farm together, with Michael Hickey, in possibly an estate car, leaving Robinson to drive to the farm, in either an estate or transit van, alone. It was alleged during the trial, that at the time of the murder on 19 September; Robinson and Vincent Hickey were at best on nodding terms, with the Irishman having no knowledge of Vincent at all. It was alleged only when mutual friend Michael Hickey suggested Robinson for the Chapel Farm armed robbery, just over two months later, that he met Vincent properly for the first time. If this were true, Molloy who was not on the Chapel Farm job would have had little or no contact with Vincent Hickey. A lot was made of this during the trial – did the four men know and work with each other before the day Carl was murdered? The testimony was flimsily to say the least and it appears that Vincent Hickey's constant local was the Dog and Partridge (Selly Oak), with Robinson and Molloy choosing to spend their time at the California (Weoley Castle) public house. It was only Michael Hickey who appeared to migrate between the two pubs.

There was no evidence to confirm the four men were close or on speaking terms for any considerable time before the murder. It was pointed out by one witness, Catherine Guy, that she saw Vincent Hickey walk past her high rise flat, just before the murder date, visiting her next door neighbours, Carol Bradbury and Jimmy Robinson. Although Mrs Guy, who was unsure when first interviewed by the police, retracted her statement later to Ann

Whelan. She claimed she was initially confused and when she finally saw Vincent at the trial, she realised she had never seen him before.

Returning to Molloy and Hickey's alleged confession about them travelling together in one vehicle, it would appear this was highly unlikely. Molloy and Robinson were best friends and seen drinking together in the California on the lunchtime of the murder day. The Hickey's were also seen at the Dog and Partridge, they were celebrating the birth of a friend's child. Having said this all four men's alibis during this time were not set in stone. However, it appears odd that if the Bridgewater Four were guilty then why didn't Molloy travel with his good friend, Jimmy Robinson? However, Robinson would have had the shotgun with him, which might lead some to say Molloy was already distancing himself from the alleged murder weapon – his pre-trial 'confession' claimed he had never seen a weapon of any kind.

When you have digested all the sightings and evidence, which surrounded those few hours on that sunny Tuesday afternoon, they do suggest a certain amount of suspicious activity.

Of course this scenario of a bumbling gang, rattling around the farmhouse ransacking the premises with little regard or knowledge of antiques, and finally blasting away a 13-year-old boy, did not fit Paul Foot and his campaigners' description of the criminal. Bert Spencer, the lone man, keen collector of antiques, and sitting in an open office in Wordsley Hospital, three miles away, should have been the last person to figure in this crime. But respected journalist Foot and his sidekick Anne Whelan had other ideas. Spencer was clearly in their sights and they were relentless in their bid to start a smear campaign of such ferocity – even today the mud still sticks to his name.

2.

The Last Coincidence

· ·

Bert Spencer has experienced the effects of coincidence on his life to a remarkable degree. This unexplained phenomenon is a quite common happening in the lives of most people. Sometimes an event of coincidental nature is so trivial that it may pass almost unrecognised for what it is. But, on occasion, the tricks played in time and space can be shattering in their effect. They can be seen to manipulate, divert and re-channel a complete life pattern. Classic examples can and do, fill volumes. Explanations range between the physical and the metaphysical – from some mystic interaction between souls to the working of some natural laws yet to be identified.

In everyday life these strange and frequent happenings can be mildly puzzling, bewildering or even disturbing, although most are readily dismissible. When the benevolence of the leprechaun syndrome shows its influence the event is accepted as a happy accident. When a strange confluence of events happens, producing inconvenience or concern, it is vaguely ascribed to bad luck. However, when similar happenings become focal points in a murder enquiry then officialdom is inclined to discount *chance, fate* and *fortune* as causal factors. When credulity is stretched beyond its normal limits of elasticity then the materialistic stance is taken and evidence is sought of some anthropocentric management.

On occasion, Bert Spencer himself has been forced to the conclusion that some Machiavellian hand was moving pieces on his personal chequerboard. Such was the extent of outside and unseen influences that at least one eventful chain of happenings could be ranked with the standard classic examples presented to students of synchronistic and time warp phenomena.

Not so startling was the demonstration of the long arm of coincidence by which Mark Roman and Bert Spencer were thrown together after a gap of almost 25 years, which by any measure, was more than unusual. Their first meeting took place one evening in the early summer of 1965. It was to set the stage for a cycle of remarkable events and coincidence which was to herald the breaking of Bert's fourteen years of self-imposed silence regarding the killing of his farmer friend, Hubert Wilkes. This refusal to speak about the tragedy had possibly cost him several of his many years in prison. It had also left an open door for speculation and had provided fuel to the hostile anti-Spencer campaigners, and given free rein to those who so fluently propagated rumours tying Spencer to the murder of Carl Bridgewater.

On that summer evening in 1965 tragedy was still a long way off; coming events were much too far away for there to be any shadows cast. Bert Spencer was, however, literally working his way towards the horror ahead of him. He was twenty-five years of age, a Judo exponent of some note and a keen body-builder. He was also working himself into the ground, a non-smoker and hardly a drinker, Bert's physical pursuits, demanding in themselves, were his answer to an abnormally stressful workload. It was, no doubt, due to his fitness, coupled with the intake of the relatively innovative training aid, anabolic steroids, that Bert was able to cope with his incredibly demanding schedule of work and play. His driving force was his obsessional desire to improve his family circumstances; to move away from the neighbourly, but decaying claustrophobic back streets of Smethwick and to relocate his wife and baby daughter in more salubrious surroundings. To this end he took as many jobs as could be crammed into his working week on top of his full-time work as a long-distance lorry driver. With his older brother, Don, he owned and worked a piggery near to his home in Stony Lane, fattening weaners for the pork market. He drove and did site work in his spare time for a Birmingham builder, built up a weekly round selling tights and stockings door to door, cleaned windows, was a jobbing driver for a local engineering firm and would sometimes fill in behind the bar at a local pub.

Equally strenuous was his 'relaxation' schedule. Three times a week he trained at different judo clubs. These included the Harry Mitchell Recreation

Centre, The Lamp Tavern and The West Bromwich Omnibus Social Club.
On Sunday mornings he ran his own judo club for youngsters at a Bear-
wood sports complex and on Wednesday night he taught his own, personally
developed, style of self-defence and unarmed combat. Even with his overly
demanding life-pattern he still found time to twice win the West Bromwich
and District Open Judo Championship. Not surprisingly, his reputation for
proficiency and instructional skills began to spread beyond his own locale.

At the time of his meeting with Bert Spencer, Mark Roman had recently
returned to his roots in Coventry after commissioned service in the army.
Army life had followed the standard military pattern, long periods of tedium
interspersed with short bursts of excitement. In rejoining the rat race of
industry and big town life, Mark found that even that small ration of adrenaline surges was missing. Even the rugby pitch, where he had played his
favourite game in his pre-army years, had been converted into a car park
by an expanding motor manufacturer. Life had taken a distinctly dull turn.
In any case, he had seen the best of his rugby playing days and had reac-
quainted himself with contact sports played out on a dojo mat.

Through the judo and karate club network Mark Roman had heard of
and contacted Bert Spencer. As Mark, with three other ex-army personnel,
drove from Coventry to the Black Country, Bert was setting off from his
home in Stony Lane, Smethwick on his BSA 650cc Gold Flash. He took his
usual route along Oldbury Road, turning right at the Home Guard Club and
over Galton Bridge in Roebuck Lane. These locations and names were to
dog and haunt him in later years as a mound of triviality was to be trans-
mogrified into a nightmare burden of mammoth proportions. This was to
happen after Roebuck Lane had been partly swallowed up in the construc-
tion of the new dual carriageway and renamed, Telford Way.

In his telephone conversation with Bert, Mark had been specific about
his requirements. Bert had been equally specific about his. It was to be a
meeting for mutual assessment. Mark had an objective in mind. Management positions in industry were deadly dull, but there was life after the
regular army. Together with a group of like-minded ex-army contacts he

had been keeping up with developments in some of the more troubled locations around the world. While the soldiers of the Queen were risking their lives and earning their shilling in Borneo and Aden, there were positive rumblings on the ex-military grapevine of more lucrative work on offer in similarly exotic locations. The rumours told of large cash amounts being distributed from the handmade luggage of mystery recruiters – advance payments for short-haul military operations.

At meetings in London hotels, Mark and his group had made contact with mercenary recruiters.

'White men,' Mark explained, 'some with South African accents, looking for trained soldiers to fight a black man's war.'

Already, so the grapevine accurately whispered, a contemporary of Mark's, Claude Couve de Murville, qualified doctor, ex-British Army Officer and practising eccentric, nephew of the French Foreign Minister, was handling himself well in the Congo civil war. Claude was serving with Mike Hoare's Five Commando, supporting Major General Mobutu's ANC (Armée Nationale Congolaise), against the Simba rebels.

For young, trained men it was an exciting prospect – a paid adventure where the worst happens only to someone else. In the preparation for such a venture a man like Bert Spencer had a part to play. In the maelstrom circumstances of Third World civil war, close quarter contact with hostile forces is an ever-present possibility and it was not overly dramatic to train against the eventuality. While the minutiae of vaccinations, money transfers, travel arrangements and insurance were being worked out, Mark's group had some waiting time on their hands. General fitness training was a daily ritual. Weapon skills had been honed during training weekends spent at a firing range situated in a remote location in the hills of the Welsh Border. All ten of the group were members of a private parachuting club. Investigating what Bert Spencer had to offer in the way of original unarmed combat techniques seemed a good way in which to round off the training programme and release some of the constantly bubbling adrenaline.

For Bert Spencer, physical excellence was a way of life and he placed a high spiritual value rather than a monetary price on his time. While he had infinite patience with youngsters and other vulnerable groups, he had little time for some of the character types that gravitate to the practice of martial arts. Before making a commitment Bert wanted an opportunity to weigh up this new group.

Like many other sports clubs in the sixties, before white tiles, chromium and multi-gyms were standard features of such venues, the Kanakwai Judo Club met in a large, showerless wooden pavilion, pervaded by the dusty, musty smell of old coconut matting. It was owned by the West Bromwich Omnibus Social Club and located on their sports field. The amenities were primitive and the mats were hard. The club was run by a colourful character, one Albert Roper. He was a short, balding figure, barrel-chested and with large eyes staring from a round face. Albert was a judo black belt, Second Dan, a veteran of World War Two and an ex-army instructor in unarmed combat. Not surprisingly he ran his club like a Regimental Sergeant Major, issuing instruction and rebuke in the rich accent and idiom of Cradley Heath. On his left hand he had one finger and his thumb only – a legacy, so it was said, from the emergency closure of a tank hatch.

At Albert Roper's self-defence factory there was little time allowed for preliminary chat. After the standard, exhausting training session, Albert, aged sixty and with only one complete hand, gave his usual post-training demonstration of multi-opponent demolition against fit men about half his age.

On this occasion the object was to establish if this new group had what it takes. And take it they did, from a man only five years away from collecting his bus-pass. The fit young ex-soldiers emerged from the testing session feeling like victims of primary shell shock. To cap off a hard evening, Bert Spencer invited Mark on the mat for a 'friendly' all styles contest. With each man feeling the need to prove something it was a bruising contest in which both protagonists were to experience a measure of surprise. Mark, already properly aware of Bert's growing reputation, had had no warning of his opponent's immense strength. He had no way of knowing that Bert Spencer could bench-press 400lbs and dead-lift even more. Bert was slightly taken aback by Mark's somewhat unorthodox competence. Finally, Bert called a halt and generously declared the bout a draw, leaving Mark feeling as though he had had a somewhat patronising pat on the back from a friendly gorilla.

As it is often the way of things, the contest established more than the initial objective. The two men became friends. After several years their different life patterns dictated that they would drift and lose contact. The break came in 1969. Bert was by then a member of the ambulance service and had added part-time farming to his overloaded working week. Mark was now works manager of Typhoo Tea in Birmingham. He had also just completed a refresher parachute course at Abingdon and taken over an airborne unit in Coventry. For both men life was jam-packed and contact with each other was lost.

In 1976 Mark was back in the Congo, now Zaire, as a staging post en route to the civil war in neighbouring Angola. As one of the one hundred and forty-seven mercenaries who made the outward trip, he was one of only ninety-seven who made the return journey. There were newspaper and television reports of the war in Angola, although Bert did not make the connection. It had, after all, been seven years since they had last had contact with each other.

It was three years later, at the end of 1979, that Bert was to make the headlines. The newspapers used his Christian name of Hubert and he, like Mark, had moved house more than once. This time it was Mark who failed to make the connection.

In a bizarre and tragic incident Bert Spencer had killed a man, using a sawn-off shotgun from close range. The newspaper accounts dwelt on the unusual elements of the affair – the absence of apparent motive and Bert's stolid refusal to throw any light upon the mystery. By his silence he virtually beat his own path to a long life sentence.

However, the element of mystery was quickly overtaken by another factor, which was to generate even more media attention than the apparent lack of motive and the bizarre circumstances of the killing itself. It was more than a year since the murder of the young paperboy and, just

four weeks before the killing of Hubert Wilkes, three men and a youth
had been found guilty of the murder at Yew Tree Farm. Pat Molloy, Jimmy
Robinson, Vincent Hickey and the youth Michael Hickey, had been sentenced to long terms of imprisonment – terms long enough to reflect the
public sense of outrage which the crime had generated. Over the years
they would be grouped together by faithful campaigners and press as *The
Bridgewater Four*.

What gave momentum to the media interest and resurrected the case
of the murder of Carl Bridgewater was the fact that Bert Spencer had shot
Hubert Wilkes at Holloway House Farm, just half a mile away from Yew Tree
Farm where young Carl too had been the victim of a shotgun murder. The
fact that to many the two tragedies were totally dissimilar in all respects,
apart from the means and proximity of location, was completely ignored.
There were media cries of a 'copycat killing'. To strengthen the point the
farms were even relocated by the press. The half a mile separation was
reduced in print to 500 yards and eventually became 'neighbouring'.

Even a cursory examination of the facts should have stilled at birth
the manufactured parallels between the two cases. After the most intensive and exhaustive investigations the police discounted any possibility of
a connection between the happenings at the two farmhouses. Regardless
of that, the pro-Bridgewater Four faction saw a thin straw blowing in the
wind and clutched and nurtured it. It was the start of a close to forty-year
witch-hunt.

*   *   *

On 14 December 1979, the eve of his fortieth birthday, normal life stopped
for Bert Spencer. There was to be no hunt for the killer of Hubert Wilkes.
Bert was at the farmhouse when the police arrived. He was arrested, charged,
remanded, tried, convicted and sentenced to life imprisonment and began
the twilight existence of a lifer. He had refused to give evidence at his trial
and maintained his stance of silence throughout his 14 years in prison. In

so doing he perhaps has lengthened the already free rein enjoyed by those who have spent those years in intense and well-orchestrated efforts to link him to a crime of child-murder.

Through the years Mark Roman was unaware that the Hubert Spencer of the headlines was the Bert Spencer of the dojo mat and the gymnasium. He was to find out in a most peculiar way.

It was March 1993. A property deal had gone wrong. 'Concrete' promises of substantial funding had been broken. Once again foreign brokers had perpetrated the classic 'up-front fee' fraud. The dominoes had fallen from Trondheim to Frankfurt, to Zurich and the USA, and England. Mark Roman, near the end of the long domino train, stood in court owing thousands and owed thousands more.

Mark's spirits had lifted as he heard the judge say, 'You took a chance, Mr Roman and you got your timings wrong...'

Maybe, he thought, standing ramrod stiff in the dock, it was going to be okay. Certainly the young barrister had explained well the unfortunate and devastating train of events.

Alas, the judge went on, '... therefore I have no alternative but to impose a custodial sentence on you to twelve months imprisonment.'

Maybe it was still going to be ok, Mark thought optimistically, just a nerve-twitching pause before adding, '...suspended for two years.'

The judge did pause, but only to display a nice command of the English language. Using the *oratio obliqua* form and the imperfect subjunctive, he decreed in a well-practised, world weary voice, 'Let him go down.'

Roman looked across at his young barrister who was too embarrassed to return the favour. With a light touch on his arm by a waiting constable, Mark Roman disappeared below and joined the army of prison inmate statistics.

For a man who had fought for Queen and country, and also by paid factions, a shared cell at, ironically, one of Her Majesty's Prison – the Victorian concrete jungle known as Winson Green, in Birmingham – was somewhat of a culture shock. After a relatively short period Mark was transferred, handcuffed to a Walsall prison officer known as Wegga, to a Category D open prison on the east coast flatlands of Lincolnshire.

Built in 1936 to the same pattern of Army camps of that era, the huddle of single storey buildings stands bleakly on land reclaimed from the sea, hidden from seaward view by a sea wall. This grassed-over bank is a hand-built rock mound, several miles long, laboriously and backbreakingly constructed by generations of young offenders, the first of whom were marched all the way from Stafford to Boston, Lincolnshire. There they were to experience real hard labour in the raw chill of the North Sea winds.

North Sea Camp houses 200 men. It is a last staging post of the prison system, one of several such establishments; it caters for men who are due for release in the foreseeable future. That also means that the camp population consists of a cross-section of the nation's prison inmates who have almost reached the end of the line. Many are sex offenders, their grim secrets locked behind a computer screen. Some ten percent are lifers, men who have killed, whose reasons are as varied as their personalities and physical appearance. Others are errant motorists or poll-tax offenders, rubbing shoulders with IRA terrorists, gunrunners and bank robbers. In order to diminish their vulnerability in an uncertain situation, many prisoners invent a criminal record for themselves and the computer fraudster takes on the mantle of an armed robber and the car thief becomes a knifeman. Like war, the shuffling anonymity of prison existence can create the most peculiar of liaisons and produce the strangest of bedfellows.

It was dusk on Tuesday 9 March 1993 by the time that the vanload of new arrivals had been processed through reception at North Sea Camp. To Mark, standing in the open air with the clean smell of the North Sea breeze in his nostrils and the familiar shapes of army-style billets around him, it was a time-travel sensation. Wegga, influenced by his own familiarity with the brick and steel of 'bang-up' thought differently.

'I'd escape from here,' he growled, 'if I knew where I fuckin' was!'

A prison officer studied his list of room vacancies and to Mark he pronounced, 'North unit spur number 211 room 12,' adding, 'You'll be all right in there.'

Mark was inquisitive and unsure of his new home. He had just spent eight days, twenty-four hours a day, with an unbalanced 18 stone old lag with a penchant for 'slashing up', 'smashing up' and 'barricading in'.

The prison officer, ex-army stamped all over him, down to his Royal Engineers watch strap, unlocked the door to room 12 and, to Mark's surprise, handed him a key. An open prison it really was he thought. One of the two beds in the room was already occupied. Lying in the half-dark beneath large hanging oil paintings was a muscular sleeping figure.

At the intrusion the occupant opened one eye to appraise the newcomer.

Without moving from the bed and obviously not overjoyed at the prospect of yet another cell-mate to weigh up, maybe one with noxious personal habits to cure or endure, asked gruffly, 'Do you smoke?'

'Yes,' answered Mark, the monosyllable reflecting his own lack of enthusiasm.

'Have you got any tobacco?'

'No,' Mark said abruptly, thinking – here we go again, another difficult cellmate to compound his misery.

The semi-dormant figure swung his legs to the floor.

'Better have this then,' he said with a grin, producing a one-ounce pouch of Hilton Dark Blend tobacco and a packet of Rizla papers – prison commodities worth gold to a smoker.

Mark smiled, outwardly brightening up.

He stuck out a hand, 'My name's Mark.'

'Bert,' was the reply, as he took the proffered hand in a weight-lifter's grip.

Mutual recognition was not immediate. After all, it had been twenty-four years. Bert was a couple of stone lighter, Mark was at least that much heavier and his hair had turned from brown to grey. The intervening years had been a kaleidoscope of places and faces for both men. Bert had been through a divorce and now spoke of Christina instead of Janet. It took all of twenty-four hours for recognition to dawn, and much longer for Bert to speak about his long running problem with the group of hostile campaigners and their assorted acolytes.

Bert had kept his case very close to his chest for nearly 14 years and had shared not a single fragment with either prisoner or screw. Of course the various tentacles of the prison medical staff, mainly stationed or visiting psychiatrists, had tried to probe his mind for rhyme or reason. Trying desperately to seek out a motive or clue to Bert's few moments of madness at Hubert Wilkes' home when he blasted him to death at close range. But they had all received a stony silence and had either come to the conclusion that Spencer was either hostile towards them, for whatever reason, or he genuinely could not recount the events leading up to the murder of his friend. True, he had batted a few letters back and forth to various legal bodies or people who had suspiciously 'injected' themselves into Bert's life. These so-called 'prison pen-pal' relationships had been treated with caution, but more of that later. Also of course, there was Spencer's old nemesis in the shape of *Daily Mirror* journalist, Paul Foot.

Now things were different. He had a confidant. A man from his past, who knew him, respected him and hopefully, trusted him.

Bert recounted his story to Mark Roman over a period of several nights. Intent as he was on delivering it with the deserved ring of authenticity, which only detail can provide. Spencer took time in the telling, stopping to validate points by producing documents, letters and newspaper cuttings and even making impromptu sketches of buildings and locations.

Mark listened in amazement at the web of intrigue into which an old friend had fallen. Any reservations he held in check, as the story was unfolded. After all, he had seen almost everything that man is capable of perpetrating on his fellow man. He had known the most gentle of men turn into enthusiastic killers once rid of the balancing factors of law and retribution. Psychopaths come with no tattoo on their foreheads and are equipped with a variety of disarming veneers. Although, Mark well knew, there is usually about them an indefinable aura that encourages caution and a wariness of approach.

Bert Spencer projects no such warning signal. He is patently open and direct. A fact that would carry minuscule weight with a distanced third party – but it was a personality sidelight, which was enough to make Mark Roman listen with more than casual curiosity. And listen he did, night after night. As the story unfolded, it gradually became clear that here was a paradox – a case to answer in that there was no case to answer. What did demand reply were the often horrific accusations, hurled in desperation by people who had taken a tiger by the tail with the predictable result. If once they were to let go it would be an admission of their having undertaken an unacceptable course of action. It would also throw possible doubt and they may look as if they were conceding that justice had already been done in the case of the murder of Carl Bridgewater. Capitulation would make a transparency of the way that some facts appeared warped and refashioned. It would demonstrate just how public opinion had been manipulated to the extent that a total non-event could be accepted as proven fact.

Despite the invidious nature and daunting impotence of his situation, despite almost paralysing frustration and troughs of deep despair, Bert Spencer had, through the long, hard years, managed to keep his head in Kiplingesque fashion – when many about him seemed to be losing theirs. He disciplined himself to keep records, despite his lack of facilities. Each episode of accusatory media exposure was logged in a copperplate hand in a prison-made scrapbook. Each letter sent or received was copied by hand and filed in a scrap cardboard box. Press cuttings were often sourced from newspapers discarded in the prison dustbins. The means were necessarily primitive but Bert was determined to amass evidence in anticipation of the day when he could begin to fight back. A day for which no date was set. But he determined that when it finally arrived, and if he were to survive the years of confinement in the concrete jungles of the prison system, he would use his collected material as the basis of a book with which to fight his corner. It would be his long awaited and forcibly postponed right of reply.

When I first read the document, which was really a bundle of handwritten notes, letters and, once they had been freed and left their prison regime, the typed words which flowed from Mark Roman. Although the references were 20 plus years out of date, there was a raw narrative that I knew could make the basis of a gripping novel. It took me many thousands of hours of research and writing to produce a manuscript that was accurate and fair, and hopefully told the story from all sides – not just Bert Spencer's.

Right from the start, to produce any details for a possible book some-time in the future, events had to be catalogued and timelines drawn up. It was a complicated process and made frustratingly difficult under the circumstances. It was a long haul project for Bert – North Sea Camp is a working prison. As a writer's working location it hardly compares with the seclusion and tranquillity of a Cornish cliff-top cottage. With very few exceptions the management and staff of North Sea Camp have enlightened and progressive outlooks, but inmate selection, naturally, does not loom large in their brief – although, thankfully, arsonists are frowned upon in the wooden hutted camp. Without the watchtowers and razor wire of the high security establishments, it is virtually impossible to prevent the traffic in drink and drugs.

Bert and Mark found it often difficult to concentrate. The noise pollu-tion discharged into the atmosphere by prisoners on a high is difficult to escape. 'Ghetto-blasters' blare the music of the moment repetitively and competitively. Pool rooms resound with chants of victory. Buildings shake to slamming doors and voices howl constant Anglo Saxon imprecations. Relief from bedlam comes only after midnight lights out or after a successful cannabis run when the smokers are reduced to the drowsy passivity, which the weed induces.

At North Sea Camp the working day is from 8.15 am to 4.30 pm unlike other category prisons where inmates exist under a 'bang-up' regime. There a prisoner can spend twenty-three hours a day lying on his steel frame bed counting bricks, watching paint peel or maybe penning his memoirs. While Bert worked outside the camp at a sports centre a couple of miles away, Mark found himself painting a mural in the prison chapel. Congenial enough occupations but the situation left no possibility of joint discussion, research or writing during the day. Formulating the chronological happenings up to the present day began each night after the teatime meal. It continued long after the midnight lights out curfew with notes being made in the dim orange light escaping into the room from a sodium security lamp outside.

Pens and pencils were begged and borrowed in the early days and the original 'manuscript' took shape on scrap computer paper and diminutive letter pads, anything with one clean side of near-white paper. This was the sum of available office facilities - no telephone, no fax, no typewriter or word processor, not even a hole punch or stapler. An attempt to obtain the services of an outside typing agency was aborted by the prison authority. Bert Spencer provided the facts, facts that are seared into his memory and kept fresh by fourteen years of constant playbacks. Facts supported by masses of contemporaneous notes and bundles of correspondence some of it colourful in its content and variety, some of it invaluable to the project by dint of its sourcing and revelatory material. Mark added an essential objectivity and third party perspective to the word pictures painted by Bert with painstaking clarity. Mark also supplied the questions, endless hours of them it seemed at the time. These extensive notes and musings were to be the beating heart of the book you are now reading.

It took six months of working days of some seventeen hours duration to finally and laboriously fashion a linear version of events. A twenty-eight year cycle of time warp coincidence had been closed. Students of the phenomenon of coincidence will be aware of the definition of this type of happening. Classed as an example of synchronicity; '... it is a contingency of events, personally meaningful, produced by the intervention of some unknown force'. Purists would add, '... perhaps Divine, but often Diabolical'. In this instance to suggest either influence would be rather overstating the case, although Bert Spencer has felt the effects of the latter to an incredible degree. The tide was long overdue in turning.

Bert Spencer and Mark Roman left North Sea Camp on the same weekend in August 1993. Life had spun a strange web around Bert and he had paid for the macabre and tragic result with years of his own life. The pressure under which the relentless anti-Spencer campaigners had placed the Establishment, had possibly added even more years to his sentence. Even now it was no case of walking away into a celluloid sunset. There was a life to rebuild. One set of lines had been written and, as the old philosopher pointed out, 'piety, tears and wit were all pointless demonstrations of self-indulgence'. Although there was one aspect of the lost years which could be redressed, if only by signposting the shifting sands upon which his long-term tormentors had tried to build a case against him. The constraints had been removed. Nothing now could prevent him from telling his story and, hopefully, stepping out from the shadow which the campaigners had cast.

When Bert Spencer left North Sea Camp he carried under his arm a large black document case containing the written elements, crude but factual, of a manuscript. As time would tell, this partially chiselled document was still only in its embryonic stage. Although it would take well over two decades, the manuscript was about to breathe life as another writer was about to pick up the baton. Once again coincidence, and this time a certain amount of luck, would roll in Bert's favour.

3.

A Gathering Storm

....

Some childhoods are riddled with trauma, incidents which implant ever-fresh memories and are on constant playback to disturb and torment. The constant recall can either be a crushing blight in later life or it can serve to stiffen the sinews and inculcate a firm resolve to protect the next generation from similar mental scarring. The causal effect of Bert Spencer's early experiences was to induce a phobic desire for self-improvement. His burgeoning philosophy, from an early age, was to fill his waking hours with work. To a degree he was successful.

From the difficult start point of a poor and unstable home background he was able to relocate his wife and daughter to fashionable suburbia. However, there was an indiscernible and sinister price being exacted in the process – the common psychosomatic response to Henry David Thoreau's famous quote, 'Most men lead lives of quiet desperation and go to the grave with the song still in them.' Unaware of any symptom of the abnormally high stress levels he was imposing upon himself, Bert's answer to his pace of life was to embrace the philosophy of '*work hard and play hard*'. This daily cramming of his hours was like turning up the gas beneath a pressure cooker and then blocking the relief valve. Eventually, already predisposed and vulnerable to psychological invasion, he was to be attacked by hostile factors. These would combine to plunge him into regions of human experience at once dark, terrifying and, even now, not totally explicable.

Bert, christened Hubert Vincent, was born on 15 December 1939 at St. Chad's Hospital, Hagley Road, Birmingham. He was the fourth and last child born to Leonard and Edith Harriet Spencer, sadly his sister, Joan, had passed away. If predestination really does enmesh us all then the sidereal influences must have augured ill on that wartime December day.

Leonard (Len) Spencer, Bert's father, was a boisterous, colourful character even in Smethwick, a Black Country town where such characters flourish. Len, driving his general dealer's cart pulled by his horse Kitty, was a familiar sight in the area. Len was an old-fashioned extrovert, well known and popular in the local pubs. An almost Dickensian eccentric, he was a very general dealer, an accomplished drinker and fairground boxer with a penchant for sleeping in the stable with his horse.

By the time Bert was a three-year-old his father had left the family home. Bert was never to see him again, despite searches made with his older brother, Don, in later years. The nearest Bert was ever to get to him was to stand at his graveside handcuffed to a prison officer. In a misplaced attempt to spread some solace, an aunt whispered to Bert, at the funeral, that seeing Leonard in his coffin had been like looking down at Bert himself. To Bert, then a Category A prisoner, in maximum security D Wing, Wormwood Scrubs, it might as well have been.

Leonard's unannounced and permanent departure from home left the hard working Edith living in her rented, gas-lit, Victorian terraced cottage with three children to support and no male wage-earner. In those austere wartime years it was an impossible situation for Mrs Spencer and young Bert found himself shunted off to one of the Dr Barnardo's Homes. The memories of his time there are limited, apart from a visual image of a Palm Sunday cross pinned above his bed and of standing in uniformed line for his mandatory dose of malt and cod-liver oil from the communal spoon.

Bert was eventually returned home when the family fortunes improved and soon he was taking his first steps into what was to be a life-pattern of intensive work. He ran errands for neighbours, smuggling suits and watches to the pawnbroker on a Monday and retrieving them for weekend use on a Friday. He collected and delivered coal in a homemade wheelbarrow and made many trips to fill jugs with beer from the local alehouse, to the twitching of the temperance-white net curtains.

At the age of nine he found himself in Smethwick juvenile court. The charge against him was wilful damage. He had been playing with friends on the local allotment and it had begun to rain. The boys had taken shelter in a greenhouse where unripe tomatoes were growing. Finding a tin of red paint, the boys brought the unripe fruit nearer to the desired shade. The verdict was guilty and the fact was recorded in the unforgiving files of the Smethwick Constabulary. To the delight of the anti-Spencer campaigners even more criminal tendencies were to be unearthed.

A second brush with the law came a few months later – Bert was now ten. The charge was that of discharging a missile. It was during a winter snowfall. Bert and his friends were throwing snowballs on Cape Hill, Smethwick. A beat policeman spotted the gang of children and called for them to stop. The boys laughed, delivering a few well-aimed shots as they ran away. The policeman slipped over in the snow and the boys laughed some more. Like a caped crusader the officer of the law set off in hot pursuit and collared the young Bert. In court the policeman gave evidence that one of the snowballs had narrowly missed the driver of an open sports car; *'an open sports car in a snowstorm?'* thought the juvenile. This would not be the first time Bert would be exposed to the dubious business of police 'verballing' – where the police gave false statements to try and secure a guilty verdict. The incident made the local headlines, 'Youth fined 5/- for discharging a missile on Cape Hill.' However, that was only part of his punishment – guilty of nothing more than hijinks, he was also sentenced to 28 days in a remand home. The 'home' was a latter day Dotheboys Hall, made famous by Dickens in his third novel, *Nicholas Nickleby*. The regime was brutal and the punishments Draconian. Random beatings were the norm and laundry work where bare hands were immersed in near scalding water was a regular punishment drill. It was not a happy time for Bert Spencer. Despite the criminal injustice of his punishment, the incident does not seem to have sown the seeds of rebellion against authority in him. The understandably predictable reaction appears to have completely by-passed the easy going Bert. This was proved a few years later when Spencer received a police commendation for assistance given to outnumbered policemen in a riot situation in a shopping precinct in Stourbridge. Many would have found their good intentions swamped by bitter memories.

Shortly after his release from the remand home Bert was badly burned while playing around a bonfire of tarpaulin and tyres. With burning rubber flaming on his back he ran in panic until he dropped. The third degree burns affected a lung and he lay in hospital initially in a life-threatening condition. Release from hospital was followed by a long recuperation in bed at home. After he had regained his health Bert resumed his work ethic, fitting in attendance at school between a host of part-time jobs. It was to be another fifteen years, aged 25, before he fell foul of the law again.

This time the offence was office breaking and larceny. The punishment was a twenty-five pound fine. The felony was committed with three friends. The wife of one of them worked at a company whose offices were a wooden shed. The cash drawer was never fastened. The wife told her husband and the husband told his friends. It was a tempting prospect to the four young, married men with commitments. They simply walked in to the empty office one evening and took the money from the drawer. The proceeds of the robbery amounted to fifty pounds – twelve pound ten shillings each. That was the extent of Bert Spencer's criminal record between 1940 and November 1979.

These blots on the Spencer escutcheon were brought up to suggest a predisposition to crime. This small catalogue of transgression, in the eyes of Paul Foot, was a criminal tendency and capable of escalating into armed robbery and child-murder.

By 1968 the Spencers, his wife Janet and daughter Janell had, by sheer hard work, achieved their ambition and were able to leave behind the streets of Smethwick and their rented home in Rupert Avenue. Moving to Ascot Gardens in Wordsley, on the very edge of the countryside, seemed like a dream come true, but it was a move that was to lead to disaster. About two miles from their new home stood Holloway House Farm. The owner was Hubert Wilkes, who Bert was to befriend and then shoot in cold blood.

Ashwood Lower Lane follows the course of a Roman road. Beside it, set in a dip in the rolling countryside is Holloway House. Today it has been impressively refashioned in rural renaissance style. It stands behind high walls and fences and the front door is approached down a long sweep of drive. Nearly forty years ago it presented a different picture. The architects had not then moved in on the traditional farmhouse and changed forever the image of an archetypal rural idyll, a façade of rustic tranquillity, typical of an England that probably never was. And so with Holloway House itself, a mirage underlain by a cauldron of emotional disturbance.

It was a busy working farm, home of the Wilkes family. The owner was Hubert Wilkes, a larger than life cartoon character – sometimes crotchety and cantankerous; he was not always a popular man. On the farm and on scattered patches of leased land sheep were raised and crops of barley, potatoes, swede and hay were grown. Close to the farmhouse, poultry was reared. There were some free-range hens, about 200, together with a small flock of cockerels and some 1,000 turkeys for the Christmas trade. Farm produce was sold outside the farmhouse.

The family consisted of Hubert Wilkes, his two adult sons Anthony and Phillip and two adult daughters, Betty and Jean. Betty was married and lived locally, the men lived at the farmhouse and Jean, an air hostess, working out of Elmdon airport, still spent some of her off-duty time back home at the farm.

Hubert Wilkes farmed some 300 acres, including about 50 acres at nearby Yew Tree Farm where he grazed sheep and grew barley, hay and potatoes. While he employed only three regular farm workers, his sons and a tractor driver, the nature of his business demanded that he take on part-time gang labour as the seasons demanded. The farm was not highly mechanised and the labour was needed to hand-pick, grade and sort the potato crops. The casual workers were also needed prior to Christmas during the frenzied period of poultry preparation. These part-time workers, mainly women, were drawn from the Wall Heath area of Wolverhampton. There was also a seasonal influx of travellers who often made camp north of the farm, at Gorse Corner, at the end of Doctor's Lane, a location that was later to feature in the Carl Bridgewater murder trial.

In the fields it was hard work in rough conditions performed by resilient people for minimal wages. No facilities or shelter was provided for these workers by the irascible and miserly Hubert Wilkes. Men and women, desperate to earn their pittance, had to urinate and defecate in the furrows and the hedgerows. Eventually, farmer Wilkes was persuaded to improve that particular situation. He had the body of an old post-office van towed into a field and dumped a few bales of hay inside as a concession to privacy and comfort.

Hubert Wilkes argued incessantly with the female potatoes pickers about their work tallies. He would stalk down the rows of filled plastic sacks in the ploughed up fields, chain-smoking his favourite Castella cigars, muttering continuously to himself as he counted and recounted, cursing at the women when he was proved wrong and getting cursed in return. The farmer made no effort to like or be liked in a sort of, 'take me or leave me' attitude. Often harshly described as peppery and sometimes publicly foul-mouthed, he could be at times unreasonable and aggressive toward his two sons.

In the way in which milestone events in people's lives are spawned in trivia, the start point identifiable only in hindsight, so did Bert Spencer first meet Hubert Wilkes. After lunching out one Sunday the Spencer's were driving home the long way, enjoying the country lanes. With only two miles to go before home they saw a sign that was to lead to several shattered lives. As the harbinger of tragedy and nightmares to come, it could have been more dramatic. It simply announced, in hand-painted lettering, on a roadside board; 'POTATOES FOR SALE'.

At the farm some two hundred yards away, the potato-seller was a short, portly figure, quite bald with a fringe of white hair above his ears. He was dressed like any farm-worker except for the leather money satchel strapped across his ample waist. The Spencer's chatted with him, telling how they had just moved into the district. Wilkes, for it was Hubert Wilkes, was naturally oblivious to the fact that his nemesis had arrived on his doorstep in the shape of this friendly stranger, Bert Spencer. Wilkes made pleasant small talk in his distinctively loud, high-pitched, squeaky voice. He presented an avuncular figure, offering no hint of the dark undercurrents, which swilled, about his sometimes over-imaginative mind. Bert, not realising that he was addressing the owner of the farm, was unable to let a potential work opportunity pass by.

"Do they take on casual labour here, mate?" asked Bert, glancing towards the working fields surrounding the farm.

The farmer conceded that he did and took a note of Bert's name and telephone number. And so was set in motion a roller-coaster which was slowly to gather impetus over the next ten years, before exploding into a scene of terrifying and seemingly inexplicable burst of murderous violence.

Bert Spencer began his part-time work at Holloway House farm a few weeks later. As just another casual worker it was some time before the strange atmosphere at the farm began to draw him in. Hubert Wilkes treated Bert fairly in a normal employer-worker relationship, paying promptly and never querying Bert's stated hours of work. The men became friends.

"However, Hubert Wilkes' attitude towards his elder son, Anthony, was quite different," explains Spencer today. "Pay-day was almost invariably a time for confrontation between father and son – an occasion for raised voices, clenched fists and aggressive posturing as the farmer went through the weekly ritual of casting doubt upon the number of hours Anthony had worked."

Phillip, the younger of the brothers, by far the quieter had less regular problems with his father, but, even so, rows still broke out. The pair indulged in two-way criticism, regardless of the company around them.

Once, provoked beyond endurance by yet another verbal attack from his father, Phillip, competent, hard-working and conscientious, was driven to shout, "You old bastard. If you died tomorrow I wouldn't come to your funeral!"

A low boiling point and a short fuse seemed to be part of the genetic pattern common to all of the Wilkes family, as Bert was frequently to

witness. However, his part-time work at the farm became increasingly regular and was to build up to some 40 hours a week, a considerable slice
of his required domestic budget. And there were other pleasing aspects
to Bert working at Holloway House Farm. He was allowed to shoot the
land, sometimes with Phillip as a companion, and Hubert Wilkes would
lend him a shotgun at times when he did not possess one himself. Gradually, Wilkes senior began to adopt an increasingly friendly attitude towards
the adaptable ambulance man, seeing in Bert someone who could turn his
hand to most things. There was a certain bivalence in the relationship that
was building up. While taking his part-time employee under his wing, the
farmer was growing to rely upon him in many ways and Bert became both
his friend and his confidant. Never once did Hubert Wilkes point his lethal
tongue in Bert's direction.

The farmhouse was comfortable and immaculately kept by a house-
keeper, a pleasant, middle-aged woman from Romsley. Wilkes' daily habit
was to take lunch in the large, quarry-tiled kitchen. The table was big
enough to seat ten people but Wilkes senior chose to eat alone. Strangely,
his sons chose or were made to eat outside, in the fields, a barn or one of the
cluster of outbuildings. This applied in all seasons and all weathers, while
the farmer himself enjoyed the comfort of the coal-fired Aga. However, after
about a year, he began to invite Bert to join him while his sons still dined
outside like the casual hired hands.

It was just another factor in the constantly demonstrated mutual dis-
like, bordering on hatred, which existed between the males of the Wilkes
family. It was quite a different relationship from that which Hubert Wilkes
fostered with his daughters. In the ten years that Bert was to know the
family no mention was ever made of Hubert's wife, there weren't even any
photographs of her on show – either as an individual or in a family group.
Local rumour had it that the lady had lived for years in a mental home. If it
was true, Hubert Wilkes was never known to make any visits.

There were other rumours too, rumours presumably more soundly
based than those about Mrs Wilkes, as they were sourced from Hubert

Wilkes himself and constantly fuelled by his repetitive bragging. Oblivious to any disgust generated in his audience he would tell the tale of bizarre sexual orgies organised by him in bygone days. He claimed that these nights of alcoholic-induced passion were enjoyed with a like-minded group of married young farmer friends at Bromsgrove.

Bert chose to ignore the local speculation and to dismiss the farmer's Pompeii-like stories as the fantasies of an old man. Holloway House Farm had become part of Spencer's life and he had no wish to sacrifice its benefits because of an old man's strange predilections. Events were to prove that it would have been immeasurably better if he had.

Bert enjoyed the general work around the farm, tending the garden, looking after the sheep in the scattered fields and creating order in the cluttered outbuildings. He played chauffeur to the farmer, who liked a drink, in his comfortable BMW car. There were crops to plant, harvest fences to mend, locks to fix, and the Polytunnel greenhouse to work in when the weather was bad. There were also maintenance and decorating jobs in the farmhouse itself. Sometimes Bert would go shooting at night with Phillip. They would hunt in the Land Rover, using a torch beam to target rabbits for the pot and foxes to reduce the losses from the poultry stock. After a year or so, Bert's wife, Janet, began visiting the farm, initially to use her secretarial skills to keep the farm accounts in order. Later on there would be social occasions with Bert who had never relayed to his wife any information regarding the darker side of the old farmer. The fact that the man delighted in telling risqué tales and kept a stock of girlie magazines in the converted coalhouse, which he used as an outside office, paled into insignificance beside the benefits Bert enjoyed from the association.

Hubert Wilkes was a lonely man, distanced from his sons and beginning to outlive some of his contemporaries. He would regularly visit the Spencer's at their home and return their hospitality in evenings at the farm. Occasionally the three would drive into the country for a drink with Bert acting as chauffeur. Hubert enjoyed the company of the younger couple and always looked forward to the visits of his unmarried daughter, Jean.

At home in his comfortable lounge, Hubert Wilkes was a tolerant host. The bottles from which he poured so generously were kept on a large, ornately carved dresser. On one wall hung an Edwardian clock with a distinctively loud tick – a detail that was to have some significance in the aftermath of the tragedy to come. A large aerial photograph of the farm decorated one wall, long before such photographs became commonplace. On another wall hung a portrait in oils of his daughter Jean – unusual only in the fact that no picture of his wife was anywhere on display, but a detail which too was to assume later significance in the analysis of the outrage yet to occur.

Gradually it became obvious that Hubert Wilkes, only in his sixties, was developing some form of dementia. Always the eccentric, the downward slide had been almost imperceptible over the years. In the six months before his death there was to be a rapid acceleration. For years the farmer had daily shown signs of strangeness, constantly muttering to himself as he walked the environs of the farmhouse, sometimes holding fierce two-way arguments with a non-existent companion. Among his phobias was his hatred of dogs – quite natural for a sheep farmer, but he also worried constantly about being robbed. He often accumulated considerable amounts of cash, after a few good selling days of farm produce, but seldom would he deposit his money in the massive safe, which was located in his office inside the farmhouse. Instead, he would get Bert to accompany him across the yard to the barn where the barley was stored.

"Across the door he kept a wooden pallet weighted down with a scrap lorry engine," explains, Bert. "I would drag this aside and Hubert would enter the barn and hide the cash in holes which he scooped in the grain. The safe remained empty. He was also highly concerned too about the possibility of a raid on his Christmas turkeys."

Instead of relying on a barking guard dog, for several weeks before Christmas the farmhouse would bristle with weaponry like some hill-billy residence in the feuding season. Shotguns were propped besides doors and windows, with loose and boxed cartridges to hand.

The armoury consisted of three 12-bore shotguns, one single and two double-barrelled, a single-barrelled 410 shotgun, a double-barrelled 410 and two air rifles. Ammunition was everywhere – beside the guns, on window ledges, in the sliding-door kitchen cabinet, in both the indoor and outside offices and in the passenger side dashboard of the Land Rover. Hubert Wilkes was prepared to repel intruders with CIA resolve, to terminate with extreme prejudice or so he was fond of paraphrasing in his usual colourful language.

Over the years during which Bert Spencer worked at the farm, the hostility between father and son, Hubert and Anthony, escalated to a serious level. Hubert constantly goaded and provoked his elder son. He displayed a constant miserly attitude towards him while he himself wore hand-made shoes, chain-smoked cigars and drove a large expensive motorcar. Hubert Wilkes made no secret of the family tensions. He would pour out his complaints to just about anyone who was inclined to listen. But it was to Bert Spencer that the farmer turned when the quarrels spilled over into violence.

Anthony Wilkes was a strong, heavily built man, about five foot ten inches in height and weighing some fifteen stone. His father was small, portly and ailing.

Bert takes up the story, "One lunchtime Hubert drove his Land Rover to the field where Phillip and I were working. Hubert was visibly bruised and in a state of distress. He claimed that Anthony had punched him, tried to strangle him and had thrown him down the stairs."

The altercation had taken place because, as usual, Hubert had queried Anthony's claim for overtime and suggested that his son had been drinking in Wolverhampton instead of working. Also there were a dozen khaki Campbell ducks, which had disappeared from the farm. There had been no trace of a fox attack and Hubert had accused his son of stealing them, heaping insult upon insult. Phillip had heard it all before. It was an oft-repeated scenario.

There was ongoing trouble about sheep stealing. Several times there
had been stock missing and it followed a regular pattern. There would be
sheep droppings on a track adjacent to one of the sheep fields, the traces
ending suddenly where the animals had obviously been loaded into a vehicle. The flocks were disappearing in sixes and dozens. Again Hubert Wilkes
jumped to the conclusion that Anthony was responsible. When his junk-
filled outer office was broken into and a paltry amount of cash taken, he
blamed Anthony for that as well. Finally, the farmer searched his son's red
Cortina and found two thousand pounds in cash beneath the spare wheel.
Hubert Wilkes raved hysterically and showed the money to Bert who calmed
him down and advised him not to act hastily, suggesting that the money
could easily have been sourced from successful betting. The farmer agreed
not to confront Anthony and replaced the money back in the boot.

So virulent had the farmer and son relationship been over such a long
period that Bert was given to wondering how it had all begun and if it had
its roots in some unspeakable past family trauma. The mother who was
never mentioned perhaps, or had Hubert Wilkes' indiscriminate and loud
bragging about his earlier sex exploits come to his son's attention? It would
have been difficult to avoid as Hubert was given to telling the tale regardless
of time, place or company, in the farmyard, in the working fields and in the
local pubs. He was surely only voicing the warped fantasies induced by the
onset of senility or fuelled by alcohol – maybe the old farmer had simply an
unusual brand of humour. Or was there even something worse which was
responsible for the constant electric atmosphere at the farm?

It was this turn of events about which Bert Spencer could not bring
himself to speak at his trial. And he was certain that if he did elect to give
evidence, all of the skeletons in the cupboard of Hubert Wilkes would have
come rattling out – with disastrous results.

Whatever the reasons behind the family feud, it continued unabated.
A few days after his finding the money in the red Cortina, Hubert greeted
Bert's arrival at the farm by brandishing a copy of the local newspaper, the
Express & Star. He was almost dancing with rage. The cause of his anger

was a newspaper account of a thwarted attempt at sheep stealing at a local farm. A farmer had been walking his land at dusk and had interrupted a small band of men rounding up his sheep.

'They had with them a lorry and a red Cortina car,' explains, Bert. 'The farmer had produced, of all things, a loaded Luger semi-automatic pistol and loosed off a round or two at the red Cortina. He proudly claimed to have achieved a hit, regardless of his own breaking of the law.'

Yet again, Hubert Wilkes associated the incident with Anthony, especially when his son failed to bring home the red Cortina, saying it was at a local garage. Wilkes' attempts to trace the vehicle around the garages were unsuccessful. When Anthony brought it home a few days later there was not the slightest trace that it had been holed by a bullet and subsequently repaired. Instead of letting the matter rest, farmer Wilkes made an assumption and promptly sacked his son. Anthony went out and returned home drunk. He physically attacked his father and turned on his sister, Jean, when she tried to intercede. That night, threatened with the police, Anthony left the farm, sacked from his accommodation as well as his job. After dark, late the next evening, when Jean was alone in the farmhouse, Anthony returned. The farmhouse was locked and bolted. He tapped on a window. Jean switched on the security floodlight. Her brother was swaying in the yard.

"Let me in, Jean," Anthony called out, adding, "I've come to give you twenty-five pounds to apologize for yesterday."

Two days later he was reinstated at the farm and had moved back into his old quarters.

Inevitably the feud was to erupt again. It was four months before Christmas and there was yet another argument over pay and hours.

"This was un-witnessed but again Hubert drove out to the field where Philip and I were harvesting barley," says, Spencer. "Wilkes senior staggered from his Land Rover, scratched, blood spattered and in a state of extreme shock. In his usual style of exaggeration he claimed that Anthony had tried to kill him, said that again he had been thrown down the stairs and that

Anthony had pushed a loaded 12-bore shotgun into his face, tearing a nostril in the process.'

Philip was unimpressed, the strength of his father's claims being diluted by familiarity.

Hubert climbed back into the Land Rover and drove off. Shortly afterwards his daughter Betty and her family drove into the field looking for her father. Philip still showed no interest in the story and Bert set off with Betty and her husband to search the twisting lane to the farm. On the canal towpath, near to Gothersley Lock, they found the Land Rover parked, empty, with the driver's door hanging open. Believing her father to have taken his life in a canal plunge, Betty was, by now, quite hysterical as the men combed the canal side bushes. Eventually, Bert found the farmer alive, crouched and hiding in a large clump of bracken. The man was pale, trembling and obviously terrified. Bert helped him into the Land Rover and drove back to the farm. The family gathered in the yard, afraid to enter the farmhouse. Anthony was still inside.

"Don't go near the bastard. He'll kill me," howled Hubert Wilkes.

Bert found Anthony in the kitchen, frothing, hyperventilating and pacing like a caged animal. Ignoring him as well as Hubert's advice, Bert made a tray of tea, added a bottle of whisky from the Edwardian dresser and took it outside, hoping to calm the frightened family. Behind him the farmhouse door was kicked shut. Inside, the telephone began to ring, unanswered and insistent. Bert went in to take the call. It was Anthony's girlfriend. Anthony muttered into the handset, rushed out into the yard, leaped into his car, reversed into the Land Rover and roared away.

On one memorable night old man Wilkes had visited the Spencer's at their cosy home in Wordsley. On leaving, while standing on the half-moon steps, bidding them goodnight, in the full light of the street lamp the old farmer suddenly turned, opened his trousers, and began to urinate on the rockery. The Spencer's, standing in shocked surprise, were torn between laughter and the need to remonstrate with the old man. Laughter won the day as the farmer waddled down the path to his Land Rover.

Bert had kept Janet in ignorance of the more shady side of Hubert Wilkes' character. Later with fuller knowledge after the tragedy, she was to remonstrate with him for letting her share the old man's company on their accounting evenings. Bert's reasoning at the time was fourfold. The old man was physically harmless – Bert was always present when Janet was in Hubert's company – Holloway House Farm was an important factor in their household economy and pre-Christmas was a busy and lucrative time of the year. Also he saw no reason to add to Hubert's own broadcasting of his strange quirks. He was quite confident that he could cope with anything that the mounting tension at the farm could generate – but Bert had reckoned without himself as part of the equation.

Bert was already toying with the idea of leaving Holloway House Farm. He loved the work, the income and he liked both Jean and Phillip. But the atmosphere was getting extremely tense, almost by the day. Without wishing to, he had obviously made an enemy of Anthony, simply by supporting his father, who was getting worse by the week. The farmer was becoming preoccupied with his memories, or what he claimed were his memories. At every opportunity he would launch into graphic descriptions of the bizarre format of the sexual social evenings, which he organized for his young farmer friends in earlier days. While pretending to participate in the drinking sessions, the men, by pre-planning, would remain sober while the women were liberally plied with alcohol. Hubert Wilkes would then mix what he called his 'special cocktail'. Devised by himself to his own formula, this combination of alcohol and a prescription drug would induce in the women a temporary semi-coma, render the recipient inhibition-free and also serve to haze the memory a sort of homemade modern Rohypnol. The after-effects were, he would say, nothing more than a mild hangover and only a dim recall of the previous night, albeit a night of wife-swapping and group sex.

With the women in a state of chemically induced permissiveness, even eagerness, the men would pick and mix their partners at will, in scenes more reminiscent of ancient Rome than modern England. So claimed Hubert Wilkes.

These wild flights of fancy, always with sexual connotations, he would share with a wink and a leer, and usually accompanied by a high-pitched laugh. It is only repeated now because it was part of the train of causal factors, which led to an evening of stark tragedy.

Whatever the reason, for what appeared to be quickening deterioration, the farmer was so much beyond the pale that Bert knew he could not continue his association with Holloway House and its residents. Christmas was the problem. It was turkey time. There was good money to be earned and there would be difficult explanations to make to Janet. His procrastination of a few weeks was the worst decision Bert would ever make. Bert's ever increasing mental turmoil was to add a raw edge to other factors and the combination would precipitate an act of ultimate violence. It would result in the ruination of the lives of both the Wilkes and the Spencer families. And it all began with a cheap, hand-painted sign, 'POTATOES FOR SALE'.

4.

Connections and Investigations

• •

Yew Tree Farmhouse was long defunct as the hub of a working farm by 1978. It had been this way since Bert Spencer began working for Hubert Wilkes in 1969. Jack Foulkes owned the land and the farmhouse. Elderly cousins, Fred Jones and Mary Poole retained the tenancy of the farmhouse. Hubert Wilkes leased the land from Jack Foulkes.

30 yards before the junction of Lawnswood Road and the A449 is the entrance to a rough and narrow public footpath, which runs past fields and woodland down to the River Stour and the Stourbridge canal. Just 30 yards in from Lawnswood Road entrance, the short driveway to the rear of the farmhouse leads off to the right. Across this driveway was a thick hedge, long removed, passable through a wicket gate.

It was at this gate that the elderly residents of Yew Tree used to stand. There was often movement of vehicles or people along the track to watch or to wave to. The footpath is a haunt for ramblers and blackberry pickers, dog walkers and courting couples. Although a public footpath it is often used by drivers as an extended lay-by or, at its junction with the driveway of the farm, as a turning point.

For the first six years of his part-time employment with Hubert Wilkes, Bert's only contact with Mary Poole and Fred Jones was a cheery, passing wave, although he had begun to occasionally shoot on the farmland with Philip Wilkes, often using a shotgun borrowed from Wilkes senior. The first time that he actually visited the farmhouse itself was in about 1974. He was working with Anthony Wilkes, trimming the protruding tree branches with a chainsaw despite the persistent deluge. The chainsaw broke down and Bert went with Anthony to ask if they could use the telephone to contact Philip, Anthony's brother, at Holloway House Farm. At that time there were three elderly people at the farmhouse, as it included Mary Poole's husband, Jack. Bert and Anthony Wilkes were asked in out of the rain. Anthony was directed to the telephone, which stood on a small table into the hallway to the right. While he spoke to his brother, Philip, Bert stood just inside the living room. This was the first of the three occasions on which Bert Spencer was to set foot inside Yew Tree farmhouse. He was to make just one more visit, regarding the shotgun for sale, before the murder and one about five months afterwards – for the auction of the contents.

In 1976 Bert made his second visit to the farmhouse. His purpose was to enquire about buying a shotgun from Jack Poole. Bert had never seen the gun, nor did he know Jack, but farm talk had it that the gun was an old, heavy 12-bore and that Mr Poole had long since ceased to use it. From time to time, Bert traded in both antiques and shotguns, as he was both licensed and equipped to do, rarely keeping one long enough to call it his own.

Mr Poole told Bert that the gun was kept 'up the hill' and gestured in the direction of Yew Tree Cottage. He said that he would think about selling the gun and invited him to write his details in the address book, which was on the telephone table. Bert went through to where Anthony had made his telephone call and made the required entry and also included in Hubert Wilkes' telephone number for ease of contact. In that hallway stood a low dresser on which stood a large, magnificent glass case over four feet long. It contained a family of stuffed foxes – to anyone with a liking for the taxidermist's art it was an object of beauty. As a part-time dealer in antiques, Bert was taken with the unusual piece.

While the whole short visit was, at the time, of less than passing importance, it was to prove to be portentous in the extreme in the analysis of the murder to come. Had Jack Poole decided to sell his shotgun on that day, and Bert's details were not required in the old people's address book, maybe the course of several lives might have been altered. Bert would have used the gun and then, as was his habit, sold it on. Bert seems to have inherited from his father, Leonard, his leaning towards the general dealer's lifestyle as well as his physical likeness. Even in his immaculately kept home, Bert would sell on and replace the antique clocks, pictures and mirrors after enjoying them for their visual and tactile pleasures.

Had Bert Spencer not written his personal details in the address book at Yew Tree Farm then a vital piece of exonerating evidence would not have existed. Had he not seen the glass-caged foxes, establishing his interest in Yew Tree Farm antiques, another link would have been severed. Also he probably would not have made his third visit to the farmhouse, some months after the murder, for the farm contents auction. A visit made in the sure and certain knowledge that the house would have the police investigators there in strength. It was hardly the sort of encounter which anyone harbouring feelings of guilt would seek, and by that time, like thousands of others, Bert had already had two interviews with the police who were nothing if not vigorous in their questioning techniques. After all, the murder of young Carl Bridgewater had sent shudders of horror through the nation and beyond. The public outcry for the speedy arrest of the killer or killers was creating quite daunting pressure at all levels. Coincidentally I did attend this auction with my parents, although I have little recollection of the event. On the day, the farmhouse was packed tight. Many at the sale were, no doubt, some of those twisted souls who delight in attending scenes of past macabre happenings – I hope I was not there for such reasons. Detective Chief Superintendent Bob Stewart was there with his team, mingling with the crowd. Hubert Wilkes made a practice of attending all local big-house auctions and he was there with his son, Philip, and Bert Spencer. Bert's obvious interest was in the display case of foxes. He had been at work on the viewing day and still had no idea of the contents of the rest of the sprawl of rooms. Again the place was packed too tightly for anyone to move about freely, but there was nothing else in the catalogue of particular interest to him anyway. He was outbid for the foxes, and that was Bert's last visit to the farmhouse.

Of course, he did know the actual surrounding farmland well, having worked on them part-time for some 10 years. None of which accounts for the unsubtle slanting of facts and the emphasis and innuendo, which Paul Foot applied in order to bolster his case against Bert Spencer.

In his book, *Murder at the Farm*, Mr Foot states, 'He (Bert Spencer) had also built up a close association with Yew Tree Farm and its tenants, Fred Jones and Mary Poole. He was a frequent visitor to the farm both as a worker and as a guest. He used to borrow Jack Poole's gun to shoot rabbits on the farm. He had been inside the farmhouse on several occasions and was known to admire the antiques in it. His name was in the old people's private telephone book.'

These inaccuracies contained in just one paragraph would be permissible trivia in any context other than a possible effort to implicate an innocent man of this heinous crime. Bert Spencer had never visited Yew Tree Farm as a guest; nor had he ever borrowed or knowingly held Jack Poole's shotgun. Ironically, in a twist of extreme fate, the gun would feature strongly in the bizarre shooting of old farmer Wilkes, which is covered in *Chapter 6 – A Cocktail for Murder*. The fact that Bert had written his personal details in the address book at the farm was actually to add great weight in his favour in the investigation into Carl's murder. As the police were to note and remark, no one would set out to rob a house, commit murder there, and knowingly leave behind a telephone book containing his name, address and telephone number, written in his own near-copperplate hand, particularly when the book lay in open view in its usual place on the hall table by the glass-caged foxes.

However, by building crafted innuendo upon inaccuracy almost any desired image can be created. The resulting vague mass of swirling half-truths and selective comment, if stirred about well enough, can be made to solidify into a passable representation of positive fact. Then, imaginative and creative 'reconstruction' can be passed off as documentary truth. All that is then required is time, repeated exposure to a wide audience and a guarantee of no possible litigation, effective protest or right to reply. Paul Foot and Ann Whelan have enjoyed all of these prerequisites to the full and have had a free hand to pass brass off as gold. The pages following show just how public opinion was moulded and manipulated in the campaigners' efforts to manipulate a case against Bert Spencer. This was at a time high-ranking police investigators repeatedly took the opposite stance on the basis of firm and positive facts.

I think to a degree the award winning journalist, Paul Foot, wrote what he believed and believed what he wrote. There was venom in his words, and a passion that reflected the hunting of a vile beast, who he undoubtedly believed was Spencer, but there was little malice in his text.

The murder investigation gathered in some 7,000 people for interview, some more than once. Bert Spencer was one such, a fact that the campaigners were to use and build on to such an extent that they were to claim that he was actually the 'prime suspect' in the case. Two things brought the police to Bert's door. Initially they arrived in the course of following up one of the stream of telephone calls, which well publicized or peculiarly horrific murders invariably cause. Such calls are prompted by a variety of factors, motives and personality traits. The reasons range from the entirely genuine wish to further the course of justice to the spirally descending ramblings of the unbalanced and the downright malicious.

According to the police, in conversation with Bert Spencer, this particular call was made by a female member of the ambulance service. After all Bert was known to work at Yew Tree Farm in his off-duty hours, he had shot on the farmland and was interested in antiques and someone saw significance in that. The facts were that, at the time of the murder, Bert had not worked on Yew Tree land for some months, nor had he been shooting there for almost a year and it was disputed, despite Paul Foot's insistence to the contrary, that Bert owned a shotgun at the time. In Foot's book, *Murder at the Farm*, Ann Whelan also claims this to be untrue. In late 1992, Whelan was visiting Jimmy Robinson, who had just completed an 81-day protest on the roof of Gartree prison. Whelan was in the visiting room of Winson Green, the prison Robinson had been moved to shortly after the protest. A man she had met occasionally at car-boot sales came over to chat with her about the case. He introduced his wife – the couple were Worcestershire antique-dealers. The couple alleged to have sold Spencer a shotgun during the summer before the paperboy was shot. They claimed to have told the police. They were directed towards Michael Hickey's solicitor, Jim Nichol. They signed a formal witness statement on 4 June 1993. Bert totally refutes this fact and certainly it was established that the shotgun associated with him was sold a year before the murder. Having said that, at the time there were 50,000 gun licenses approved and this was sporting country.

It had been some six years, before the murder, since Bert had traded seriously in antiques. Six years since he and his then partner, Ken Farndon, had closed their shop in Wordsley High Street.

However, all that was beside the point. Bert Spencer had a solid alibi, an alibi, which was to be checked and rechecked and found to be pretty watertight. He was at his workstation in an open-plan area at Corbett Hospital.

The next police visit to the Spencer household was occasioned by the vehicle sighting report made by Mr Roger Edwards, although it was relatively early in the afternoon, 2.50 pm - one and a half hours before the murder. There were a further nine, possibly ten, more significant sightings between then and the estimated time of the murder. However, Edwards view was one of the clearest sightings of the day, although it was to pale into insignificance beside the weight of eyewitness evidence, which combined to push sightings of quite a different vehicle to the forefront of the investigation.

Roger Edwards had turned into Lawnswood Road off the A449 just as a pale blue Vauxhall Viva was turning left into the track way leading past Yew Tree Farm. The opening was approximately 30 yards from the junction with the A449. Mr Edwards described the driver as male, about 55 years of age, with dark, greying, wavy hair. He was wearing a dark blue uniform with a single pip on his tunic epaulette. He also wore no headgear. Together with Mr Edwards' particular recall of the driver's hair and apparent age, he also remarked that the car was reasonably new.

Bert Spencer's Viva was in anything but good condition. It was five years old and sold a few months later for a mere £175. Bert himself had brown hair, worn short, combed forward and without a hint of a wave or bend. It was confirmed by colleagues at the hospital that Bert Spencer never drove with his tunic jacket on and that at the first sign of sunshine he invariably drove wearing Reactolite lenses. The 19th of September, 1978, was sunny and his driving glasses would have been quite dark and very noticeable. Bert's jacket had not one but two pips on his epaulettes. He was also given to driving in British school of motoring style, hands at 'ten-to-two', making turns by threading the wheel through his hands: an incredibly small triviality, until played out in a future documentary surrounding the case.

It was years later, in March 1987, when Thames Television screened a pseudo-documentary on the Carl Bridgewater murder, based on Paul Foot's book, *Murder at the Farm*. The objective of both the book and the programme were aimed at exonerating the four men who were given long sentences for the killing of the paperboy – although Molloy had since died in prison in 1981. The main thrust was a somewhat far-fetched, but nevertheless effective, attempt to implicate Bert Spencer in the murder in the face of logic, reason and evidence to the contrary. In 'reconstructing' the Roger Edwards sighting, an actor was used to play the part of the driver of the Vauxhall Viva. He was wearing an ambulance service uniform with two shoulder pips, borrowed from a helpful ambulance officer. As he made the turn into the farm track he made a right arm movement as he turned the steering wheel. With the rising of his right shoulder only one-pip was visible.

Paul Foot was exultant. He hailed the scene as a dramatic discovery, which constituted 'new evidence'. The one-pip/two-pip factor became a pivotal point in the application for an Appeal Hearing in 1988, 10 years after the murder. At that hearing Paul Foot was accused of misleading the public. But, of course, by then some seven million members of the viewing public had seen the 'documentary', although relatively few would have heard or read the courtroom comment on Mr Foot's conduct. At the same hearing he was to suffer further disappointments, but that is leaping ahead in the saga.

Bert Spencer was to be involved in a curious incident, which was to have a delayed, but major impact upon the whole affair. It was to be a story of small beginnings but it was to endure as a setback and a question mark for Bert of the next 10 years. The incident took place on the evening of

Saturday 23 October, 1978 and was forgotten for over a year until it was exhumed by events. The extraordinary and peculiar incident is covered in full during *Chapter 5 – The Piece of Card*.

In the meantime the police investigation continued unabated, having discounted any connection with Bert Spencer and the murder of young Carl. He had been interviewed three times, the last time at Corbett Hospital. His friends and his work associates had been interviewed – even his previous partner of six years. His alibi had been the subject of multi-checks and found to be sound. He was eliminated from the inquiry to the satisfaction of the police and to that of the Director of Public Prosecutions. The only dissenting voices were to be those of Ann Whelan and Paul Foot's at a later date. The existence of a *Spencer Factor* in the case was stilled at birth, only to be unearthed by the campaigners.

Nine weeks after the murder at Yew Tree Farm there was yet another clumsy and violent robbery at a farmhouse occupied by elderly pensioners. While Vincent Hickey acted as driver and lookout, Michael Hickey, then only 16, and Jimmy Robinson, who was armed with a shotgun, carried out the attack. Their target was cash. Vincent Hickey and his girlfriend, Linda Galvin, had earlier conned the old people out of £350 by pretending that they would supply cut-price coal. The idea had come from coalman Alan Murray, who lived at Linda's flat, who had told the pair that the old man had paid for the coal from a tin full of money.

The tin became irresistible to Vincent Hickey, who recruited his young cousin, Michael Hickey. Michael recruited Jimmy Robinson with whom he had committed the armed robbery on the Tesco store at Castle Vale just a week before. In that violent affray, pick-handles were used and a shotgun was discharged.

Now the team of three were to attack Chapel Farm at Romsley, similarly armed despite their knowing that the residents of the farm were an 83-year-old man and his three aged sisters. Michael Hickey and Jimmy Robinson burst into the farmhouse. The masked pair then abused, terrified and assaulted the four old people, knocking one old lady to the ground when their demands for cash met with resistance. Finally they made their getaway with a haul of several hundred pounds, leaving the old people in a state of shock and distress, some physical injury and a lifetime of nightmares.

An alert window cleaner had seen Michael Hickey and Jimmy Robinson running to the getaway car and noted its number. The car was traced to Linda Galvin. Miss Galvin lived with Vincent Hickey, and Michael Hickey had already been interviewed during the investigation into the murder of Carl Bridgewater. Vincent's criminal record and ownership of a blue Ford Cortina estate had also drawn him into that net. Now, the similarities between the two crimes, at Yew Tree Farm and Chapel Farm, were screaming of a connection. Within a few days Linda Galvin was arrested and Vincent Hickey was now a wanted man.

While Vincent was trying to dodge the police (they had already raided his distraught mother's house) he claims a seed of an idea struck him. He had bought a lunchtime edition of the *Birmingham Evening Mail*, the leading headline screamed at him; 'CARL LINK IN FARMHOUSE RAID?' Anxiously, Vincent read the article, which linked the Chapel Farm armed robbery, which he had masterminded, with the murder of the paperboy at Yew Tree Farm.

After spending a few days on the run Vincent Hickey gave himself up to the police. He quickly realised that this time, like with his recent brush with the law, grassing up his fellow accomplices would not help. In that instance, when cornered, although he had received his monetary share of the robbery, he had given the police all the names of those involved – including three cousins. However, this was far more serious. This was armed robbery, even if he was only the driver he was looking at a long stretch. As a gesture of goodwill, Vincent Hickey offered some names. He correctly named his cousin, Michael Hickey and Jimmy Robinson as having been on the robbery at Chapel Farm, Romsley. Alas, he offered John Burkett as the third member, saying he had nothing to do with it and only lent them his girlfriend's car. Burkett was a good choice as he was a known associate of Robinson and seasoned crook. Vincent went further. He also offered them the Tesco armed robbery that Burkett, Robinson and Michael Hickey had been a part of, in which a shotgun had been discharged.

It was not long before the detectives realised that Vincent Hickey was deliberately painting himself in a good light regards the Chapel Farm robbery. Eventually he crumbled and admitted being the driver. Hickey was once again in a corner. It may have been at this point, according to his testimony, he remembered the 'link' report in the *Birmingham Evening Mail*. The questioning had taken hours and it was now well after midnight. However, the detectives were interested in the team that informer Hickey, had given them.

Sergeant Dickens continued, 'What other jobs have they done?'

'I think they did a job at a jeweller's shop because they had a load of silver bracelets,' offered, Vincent.

'Anything else?' asked the sergeant.

At what would appear to be a routine line of enquiry and somewhat innocent question, Hickey paused, before saying, 'Our Michael says the older one did the Bridgewater murder.'

The other detective in the interview room, Superintendent Knight, could hardly contain himself.

'What's this?' he asked. 'Tell us about it.'

Hickey, holding court, obliged and went on, 'Our Michael told me that he'd told him he'd done the Bridgewater murder and one day I was with them when Michael said to him about it. That he'd done the murder. And he got rattled which isn't like him. He's not the type who gets rattled easily, but he was then, and he said, "turn it in" in that sort of voice.'

DS Dickens asked, 'Which is the one, the junkie (Burkett) or the other chap (Robinson), the one you know?'

'The other chap,' Vincent replied.

The ever helpful Vincent Hickey, the following evening, pointed out the flat where Robinson lived with his girlfriend and then took the police to the flat of Michael's grandmother where, he told them, Michael would be hiding out. The police did not move straight away, but kept the properties under surveillance.

The news of Hickey's statement had reached senior officers at Wombourne police station. They were greatly excited by the news. Rudimentary checks on Jimmy Robinson made him an ideal suspect. Here was a known armed robber, who had robbed a lonely farmhouse with the help of a shotgun, being named by Hickey as the Bridgewater murderer.

On the afternoon of 6 December, 1978, the day Vincent had pointed out Robinson's house, he was visited in Bromsgrove police station by Detective Chief Superintendent Robert Stewart, the officer in charge of the whole Bridgewater inquiry. He was flanked by other big guns, Detective Superintendent Eric Lycett and DCI Weslea Watson.

'I understand you have been saying things about who may be responsible for the murder,' said DCS Stewart, getting straight to the point.

'Well, it's nothing really, 'replied Hickey. 'Only what I've heard.'

Stewart wanted names of all those involved at Yew Tree Farm.

Once again Vincent was only too happy to supply more information.

'It's Jimmy Robinson and that other one,' he said. 'The one with the bad teeth. They know who he is.'

'And Mickey (Michael Hickey), of course?' asked DCI Watson.

'Well, yes, he had been involved with Jimmy and that older man. Someone has mentioned his name I think. Mickey has only been with them a short while. I think he replaced somebody on the team.'

'What are you saying, then?' Stewart interrupted.

Hickey replied, 'I think they did your job. Mickey is very young, you know, and talks a lot. He told me Robinson had done the shooting. I didn't believe it, but then another time Mickey said it when Robinson was present. He went bloody mad.'

The interview lasted only 15 minutes, but it impressed the officers enough to realise how important Hickey's information was. The excitement reached another level when an hour later Vincent identified Pat Molloy, an associate of Robinson's, as 'the man with bad teeth' who had taken part in the murder at Yew Tree Farm. Later that day both Molloy and Robinson had been arrested, although Michael Hickey slipped through the net.

Little by little, Vincent started to offer morsels of information about the Bridgewater murder. Quite often, which was exasperating to the detectives, he would contradict himself. He also rarely elaborated on his information, leaving loose ends that were often impossible to follow up.

Hickey was desperate to get off the charges from the Chapel Farm robbery, in Romsley; the police now knew he was the driver. Halfway through one interview, Vincent insisted on ringing DCI Knight. He demanded an assurance that charges would be dropped for the Chapel Farm job. The DCI explained that if Hickey helped them fully with the Bridgewater murder, he would personally submit a favourable report to the Director of Public Prosecutions recommending leniency. However, the detective stressed that if it was discovered that Vincent had been involved at Yew Tree Farm, there was no hope of any immunity with regards the murder.

This seemed to cheer Vincent up. Again he offered more rambling statements, most of which were public knowledge and had been written in the papers or broadcast on TV.

Sergeant Lessemun was getting more and more exasperated, 'You haven't told us a single thing that makes me think you know.'

Vincent retorted that the newspapers had claimed that the vehicle was parked in the driveway of the farm. That was incorrect he said. It had in fact 'floated about', as he had done in Linda Galvin's car at the Chapel farm robbery. However the police were not impressed. Yes there were conflicting sightings of vehicles around Yew Tree Farm, on the afternoon of the murder, but evidence certainly pointed to at least one being stationary at the farm for some time. Again they pressed for more information.

'The farmhouse has no hallway,' replied Hickey. 'You go through the back door and the living room is on the right.'

At last the officers showed interest and some respect for Vincent's information.

'How do you know that?' asked Sergeant Lessemun, excitedly.

'I know a lot more than that,' boasted Hickey, pleased at last to have the detective's attention. 'But give me what I want and I will give you what you want.'

Actually this particular snippet was in the public domain. During a reconstruction of the paperboy's last movements, a camera crew had followed Carl's school pal into the farmhouse and its topography could be plainly seen. Clearly moved by Hickey's knowledge of the inside of the farmhouse, they moved on to the gun. Robinson had almost straight away confessed to the Chapel Farm robbery, and, one would assume, hoping to clear himself for the Bridgewater murder, told them where to find his buried weapon.

'It could be the same as the one used on the Romsley job,' offered Vincent.

He then asked if the gun retrieved from Jimmy Robinson had been the murder weapon. The detectives explained that they had not had the ballistics report yet. Hickey went on to explain that the gun he had seen had 'silver engraving' on it. The gun recovered had no such markings.

After a prolonged game of cat and mouse, they would not give him bail and he was becoming more and more desperate, Vincent claimed to be feeling ill and was shown outside the interview room to have a glass of water. As he was drinking, Sergeant Lessemun asked Hickey if he was on the Bridgewater job. Hickey nodded in the affirmative.

Lessemun then asked, 'Were you the driver?'

Again Hickey answered yes. He started shaking and reeling, and he was shown back to his cell. It was 3.20 pm, 8 December, 1978. There was a natural sense of optimism and relief amongst the officers – after all, Hickey had collapsed and admitted his involvement at Yew Tree. That initial admission would have catastrophic consequences for the Bridgewater Four. However, over the next 16 hours Vincent added nothing more as regards the murder inquiry. Again he asked for bail, but was once more refused.

Although the officers were patting each other on the back and extremely relieved at the decisive breakthrough, Vincent had only made a verbal admission. He would not sign the statement to having been the driver on the Yew Tree Farm affair. Added to that, everything he had said was public knowledge. Slowly, the interview team of DS Lessemun and the truculent DC Millington started to run thin.

After one fruitless exchange, where Vincent stated he would make no further comment, DC Millington snapped, 'All right then, just tell me what happened to the lad's paper bag?'

'I can't,' Hickey replied at once.

'Why not?' barked Millington.

''Cause I wasn't there,' Vincent replied.

'That's a turn around,' said a surprised Sergeant Lessemun.

'Yes,' replied, Hickey, simply.

He still insisted that Jimmy Robinson was the one they wanted, but insisted he had nothing to do with the murder and was not at Yew Tree Farm. This was possibly the lowest ebb for all the officers involved. Then, suddenly, when all seemed lost, a phone call came through from Wombourne police station. A jubilant officer explained that Molloy had confessed to being at Yew Tree Farm. He named three men who had been with him – Jimmy Robinson, Michael Hickey and Vincent Hickey. Also, it was not just a 'verbal' confession, as was Vincent's, but Molloy has *signed a statement*.

Pat Molloy was not a violent criminal. He had already steered clear of two armed robberies – Castle Vale Tesco store and Chapel Farm. It had been a habit of the Irishman to admit, when caught, what he had done and plead guilty. He was not a surly criminal like Vincent and Robinson, who were openly distrustful of authority. Pat, when interviewed by the police, wanted to help and please the officers.

After his arrest they had left Pat Molloy to stew in his cell, without contact, for twenty-four hours. Two seasoned Staffordshire detective constables, John Perkins and Graham Leeke then started to interview Molloy about the murder at Yew Tree Farm.

'I'd like to help you,' offered Molloy, adding, 'but I don't know anything about the matter.'

Perkins responded immediately, 'We believe you do. You're involved with men who have committed a similar burglary at Romsley.'

This went back and forth for some time with Molloy denying any knowledge of Yew Tree Farm and the murder. It appeared that the firmer his denials were, the more certain the officers became sure of his guilt. Following the original verbal confession made by Vincent Hickey, the detectives believed that staring back at them, in the shape of Pat Molloy, was a child murderer. Their anger began to rise.

They would leave it an hour and then go back in to his cell to interrogate the Irishman. Unbeknown to Molloy, DC John Robbins was seated outside the cell taking notes. There were no sophisticated recording devices used in those days. Often they would simply make notes and rested heavily on those to make out their reports and to reproduce statements. Not a very reliable system and obviously open to abuse – which was often the case. There is some confusion during the latter part of Molloy's interview sessions. It appears from the police notes that Molloy was not told of Vincent's verbal confession, where he named the Irishman as being part of the team at Yew Tree Farm.

At one point, recorded in the notes, Pat says, 'If others have told you I was there, they are telling lies.'

Certainly, when Molloy came to write and talk about those interviews later, he said the police had made it perfectly clear that he was only a major suspect because Vincent Hickey had named him.

On 10 December Detective Inspector Jeffrey Turner, who had been masterminding the Molloy interrogation from his upstairs office at Wombourne police station, started his interview with the Irishman.

'You have not told anyone that you were at Yew Tree Farm when the boy was shot,' he began.

'I wasn't there, Sir, I don't know anything about it,' offered a tired and somewhat bewildered Molloy.

'I know you were at the farm, Pat. Why do you think we are here?'

'If anyone has said anything about me, it must be because they want to protect someone.'

And later, 'I don't believe you because I know you were on the job. Why don't you tell the truth and get it off your chest,' offered Turner.

'You just want me to admit it to make it easy for you. You just want the job cleared up,' was Molloy's response.

'Patrick, we would not be doing our duty if we accepted a false admission from anyone just to clear the job up, and leave the killer free. You must realise how important it is for us to find those responsible.'

'I wish I could help, Sir, but I can't,' said Molloy sounding like a stuck record.

'You can't or you won't?' fired back the detective.

'I can't, Sir, believe me... You don't expect me to admit to something I haven't done.'

On and on it went, the same tough questions from the detectives and the same denials from the Irishman. The questions grew more and more repetitive, and more and more insistent. Molloy sank into long silences, which fed his interrogators some hope, as they believed they were getting closer to Molloy breaking down and confessing. They were about to be rewarded.

Following one fruitless path of enquiry, Inspector Turner stormed out of the cell. Sergeant Walker, who was left with Molloy, remembered that the suspect was, 'utterly shaken, licking his lips'. Molloy asked for a glass of water. He then asked to speak to the boss, meaning Chief Superintendent Stewart, and was told that that would take some time. Eventually Molloy asked if he could see 'the chap with the beard on his own'. Almost at once the bearded DC Perkins arrived in the cell. Walker left, and joined DC Leeke in the passage outside, who was making notes.

'I need advice. I need help. I'm in a terrible mess,' began Molloy.

'Pat, the only advice I can give to you is to be honest and straightforward. It's up to you,' replied Perkins.

Molloy dropped his head and sighed, 'I was there at the farm when that lad got shot, but I didn't know about the gun until after. I was told that it was Jimmy who did it, and it was an accident.'

Perkins said, 'Are you saying that you were involved in the burglary, but took no part in the murder?'

'Yes, Sir, that's right. I was upstairs looking for something of value. I was upstairs and heard a bang. I knew that it was a gun being fired. I went downstairs. They were still in the room. I heard Jimmy say it went off by accident. Then I ran out.'

As Molloy uttered this last sentence, DC Graham Leeke burst into the cell.

'You know Graham, Pat, don't worry,' said Perkins soothingly.

'I am worried. I'm terrified of the others. They have threatened me with personal injury,' blurted out Molloy.

'Who are the others, Pat? Do you mean the persons that were on the job with you?' asked Leeke.

'Yes, Sir,' replied Molloy.

'Well, who are they? We need to know the complete story,' asked Leeke, pushing home the advantage.

Molloy, head still bowed, responded, 'Vinny Hickey and his relation Mickey and Jimmy.'

It was after this outburst that Molloy agreed to make a full statement (4.00 pm, 10 December), to DC Perkins, commenting, 'I have been threatened by Vinny and Jimmy. I was told never to admit anything to do with this job, but to turn others in and the police would be satisfied.'

There was obvious jubilation and relief having secured this signed statement by Molloy after 80 days of relentless enquiry. He had cracked under intense interrogation. The story he had told corresponded in several crucial respects with the initial information from Vincent Hickey.

Following a hurried discussion, DCS Stewart decided to challenge the other two suspects in custody – Vincent Hickey and Jimmy Robinson – with Molloy's signed statement. Stewart reached Robinson's cell at 9.10 pm and dramatically produced the damning statement, which he read at once. Straight away he declared it was 'fucking rubbish', and 'a load of bollocks'. Vincent, when shown the same document, uttered more or less the same words. Robinson was in for a very rough ride and almost all of that Monday, 11 December, was taken up by various detectives, trying to make him admit he was involved in the murder of the paperboy. At one point Robinson got on to his hands and knees in the interview room floor, literally praying to be left alone on the murder charge.

I am not sure what happened to change Molloy's strong stance, in a relatively short time, with regards the 'confession'. We know initially his change in direction was fuelled by revenge and anger at being placed in the frame by Hickey. It is pretty apparent that Molloy was threatened, and probably physically attacked by one or more of the officers. It has also been established that Molloy was shown a forged, false statement from Vincent, naming the Irishman as being present at Yew Tree Farm. Serious doubt has been placed on the validity of the so-called verbatim statement. At least four leading experts, over the years, would more or less destroy the statement.

It is true that Vincent had made a verbal confession, in the early days of his arrest, which he says he made in an effort to secure bail. He never challenged this early confession, but he certainly withdrew it when he real-ised the Stafford detectives were not going to do a deal.

Following these early confessions by two men who alleged to be there on the afternoon of the murder – it should have been an easy downhill run for the police. Instead, they found themselves wallowing in a morass of con-flicting statements as Vincent Hickey made small offerings admixed with a welter of confusion. To add to this Pat Molloy's lack of substantial backup material made his constantly changing accounts seem like the offerings of a drink-befuddled amnesiac.

Michael Hickey was finally arrested in Birmingham after spending the night at a friend's house. Strangely, it was his own father, Joe, who brought the police to the door and it was Joe Hickey who entered the house, roused Michael and told him to get dressed as the police were waiting outside. There could be other explanations but it did appear that Joe had organised his biggest ever trade-off with the police. Perhaps he was prompted by the belief, shared with Michael's mother, that Michael could not be guilty of child murder. Joe knew that Michael had been party to the armed robberies at Tesco's and Chapel Farm and that his son could not stay in hiding from the police forever. On that basis, Joe, who undoubtedly loved his son, may have decided to manufacturer some credits out of the inevitable. It was 21 December, 1978.

The 17-year-old Michael Hickey was incredibly robust for his age – as his future rooftop protests would attest to. The police started their relentless questioning and he stood firm, saying over and over again, he knew nothing about the murder at Yew Tree Farm. Eventually Michael was shown the signed statement by Pat Molloy.

He read it and described it in the same way his cousin Vincent and Jimmy Robinson had used, 'That's a load of fucking bollocks.'

On 28 December Patrick (Pat) Molloy was charged with the murder of Carl Bridgewater. On 9 January, 1979, Vincent Hickey too was charged and nearly a month later, on 7 February, Jimmy Robinson and Michael Hickey were taken down the same road.

The men, who would later be forever known as The Bridgewater Four, passed committal and eventually a lengthy trial at Stafford Crown Court. On 9 November, 1979, Molloy was found guilty of manslaughter and the other three of murder. Public and judicial attitudes to child murder were reflected in the sentences. In most cases that would have been the end of the story of the gang-of-four but the convoluted tale was just beginning.

We have backtracked to the previous year to see how Bert Spencer himself unwittingly took a major step towards setting himself up as fodder for hostile guns. This he did in a simple public-spirited action, overshot with bewilderment and curiosity. It seemed that the police report was filed in some tray marked, 'permanently pending'. It was to take a second murder to resurrect the peculiar incident and for the pro-Bridgewater Four campaigners to convert it into a linchpin – fallaciously as it transpired, but it took almost 10 years for the fallacy to be publicly exposed. Even then, as Paul Foot's letters to Bert Spencer show, it was still to be waved in front of Bert as though its evidential value had not been thoroughly scotched in court.

Before examining that strange episode, some odd aspects of the tragic day at Yew Tree Farm demanded attention. While the murder of the 13-year-old paperboy is impossible to forget it is almost too horrific to contemplate dispassionately. It is difficult, therefore, to be objective about the analysis of the build-up and aftermath of events at Yew Tree Farm on that day. Time, paradoxically, does provide perspective but it also serves to blur the memory and to create distortions of convenience. However, emotional peaks do subside, if only in small measure, although the key facts remain unaltered.

In considering the events at Yew Tree Farm no attempt is made here to weigh the case against the Bridgewater Four – whose names were rightly cleared in a successful appeal in 1997. To a reader of discerning eye and analytical mind it may be that Paul Foot's own book, *Murder at the Farm*, provides ample damning pointers in that direction. It may be an unintentional by-product though and very far removed from Mr Foot's main aim. It is a simple matter to reshape, modify and blur past events through the medium of the small screen as Foot has demonstrated so successfully and possibly so unethically at times. Using the medium of cold, black print, devoid of emotive heartbeat thuds as a background to terse and dramatic narrative, like Don Shaw's movie, *Bad Company*, leaves invention at the leisured mercy of the questioning mind. Careful reading and an absence of tunnel vision are the only prerequisites in the game of spotting the potentially flawed argument, the non sequitur and the manifest weakness of Foot's chosen lines of narrative.

The passage of time leaves little chance of great addition being made to the key facts; solid conclusions cannot now be drawn. Some key figures in the case are dead and main locations have been pulled down or altered to a considerable degree. Lines and angles of vision have been obscured by luxuriant foliage and witness sightings cannot be faithfully replicated. Although some reasoned surmise can be made. There remain questions to be addressed and possibilities to be explored, or perhaps overridden at the time by the main aim of identifying the killer or killers of a young boy. Yew Tree Farm was demolished some years ago and a modern building was erected on the site and still stands today. Fortunately, a friend of mine, Alan Smithyman, conducted all of the building work. Alan was still in possession of the original plans for the farm buildings, outer buildings and surrounding farm area. His son Ben, who oversaw the actual work, very kindly walked me through the alterations and we viewed the many, many photographs taken before work began on the old farm.

Sidestepping the horrific murder itself, one of the strangest aspects of the whole affair was uncovered by the police search of the farm surroundings. As we have seen, items from the burglary – for a burglary it was before it became murder – were found, hidden rather than discarded, in scattered locations around the farmhouse. Two were items of china, one of silver plate, one of copper and a brooch. These articles were of at least the same value as others, which were stolen from the house and never subsequently traced.

Paul Foot hypothesises about a man; 'chucking the goods out of the car in a panic'. He goes on to suggest that perhaps only one vehicle was used by the robber and that items were discarded in view of their bulk and the difficulty of fitting them into one car boot, alongside the other missing and unrecovered articles. This he does in the hope of strengthening his deduction that the crime at Yew Tree Farm was effected by one man and one car.

The facts shout out a scenario altogether different. The directional scattering, the awkwardness of the terrain and the distances involved make a *panic discarding* a less than likely happening. It is hardly imaginable that anyone would discard a brooch on the grounds of excess bulk. A china jug and basin set was found undamaged some 20 yards away, the brooch slightly further, from the farmhouse in the thick undergrowth of the disused cattle yard. Further away still, an unbroken delicate china teapot was found; it was located about 40 yards from the farmhouse door, in front of a large damson tree in the same cattle yard.

True, the brooch could have been hurled the 30 yards and still have landed safely, cushioned by the ample undergrowth. However, to position the teapot and the jug, plus the bowl set, would have involved maybe more than one person or two journeys, or a specialist balancing act. The bearer

had to trudge across the debris-strewn old pig yard into the veritable jungle of waste-high nettles in the disused cattle yard with its hidden traps of
rusting farm equipment. Also nearer to the house a silver teapot had been
tossed over the hedge into the untended orchard. Across the drive a copper
kettle was found in the tangle of weeds beside the garage wall. This all took
time and a degree of planning.

The question which arises is why? Why would anyone go through such
an awkward and time-consuming procedure after ransacking a house with
at least one estate or even a saloon car and possibly a van available as transport? The total mass of the items missing from the house would have fitted
into almost any car boot. It is hardly possible that the items would have
been so carefully hidden in the aftermath of a horrific child-murder. However implausible surely such unnecessary activity would have taken place
before the murder.

It could be that the copper kettle and the silver teapot were discarded
in panic when the intruders were disturbed while carrying them to getaway
transport. Such transport could not, as has been stated in several accounts,
been backed up to the door of the farmhouse. Some 15 years after the murder, during the mid-nineties, that would be possible as the hedge, which
then divided the drive, had been removed. The hedge was breeched only by
a small wicket gate and stretched from the wall of the garage to the perimeter hedge of the orchard. From the gate, 10 yards of pathway led to the back
door of the farm, bordered by flowers and shrubs. A panic reaction could
well have seen these metallic items hurled to either side of the path – maybe
at the first hint of the approach of the paperboy.

However, nothing connected with a disturbed robbery can account for
the placement of the items in the cattle yard. Add to that the fact that
unidentified fingerprints were found on the broken roadside window at the
front of the house and a train of events is strongly suggested.

No fingerprints or other forensic evidence of any kind was found inside
the farmhouse, despite the state of chaos left by the killer or killers of Carl
Bridgewater. Presumably gloves were worn during that intrusion. But does

the evidence point to an earlier and unconnected break-in and burglary? Were some or all of the missing items taken by an early thief on that day? Certainly the Bridgewater Four and Bert Spencer were eliminated from the ownership of these unidentified fingerprints – as were household members, visitors, cleaners, police etc. Was the haul originally stashed in the cattle yard with the object of return collection trips being made? The cattle yard is not totally enclosed. The quadrangle has an impressive archway, large enough to accommodate loaded hay-wagons. This leads to open fields and a virtually straight run of some 800 yards towards the thin tree line, which is Lousy Wood and onto the Stourbridge canal, a cross-country journey taking about 10 minutes.

The list of items missing from the farmhouse was quite short. Some were of pocketable size, the ladies antique watch, the gold and silver cuff-links, plus a silver watch-chain. Others were moderately heavy and probably too bulky to be contained in the green canvas shopping bag, which was also stolen. The full load would have included; a pair of brass candlesticks, an oak tantalus with three cut-glass decanters, a set of brass fire irons, a second copper kettle, a copper warming pan, a glass biscuit barrel and two brass meat hooks.

Could it be then, and it is Spencer's view, that the full sequence of events at Yew Tree Farm on Tuesday 19 September, 1978, ran like this? A thief, may be an opportunist or perhaps with prior knowledge of the old couple's planned absence, breaks in through the front window, disregarding the problem presented by Mr Jones' constantly parading flock of geese. He, if it was a he, leaves his fingerprints on the window-frame. From the house he selects some items for immediate removal and hides other articles in the disused cattle yard. The thief possibly has second thoughts about the readily identifiable brooch and drops that too. To avoid being seen, he takes his easy cross-country stroll down to the canal bridge, below Primrose Hill and a waiting boat, or maybe walks the extra few 100 yards to a waiting car in Prestwood Drive. He returns to the cattle-yard to recover the hidden items but encounters human or vehicular activity at the farm. He retreats back through the archway and across the fields, believing his haul to be safe from discovery until he can make a future collection trip. But he has discounted the possibility of perverse coincidence in his calculations. And as the story will show, far more powerful and seemingly far-fetched coincidental influences invade the saga and are later proven beyond doubt to have been just that. Maybe this possible scenario of the first thief's collection mission had to be aborted because the killer or killers had arrived on the scene. Perhaps the back door of the farm had already been smashed open or maybe the 'second' band of thieves were loading some of the unrecovered items into their vehicle.

Surely it is uncertain that the same person or persons did not both smash the window to gain entry and then tear open the back door from the outside with the spade.

The subject of the topography of the farm layout was mentioned at the 1997 Court of Appeal hearing:

'... the window of the living room through which entry to the house had been gained was on the south aspect of the house, that is to say the old front of the house. An approach to that window would have involved a person who had used the drive to the house going round the house to the side furthest from the drive. It was the back door of the house, which showed the marks of an attempt to force it. At the scene the police were to find a spade with traces of paint on it, which matched the paint of the back door. The marks on the back door could have been made by that spade. The third outside door into the house was a door to the left of the back door as approached from the drive, which gave direct access to the washroom.'

The window evidence was also looked at during the appeal and Vincent Hickey's initial alleged 'verbal' confession covered this aspect of entry to Yew Tree Farm:

'... DS Lessemun put to Vincent Hickey that he was in the house, to which Vincent Hickey replied 'I may have been'. A short while later Vincent Hickey admitted being there in the house. He said 'I'm too fat to get *through the window' and 'I walked in'. He also told the police, 'The person who went in the farm first did not shoot the kid'. He was asked how he knew that and answered 'I was there, wasn't I'.'*

During Pat Molloy's statement to DC Perkins, alone in his cell but with DS Robbins, DC Leeke and DS Robbins making notes in the corridor, he also mentions the window. Molloy stated that, '... the vehicles were parked away from the farm. Vincent Hickey and myself walked to the farm first. James Robinson broke in through a window and let the others in.'

This of course we know is incorrect as the police found the spade, which was used to break into the farm from the *outside*.

It is possible that a burglar may have broken in through the window, but was unable to open the front door – so anyone on the outside was forced to break in. Albeit that this scenario never appeared in any of the early statements made by either Vincent Hickey or Pat Molloy.

One piece of evidence to go with the unknown fingerprint, although that could have been placed there by an innocent person and simply not eliminated, was a button found at the scene. During the appeal it was stated that, '... Patrick Molloy told the police that two days after James Robinson was released on 23 October he had got rid of a fawn duffel coat which had a button missing, a biggish, brown button. A button had been found at Yew Tree Farm on the windowsill of the living room through which access had been gained, but that button did not fit the description given by Patrick Molloy of the button missing from the duffel coat.'

Of course, with all the evidence pointing to police corruption in securing various confessions, none of the alleged statements made by the four men can be relied upon. Certainly from quite an early stage Molloy states that his written statements were more or less dictated to him by certain police officers – one of those would have been DC Perkins. DC John Perkins, who died in October 1993, was involved in 17 of the 97 cases investigated by the Police Complaints Authority (PCA). He openly boasted that his fist was a 'truth drug'. At least four experts have cast grave doubt that the Molloy signed 'confession' statements – the words used and the interview time constraint proposed by the detectives – were unlikely to be Molloy's dialogue. A police officer also certainly forged a signature of Vincent Hickey, together with a 'confession' statement, and shoved it under the nose of Molloy. There is no doubt that some members of this now disbanded West Midlands Serious Crime Squad were rotten apples. There was almost an unwritten code between various police officers in the squad that they would not let a small thing like evidence get in the way if they were positive their suspect was guilty. To be fair the criminals were not playing by the rules and I am sure some police officers just thought they were levelling the playing field.

If indeed the first and second robbery did take place, it would, from a consideration of the log of sightings and movements around the farm, have had to have taken place between 11.30 am and possibly 3.00 pm. If the first robbery scenario never did take place, how else can the unidentified fingerprints and the two means of gaining entry be accounted for? And just who was eliminated in the course of the investigation by having their fingerprints taken and compared? If this is correct, who could the first intruder have been?

The fact that the back door of the farm was closed on such a fine day was a signal to anyone who knew the habits of the occupants that the farmhouse was empty. Fred and Mary probably had notice of their intended day out and would no doubt have passed the information on, with the subsequent ripple effect acquired by the most mundane of information snippets. The footpath, which runs past the back of the farmhouse, was well used for both work and leisure purposes. A few people must have been aware of their planned absence from the property. Given notice, someone with access to a boat could well have moored up on the Stourbridge canal at the base of Primrose Hill or, again, a car waiting in Prestwood Drive and carried out the initial break-in.

Equally easily, the thief could have taken the low road, the path which is the extension of the Roman road (now Ashwood Lower Lane), from Yew Tree Farm to Newton Bridge, where Prestwood Drive meets the canal towpath – a straight line stroll of some 1,000 yards taking less than 15 minutes. There was a labyrinth of ways to access the farm and any knowledgeable local thief would have chosen any possible retreat apart from the front driveway off the busy farm road. Strangely enough, Nicholas Holden, who had reported a sighting of a blue Ford estate at about 3.00 pm in Lawnswood Road, had continued his journey along the A449 and had spotted another blue Ford estate leaving Prestwood Drive a minute or so later, just after 3.00 pm. This vehicle contained two men. While all of this is irrelevant to the central question of who killed Carl Bridgewater, it does, perhaps, explain some puzzling aspects of that fatal afternoon.

At 3.15 pm a man with long, corn-coloured hair was seen in the yard of Yew Tree Farm. 10 minutes later (and the time gap could well have been shorter) two men are seen leaving their Ford estate in Lawnswood Road, crossing to the farm side, one carrying a gun and peering over the hedge at Yew Tree land. From their position, the gate opening onto the field opposite the driveway to the farm is clearly visible. Was the man with corn-coloured hair the outrider of the killer group, a doorknocker checking whether or not anyone was at home at the farm? And were the two men with their gun looking for a hand-signal from their accomplice at the farm? All that can be said is that it would seem to be quite likely. As speculation it fits the facts. It also exonerates any earlier robber or robbers from the charge of murder.

It appears that, in the course of the day, the farm dog had been moved from the kitchen, where Fred Jones had left it, into the scullery.

The inference drawn from this by Paul Foot was that, 'Once again the evidence suggested that whoever broke into Yew Tree Farm had some knowledge of the place and was well enough known to the dog to move it without it barking'.

Indeed, Mrs Gladys Jones had stated that she had not heard the dog bark '… while she was in the garden …' In fact the lady also affirmed that the dog barked at each and every caller, known or not – including herself, even after her long association with the animal. Certainly the dog would have barked at the sound of breaking glass, as the first window entry point was breached, or at the back door being noisily forced. However, the dog was a small, yapping terrier, not a bellowing mastiff. At a range of around 20 yards, Mrs Jones would probably have heard the dog if she were standing in her garden and the dog was outside in the yard. But, if Mrs Jones was inside her cottage with distracting household noises inside and traffic noise outside, and if the dog was confined inside the farmhouse then it is doubtful that the terrier's protests would have been audible at that distance. Certainly Mrs Jones did not hear the later roar of the 12 bore shotgun. And yet Mr Foot was adamant, 'The dog had not barked'. Alas, a supposed familiarity with a farm dog is to crop up again in Bert Spencer's story. Merely the existence of dogs at Yew Tree and Holloway House farms was enough for Mr Foot to draw an explicable link between both murders.

An early line of enquiry in the case that the police followed was that the paperboy had recognised his killer, and this is why he was shot in cold-blood. The link between Bert Spencer and Carl Bridgewater was also a beacon for Foot and the campaigners. In 1970 the Spencers moved to 21, Ascot Gardens, a newly built housing estate in Wordsley. At 25, Ascot Gardens, just three doors away, lived Brian Bridgewater, his wife Janet, and their three children, Jane, Philip and Carl – who was five. When they moved to 42, Kingsley Road, Kingswinford, Carl Bridgewater was 10. At the time of his murder, Carl was 13. Perhaps Bert would have recognized the teenager, perhaps not. There can be some change and growth in a child in these passing three years – although one assumes nothing significant. Having said that, it would be consistent to assume the paperboy would have certainly recognised Spencer – he had obviously come into contact with the young boy. Although all the children attended the same school, it was the daughters who became friends, Jane Bridgewater and Janell Spencer, as they were of similar age.

'I did not know that Carl was the newspaper delivery boy at the time of the murder but I certainly did know the evening papers were delivered by a "paperboy" and I would also have known the approximate time,' explains Bert Spencer, adding, 'Even though I was not working there on that particular date I had, during the seasons seen most of the visitors come and go. The Foot allegation seems rather silly, but he did at times display "tunnel vision" and failed to dig deeper to try to back up his allegation theories.'

The point made by Paul Foot and the campaigners was that Carl died with his tear ducts shut. Therefore, they conclude, Carl must have known his killer or killers. This glaringly fallacious assumption could be swamped by many alternative explanations and possible scenarios, including Carl being surprised or reassured. Even if such a scene were true any 13-year-old boy faced with a loaded shotgun, whether he knew the assailant or not, would be terrified, as would any adult. Whatever the reasons for this extraordinary fact we shall probably never know. Incredibly, Carl's lack of tears was later to be used to draw yet another implausible parallel with the later killing of Hubert Wilkes.

Undaunted by non-facts and cobweb reasoning, Paul Foot was to describe Bert Spencer as the 'prime suspect' and to launch a campaign of harassment against him which only truly ended when Foot passed away in 2004. Although, to be fair, most journalists have picked up the gauntlet and have happily linked Spencer to any article surrounding the Bridgewater murder. This is despite the fact that they have continued to fly in the face of all fact and opinion to the contrary. Even after the results of high-flying police investigations, the considered opinions of the Director of Public Prosecutions, those of eminent members of the judiciary, and in the face of all logic and reason.

Bert Spencer was, however, unintentionally and in the most improbable way, to project himself into the firing line just four weeks after the murder of Carl. It was to prove to be the most bizarre episode in the whole convoluted story and an event, which would cast a dark shadow over Bert Spencer, lasting up to the present day.

5.

The Piece of Card

....

It was five weeks after the murder of Carl Bridgewater and thirteen months before the murder of Hubert Wilkes when there began a strange and prolonged saga. The focus of unusual attention could have been a scrap of refuse, spillage from a plastic rubbish sack awaiting the casual attention of a street cleaner. It was a piece of cardboard, which perhaps was torn from an empty tissue carton, an inconsequential fragment of domestic rubbish – but for the cryptic messages written on both sides. Their content could well have been devised for the opening chapter of a Sherlockian mystery. On the card, printed in capital letters, read;

'BERT,
THAT CHAP WHO DISGUISES ISSELF WAS SEEN AT THE FARM
WHERE CARL BRIDGEWATER WASSHOT. TED SAYS HE LIVES IN
VICARAGE ROAD SMK. HE SCARES THE WOMAN. JOE.'

On the reverse of the card was printed:

'HE SCARED DON'S MISSUS, 107 OR 108 STONEY LANE. UWP 751R.'

The finding of the piece of card was to prove to be the most peculiar example of synchronicity in Bert Spencer's coincidence-ridden life. It was strange, puzzling and even sinister in its implications and it was to haunt and create incalculable stress for Bert for many years. For Bert himself was present when the piece of card was picked up in the street, at night, 14 miles from his own home.

Paul Foot and his co-campaigners were to seize upon the oddness of the situation in which Bert was to find himself and, ten years later, were to use it against him. They would make it the focal point of an Appeal Hearing by the men convicted of the killing of Carl Bridgewater. But 'experts' were to be publicly discredited and pointers were to emerge as to the true author of the card's cryptic messages. The finger of suspicion had been pointed at Bert Spencer for 10 years, back in 1988, before the cavalry finally came over the hill; and when it did, it came in a surprising form.

A young woman, a young girl at the time of the finding of the card, possessed of intelligence, powers of observation and a sense of duty, came forward publicly to throw some revealing light on the mystery. Ironically, after a decade, the issue of the card was brought to her mind by her watching Paul Foot's *own* television documentary, *Murder at the Farm*.

Bert was to be allowed at last a sigh of relief after years of ill-founded pressure. Part of the mystery was to have a rational explanation. But, having been able to cancel out any *Spencer factor*, we are still left with unanswered questions and a heavily perverse stroke of the invariably inexplicable long arm of coincidence.

It all began on a drizzly Saturday evening, 23 October, 1978. It was a family outing for the Spencers with a visit to Bert's brother, Don and his wife, Val, in Smethwick. The evening often ended with a stroll to a local social club and a few drinks in comfortable company. However, it was to end with a strange and discomforting happening, although there was no hint at the time of the nightmare quality of the interpretation which was to follow – or that it would be 10 years before Bert would be free of its haunting shadow.

The trip started normally, although quite often these visits happened irregularly and without structure. Bert, Janet and their daughter, Janell, would travel from their home in Kingswinford to visit Bert's brother Don, and his family at their home in Great Arthur Street, Smethwick. As usual, the intention was to spend a social evening at the nearby Home Guard Club in Oldbury Road. The seven-strong family group, comprising of the two couples along with their three respective teenage daughters, walked the few hundreds to the club accompanied by Don's next-door neighbour. They spent an uneventful, pleasant evening, leaving at about 10.45 pm for the walk back.

From then on, trivial details were to achieve elevated status and the inconsequential was to assume major proportions as the spotlight of publicity was later to be directed towards a piece of cardboard, but that discarded scrap of rubbish was to achieve the status of 'evidence'.

Still raining, the group were on their way back to Don Spencer's home on the opposite side of Telford Way to that which they had walked on the outward journey. They were in a happy mood, spread out in adult couples with the children making a crocodile formation in the middle. Bert and Janet were bringing up the rear, about 100 yards behind the group leaders. Val Spencer's attention was caught by a piece of cardboard. It lay on the inner edge of the pavement, about 10 feet away from a wooden gateway. This led to a patch of scrub and woodland, which ran parallel to the two canals which themselves ran beneath Galton Bridge in Telford Way.

Some unexplainable compulsion led Val Spencer to pick up the card and it would have been easier all round had she not done so. Astonishingly, the card was headed in bold hand printing and simply read, 'BERT'. It made mention of a 'DON', Bert's brother, and gave an address called 'STONEY LANE'. Despite the spelling error, this was to turn out to be intended to indicate 'Stony Lane', where Bert and Don had been brought up but had left years before. The message carried by the card was intriguing, but what gave the party a jolt was the mention of the shooting of Carl Bridgewater – the crime which was currently on everyone's lips and about which Bert had already been interviewed, as had many others.

At Don's house the peculiar incident was discussed at length while the wet piece of cardboard was placed on the mantelpiece to dry off. Bert decided that he ought to deliver the card to the police, thinking that it could link in to their ongoing investigation. At Smethwick police station Bert suggested that it could be helpful to the Bridgewater enquiry if the card bore any discernible fingerprints. The desk sergeant, Philip Rich, replied that this was not possible as the card was still damp. This was a small fact that was also very questionable.

The policeman said he would pass the card on to Wombourne police where the enquiry was headquartered. Desk sergeant Rich then performed a natural and commonplace action, but it was to create years of soul-destroying problems for Bert Spencer. The police sergeant flipped to and fro in his ledger to find the appropriate place in which to record this apparently trivial event. Finding his place, he made the entry and also filled in a slip with Bert's details; name, address and telephone number. This he did on top of the damp piece of card, so leaving an impression of those personal details on the card itself.

This later was to add weight to the contention of the campaigners that Bert Spencer was himself the author of the card and that he had planted it for a member of his family to find on their homeward walk, even though the routes to and from the pub were random and unplanned. Bert's objective, so claimed the campaigners, was to divert suspicion from himself and to implicate the owner of the vehicle whose registration number was written on the card. Although such accusation was ridiculous on the face of it – a simple anonymous telephone call or letter to the police would have been the obvious means of passing on such information – the piece of card was to become the cornerstone of an Appeal by the men convicted of the murder of Carl Bridgewater.

This Appeal Hearing was heard in December 1988 and continued into early 1989. It was to be marshalled by Paul Foot and Michael Hickey's mother, Ann Whelan.

Prior to this, the then desk sergeant at Smethwick police station, Philip Rich, allegedly made a sworn statement, eighteen months after Bert had handed in the card, to Paul Foot.

In the statements, dated 22 May 1980, he claimed, 'At this time it was raining heavily for some hours. I noticed, however, that the cardboard was completely dry.'

A year and a half is a long time, even for a policeman, to produce perfect recall of a very minor incident in a busy environment, or to retain a clear memory of the weather conditions at the time. It is true that there was intermittent drizzle in the Smethwick area on the night of the 23 October, 1978, and that the piece of card was quite damp when Val Spencer picked it up. But it is also true that, despite being partly dried in the Spencer's house, it was still damp enough for the sergeant to pass comment on the fact.

What may appear to be a niggling detail, however, was far from being that. In saying that the card was dry, the sergeant was in fact opening the door on damaging suggestion – damaging for Bert Spencer. Paul Foot's inference was to be that Bert Spencer did write the card himself and that further strengthened the campaigners' assertion that Bert Spencer was guilty of child murder. To that end Mr Foot was to go to extreme lengths.

Critical to the focus of attention given by Mr Foot to the whole affair is the detail of the routes followed by the Spencer party to and from the Home Guard Club. For Bert Spencer to have planted the card where it was picked up, the party would have had to take identical inward and outward routes and the card would have had to remain in place, in the open street for several hours. In fact, on the outward walk, the Spencer party crossed Telford Way before reaching the gateway to the woodland.

In order to create the certainty that the Spencer party did go near the gateway, Mr Foot, in his book, has them actually passing through the gate, via an almost impossible route.

Referring to the walk he states: 'This involved a walk from the back of Don's house through some scrub and woodland onto a dual carriageway, Telford Way.'

Referring to the return journey, he incorrectly quotes Don Spencer as saying, '… and then we crossed over to go through the gate to the footpath. We had gone to the pub exactly the same way.'

Such comment would be quite laughable if it did not verge on almost maliciously criminal – for the following reasons. There was no exit from the back of Don's former house. For safety reasons, the properties on that side of Great Arthur Street, Smethwick, were enclosed at the rear by six-foot high chain-link fencing. Beyond that, for anyone following the 'Paul Foot' route, is a 75-feet drop to a canal, which is situated, in the deep cutting that runs in parallel with Great Arthur Street. After having negotiated both the fence and the waterway there is then a 75 foot climb to the strip of scrub and woodland. There then is required a walk of some 150 yards through dripping trees, mud and wet grass to reach Telford Way. In all, it would be an assault course to test a fit soldier.

The alternative route is the one actually taken; out of Don's front door, along Great Arthur Street, into Telford Way, cross the dual carriageway at the gap in the central reservation and continue in a straight line to the Home Guard Club. The return journey was made on the opposite side of Telford Way and did, as we know, take the Spencer family past the gateway to the woodland where the card was found.

Although relatively little interest in the piece of card was shown by the police, Paul Foot and some of the campaign acolytes were to pursue the matter with unrelenting fervour, without any accompanying in-depth analysis of the strange memo. A Mr Derek Davis, Flauden Lane, Hemel Hempstead was employed to use his skills as the country's self-proclaimed leading graphologist in order to determine whether or not Bert Spencer was the author of the card. In an attempt to bolster Davis's impartiality and credibility, Foot wrote the following after the hand-writing expert appeared in the Thames Television documentary reconstruction, *Murder at the Farm* (first broadcast 25 March 1987), in which he categorically stated that Bert Spencer had indeed written the card, 'There was, however, much more weighty evidence in store for the Thames TV programme. Justice, the British section of the International Commission of Jurists, had sent the photograph of the card which had been found by Hubert Spencer in the road at Smethwick, four weeks after the murder, to Derek Davis, the country's leading handwriting expert.'

By the beginning of March Davis had reached his conclusion. The journalist continued, 'Beyond doubt, Spencer had written the card. In spite of all his denials and protestations, he had, for reasons that were entirely unclear,

himself written a card which his family had then 'found' by the side of the
road and which linked someone else with the Carl Bridgewater murder. Mr
Davis's verdict, which he reached for no reward (he refuses all criminal
work save for organisations such as Justice, which doesn't pay him), profoundly altered the balance against Spencer, who reacted with more furious
denials of what was now established fact.'

In implying that Mr Davis had been employed by Justice and had made
his study of the card for no reward, a degree of respectability was conferred
upon his findings purely by suggested association. In fact, as the following
letter shows, Mr Davis was hired by an agency quite different and with quite
definite partisan leanings:

JUSTICE

(BRITISH SECTION OF THE INTERNATIONAL
COMMISSION OF JURISTS)
95a, CHANCERY LANE, LONDON, WC2A IDT

(Council information)

LL/RC 22nd   March 1989

Mr H.V. Spencer
C21543
H M P Kingston
Portsmouth
PO3 6AS

Dear Mr Spencer

We have received your letter of 7th March 1989. Mr Derek Davis was instructed in this matter by the solicitors acting for Michael Joseph Hickey
and the family of Patrick Molloy. He was not employed by JUSTICE.

We have noted your proposals but in the circumstances have no comment to make.

Yours sincerely

LEAH LEVIN

Having no crystal ball, Mr Foot was not to know that the credibility of Derek Davis was to be shattered in open court at a later date. Based on the premise that Bert Spencer was the author of the card, another 'expert', this one in the field of psychiatry, was produced to build upon Derek Davis' accusation about the authorship of the card.

The 'expert' psychiatrist was to state that the card was written, '... as the irrational act of a psychopath trying to draw attention to his crime'.

And well it may have been, as it was later to be proven that Bert Spencer neither wrote, nor could he have planted the card. The compounding of wishful thinking and the suspension of analytical thought, along with the damaging falsehoods, were shortly to wither and die.

At the time, Paul Foot had, no doubt, far more lofty reasons for his ongoing harassment of a man, held helpless in a prison cell, without recourse to the normal retributive channels of the law. Although it cannot be denied that over the years the case of the murder of Carl Bridgewater has provided a dependable and regular filler for his time and topic-consuming newspaper column in the *Daily Mirror*. He continued to gnaw away at the affair of the piece of card and in 1987 was still wagging the stick at Bert Spencer in a manner both petulant and aggressive.

In the following extracts from Paul Foot's letters to Bert Spencer, then in Kingston prison, Portsmouth, mention is made of a Janet Cotter. This lady, who features later in this story, in 1984, six years after the finding of the card, initiated a peculiar correspondence with Bert Spencer. A correspondence which, without very much stretching of the imagination can be shown to bear a relation to a known armed bank robber, still wanted after a prison escape in Southern Ireland. Ms Cotter's first letter to Bert was dated two days after the man had made a terrifying visit to Bert's wife and young daughter.

Extracts from letters written by Paul Foot on *Daily Mirror* headed paper to Spencer,

14 May, 1987. Ref: MY/102.
'*... But the most striking piece of evidence of course was that you wrote the piece of card, which you found in Smethwick. You have consistently denied writing this card. Why have you lied about it? Why did you write the card?*'

4 June, 1987. Ref: JN/91.
'*... I have never met Janet Cotter. She was the girlfriend of Harry Rushton whose van number you included on the piece of card you wrote and handed in at Smethwick. She also lived at the address on the card in Stony Lane. I have spoken to her on the phone a few times in the course of my enquiries into the murder. She has been very helpful.*

'*Have you seen a copy of my book on the case? If not, would you like me to send you one?*'

1 July, 1987. (no reference given)
'*... Mr Davis (Derek Davis) by the way, does not make mistakes. When he says that someone wrote something, it is as near certain as anything can be that that person did write it. In other words, you wrote the card.*

'*You suggest that Janet Cotter wrote the card – though Janet Cotter had no idea who you were before she wrote it. I have no doubt*

that she is a remarkable woman – I have never met her – but I don't
think she has powers to see into the future ...'

3 August, 1987. Ref: AV/16
'... It will certainly go to the Home Secretary, who will analyse it.
You need have no fear at all that it will prove conclusively that you
wrote the card, and I understand there are more than 200 simi-
larities in handwriting (a quite extraordinary case of correlation,
which leaves no room for doubt whatever). Your continued allega-
tion that Janet Cotter wrote the card when she did not know you or
Don or any of your family is so ridiculous as to suggest that you are
slightly off your rocker ...'

In fact, the piece of card *was* to be the subject of analysis by Home Office experts but their conclusions were to take the feet from under Paul Foot's barrage of misguided accusation. Mr Derek Davis' credibility was to be brought into question, his own analysis of the card was to be ridiculed in court and Paul Foot was to be accused of misleading the public.

There was to be no follow-up correspondence from Mr Foot to Bert Spencer in appropriate apologetic vein. Past venom was left undiluted, despite its proven misdirection, and the long persecution was to be continued, even after Paul Foot was publicly seen to be hoisted by his own petard. This happened at the Court of Appeal hearing, which started on 23 November 1988, into the convictions of the Bridgewater Four. A hearing for which Paul Foot had fought, in collusion with Ann Whelan, for so long and so hard.

The three main points of focus were prosecution witnesses who had later retracted their statements, the two-pip/one-pip theory (Roger Edwards' sighting) and the campaigners' interpretation of the significance of the piece of card.

On all counts, the campaign group were to be doomed to disappointment, for this appeal at least.

Val Spencer, who was present at the hearing, summoned as a witness, wrote to Bert, her brother-in-law, in prison,

'I don't know if you are aware that the verdict on the Hickeys and Robinson appeal will be made public on 17 March (1989). We are all hoping and praying that will be an end to all the insinuations once and for all ... I had to go because of that blasted card I picked up that night coming from the Home Guard Club ... It wasn't until the end of the first day that I was there that I found out that I was not the first person to pick it up. Apparently, it was first picked up on Oldbury Road, two days before I came upon it, by a 12-year-old girl. She was with her brother and some friends when she found it. She and her friends read it and carried it round onto Telford Way where she dropped it, somewhere by the entrance to the woods. She went home and mentioned it to her parents but they took no notice ... nine years later, now aged 21, she was in her married sister's house in Ironbridge when, GUESS WHAT – our friend, Paul Foot's documentary 'reconstruction' *Murder at the Farm*, was shown on the television. The young woman said, "That's all wrong, what he is saying. That's the piece of cardboard I found that I told you all about." Thank God they all realised that what was being said was wrong. So next morning she went to the police and told them her story. So the theory that you wrote that card or the theory we concocted the story was shot to bits ... I can only hope that that is an end to it all ...'

The Court of Appeal hearing lasted just over a couple of months, with three days dedicated to the mysterious piece of card. The witness Valerie Spencer refers to in her letter was Judy Gadd, who was one of the few new witnesses during the whole appeal hearing. It was established that Gadd did know the Spencer family, but she rigidly stuck to her testimony and was a strong and believable witness.

*   *   *

With all association between the piece of cardboard and Bert Spencer now more or less to be nothing more than far-reaching and grim coincidence, the very existence of the card itself begs questions. Was the mystery posed by the content of the cryptic messages ever to be fully unravelled and would new light be thrown onto the murder of Carl Bridgewater at Yew Tree Farm?

The crudely written message provides enough information of substance to fund endless speculation about its origin and intended purpose. Was it the intention of the author, by providing those tantalising glimpses of suggested hard-core fact, to incriminate someone in the murder at Yew Tree Farm? If so, was that someone actually involved or was he innocent? Was the motive of the author to further the course of justice or was the card written out of pure mischief? Was it written by someone devilishly clever or was it a genuine, if naïve, attempt to pass on a warning? Was it lost in Oldbury Road by the author or had it reached its intended recipient, only to be read and then discarded in the gutter?

The card began, 'BERT, THAT CHAP WHO DISGUISES ISSELF ...' It is a fact that a known criminal, a member of Birmingham's underworld, made a terrorising visit to Janet Spencer and her daughter on 19 November, 1984. He posed as a police inspector and he was wearing stage make up at the time. *Chapter 8 – An Inspector Calls*, tells how Bert Spencer, from his prison cell, tracked the man down and was able to reveal his true identity to the police. This man, a prison escapee, wanted in Southern Ireland, was sentenced to 15 years in the early seventies by an Irish court for a series of armed robberies carried out as part of an IRA team. He made a sophisticated escape attempt, after serving just three years of his sentence.

Information gleaned during the bogus inspector's visit to the Spencer women was recorded by means of a tie-pin microphone and appeared in Paul Foot's column with little delay. A letter written by Bert Spencer to this man, who, by then was using yet another alias – Inspector Curry, had become Alan Johnson – was printed in its entirety in Paul Foot's column. The piece, in the *Daily Mirror*, Thursday, 5 September, 1985, went under the banner headline, 'DEATH OF AN ALIBI', (it was, of course, no such thing). Mr Foot omitted to mention just how and where the letter was sourced. But, certainly the bogus inspector's girlfriend at the time was a friend of Ann Whelan, mother of Michael Hickey. While no assertion is made here, it is difficult to avoid certain conclusions.

However, there is an even more interesting connection between the stage make-up wearing impostor and the piece of card. At the address given, 107, Stony Lane, Smethwick, lived Janet Cotter – a lady whom Mr Foot acknowledges in his book as having 'helped me a lot with the Spencer mystery'. Just how, he leaves unspecified. However, just two days after 'Inspector Curry', later to use the name 'Alan Johnson', made his visit to the Spencer women, Janet Cotter wrote a letter to Bert Spencer in which she offered the hand of friendship in pen-pal form. She also demonstrated an in-depth knowledge of Bert Spencer's own interests and pastimes.

Later the correspondence was to become rather more acrimonious with Ms Cotter showing an obsessive interest in the piece of card that had been found in the street so long ago.

This was perfectly natural as her address and the registration number of her boyfriend's van had been included in the information presented on the card, together with the name of the road (Vicarage Road), where her boyfriend lived. But what could account for the time gap of six years? And is it just coincidence that she made her first contact with Bert Spencer only 48 hours after the disguised impostor had visited Bert's family?

To test for a connection, Bert Spencer wrote to Janet Cotter requesting that she place an advertisement for him in the *Express & Star* newspaper. The advertisement never did appear, or if it did it was sometime after an immediate response by letter from the disguised and bogus 'police inspector'. The nature of the letter was such as Bert would have expected had the advertisement actually been printed and then read by the person at whom it was aimed – 'Detective Inspector Curry'.

Coincidence maybe, but, as Al Capone was fond of saying, 'Three coincidences is enemy action'.

And so we have mention on the card of a man who disguises himself and we also have identified a man who has used disguise at least once and who has a fringe association with the Hickey family. This man with a violent past is not above terrorising a defenceless woman and her daughter. The message on the card goes on to state that a man who disguises himself, 'WAS SEEN AT THE FARM WHERE CARL BRIDGEWATER WAS SHOT'. Although not stated, the message would seem to suggest that the sighting took place on the day of the murder, otherwise there would be only slight significance in that particular piece of information. At 3.15 pm on the day of the murder, witness Mr Leonard Bick saw a man in the yard of Yew Tree Farm. The man's hair was shoulder length and bright blond, the colour of corn. Could this have been a wig? Who was the unnamed witness, mentioned on the card, who saw the man who wore disguise at the farm? This person surely can identify the author of the card, having transmitted this information to him or her. Again, was this sighting made on the day of the murder? If so, at what time?

Mentioned on the card are two road names and one uncertain address, 107 or 108 Stoney Lane. Paul Foot places Janet Cotter at 108 although Ms Cotter, at that time, was heading her letters as coming from 107. The road name, with an 'e', is incorrectly spelt on the card; perhaps deliberately as a miss-direction ploy to help conceal the identity of the writer. The other address, Vicarage Road, SMK, is given as the location of the man with a penchant for disguise. Presumably 'SMK' is an abbreviation of Smethwick, included to distinguish the road from the many other Vicarage Roads in the Birmingham area – or maybe from the Vicarage Road, which is just a countryside footpath walk from Yew Tree Farm.

Maybe the disguise artist did live there at the time but after so long, and in an area dominated by bed-sits, it has proved difficult to establish. But what is known is that there is a connection between the two addresses. While Janet Cotter lived at 107, Stony Lane, her boyfriend of the time, one Harry Rushton, lived in the adjoining Vicarage Road, at number 76. The vehicle registration given on the card belonged to the works van which Harry Rushton drove and in which he delivered, for his laundry firm employers, dry-cleaned ambulance service uniforms. His delivery run on Tuesdays included drops in the area near to Yew Tree Farm. So this was another line of enquiry and a possible reason someone was either trying divert attention away from themselves, maybe to simply make mischief, or to direct police to a possible suspect. The inclusion of the printed words 'DISGUISES ISSELF' could obviously purport to someone who was to dress up as an ambulance man, which would be a disguise, to hide his or her identity.

Both Stony Lane and Vicarage Road lead into Oldbury Road, where the piece of card was first found by the young girl. The address of the disguised 'Inspector Curry', to which he was traced, turned out to be, at that time, a down-market snooker hall in Saltley, Washwood Heath Road. Where he actually lived at the time is not known. Was the author of the card attempting to incriminate Harry Rushton in the murder at Yew Tree Farm? Or was the intention to point the finger at the man who used disguise and, in so doing, mistakenly suggested that that man was Harry Rushton? If the writing of the card was a serious attempt at creating mischief, how did it come to be found discarded in the street?

In view of the unusual choice of writing material, could this indicate a spontaneous and hurriedly scribbled warning, passed, maybe, across some pub table by a hand possibly made nervous by the presence of near and frightening company? If not this or some similar scenario pertains to the origin of the message then under what sort of conditions could it have been written? The argument for spontaneity is offset by the deliberation, which is apparent in the unsubtle misspelling of 'himself' (spelt 'ISSELF'). It suggests this was hardly written in error by someone who can correctly spell 'disguise'.

At the time when the card was found, Bert Spencer's name was not public knowledge. He was no 'prime suspect' but just one of many who were to be embraced in the murder enquiry. And it was addressed to Bert and not his Christian name of Hubert. But, despite the fact that any association of Bert Spencer's was to be publicly refuted by both Home Office and police authorities at a future date, there was a strange and very tenuous connection to be made. Harry Rushton had a brother, Jim.

Jim Rushton was a member of the ambulance service and knew Bert Spencer. He also knew Bert from using the same judo club and their relationship was friendly, if not particularly close.

Although Bert Spencer has no recall of the incident, Paul Foot asserts that Harry Rushton had once visited Bert's home in Kingsley Road, Kingswinford, with his brother Jim, in order to collect some DIY material. Foot makes the point that the visit was made in the same works van whose registration number was written on the piece of card, presumably implying that Bert Spencer had noted the vehicle – although this was before the murder had yet happened. He later then sourced the number in order that he might use it on the card to confuse the enquiry.

Had Bert Spencer thrown away that wet piece of cardboard he would have saved himself 10 years of added stress and denied the campaigners a stick with which they beat him until it finally broke.

'But I did not throw it away,' explains Spencer. 'I handed it in to the police. I thought that it might be helpful, and its content baffled and intrigued me. The questions remain and they are intriguing still. Who wrote the card and for whom was it intended? Who was the man who disguised himself and was said to live in Vicarage Road, Smethwick?'

More questions flowed from Bert, like, 'If not Ms Cotter, then who was "Don's Missus" who was said to live at Janet Cotter's address? Why was the registration number given of a van which was used to carry ambulance service-uniforms and which travelled the area adjacent to Yew Tree Farm, bearing in mind that the campaigners were to make so much of the Roger Edwards sighting at Yew Tree Farm? Who were "Ted" and "JOE", from whom the message was purported to originate? Surely not Michael Hickey's father, Joe?'

The card may have been given more interest than it deserved. Personally, I was interested in what was written on the card, even more than that of the card's origin. Obviously there were some striking points as to why anyone would want to disguise the authorship in the first place – unless, of course it was Spencer who wrote it. There was no information shared in the printed message, which carried any possible criminal charges. It was in the shape of a warning to Bert Spencer – but a friendly warning, so it was someone watching Bert's back. It was someone who obviously knew Bert quite well. He used his shortened name for a start, 'BERT' and not 'Hubert'. It was someone who knew Spencer was a suspect in the Carl Bridgewater case and feared he might end up getting charged or embroiled in the murder. One assumes the author also knew of Roger Edwards' statement claiming that the person driving the Vauxhall Viva was wearing a navy uniform with a pip on the shoulder, which the police deduced this to be an ambulance man's attire. The card states, 'THAT CHAP WHO DISGUISES ISSELF WAS SEEN AT THE FARM WHERE CARL BRIDGEWATER WAS SHOT.'

The author also knew that the registration number on the card, 'UWP 751R' belonged to a van owned by Somerfield Laundries, of Smethwick, and that the driver was Harry Rushton who lived in Vicarage Road. It was also established the writer knew the laundry van travelled close to Yew Tree Farm on the day of the murder and carried ambulance men's uniforms – the inference being that the driver possibly disguised himself in one of these uniforms when robbing the farm. Also on the card was the knowledge that Rushton's girlfriend, Janet Cotter, lived round the corner at 108 Stony Lane, where the laundry van was often parked. Added to this was the information on the reverse, that not only did the author of the card know that Bert had a brother called Don, but he also knew about a previous incident when someone did in fact scare Don's wife – 'HE SCARED DON'S MISSUS'.

A simple puzzling feature is how the message was ever intended to get in the hands of Bert Spencer? As previously mentioned there are numerous ways to convey this information to Bert. Apart from mailing it, anonymous call to the police, placing it through Don's letterbox, actually telling Bert themselves … the list goes on.

There is one other odd factor to the whole mystery that surrounds the piece of card. The card came to light before the Bridgewater Four were suspects in the case and *after* Roger Edwards' statement was common knowledge in the media. At that time the police were making enquiries into, together with many hundreds of other leads, possible suspects who drove a Vauxhall Viva, wore an ambulance man's uniform and held a shotgun licence. Now if this was an armed robbery of a security van or a raid on a bank – then a disguise of any kind would have been of vital importance. The police would be out in force as it would most likely be high profile offence with members of the public at risk and high sums of money stolen. But surely in this case, especially if it was the laundry driver Rushton – who knew the area, it would have simply been an opportunist run-of-the-mill burglary – so there was little or no need for any kind of disguise. It was only when this burglary went tragically wrong when the paperboy stumbled across whoever was robbing the place and it turned into a horrific child murder. It was at the point that the case was taken up at the highest level. The West Midlands Serious Crime Squad was involved and over 200 police employed to find the murderer.

Another conundrum for the interested sleuth, be it armchair or professional, is that two names are mentioned on the card – both 'JOE' and 'TED'. It would appear odd, after the author has gone to such extraordinary lengths to disguise his writing by somewhat amateurish and childlike spelling and using printed letters, that he should attribute one sentence to a 'living' name. The card states, 'TED SAYS HE LIVES IN VICARAGE ROAD SMK.' Ted is not that common although the name originates in England. Although in America the name Theodore (Greek), is often reduced to Ted – in England it is normally an old English nickname from the Christian name, Edward. One assumes the author is somewhat devious and this is a name to possibly confuse or mislead. At the time, which may be a complete coincidence, but the American serial killer, Ted Bundy, dominated the headlines worldwide with his capture and escape during 1977 and 1978.

The second name, 'JOE', appears at the end of the sentence, 'HE SCARES THE WOMAN. JOE', which appears somewhat of an irrelevance or an added afterthought. Maybe Joe was the author, or this was part of the smoke screen, and it was placed at the end as if finishing a letter?

Whatever views one has with regards the author or the information contained on that piece of card – its significance will almost certainly never be truly understood. It is not unusual for answers to be revealed in celebrated cases, long after the event. But what will never be known is by what malign influence Mrs Spencer's attention was drawn to a piece of cardboard, discarded innocently by 12-year-old Judy Gadd, lying on a pavement on a dark and wet night on 23 October 1978.

6.

A Cocktail for Murder

••

In the nature of things, the build-up to any event is a complex mass of interacting feed lines. The most difficult timing to determine in a retrospective analysis is the start point. In a motiveless murder, even with the advantage of hindsight, the search for a finite beginning is even more perplexing. And motiveless is exactly what Bert Spencer's killing of his friend and employer, Hubert Wilkes, was. Of course, there were reasons; the law of action and reaction is inescapable. But, in anatomising a killing, emotion and shock generate their own spontaneous smokescreens for participants, witnesses and their subsequent interrogators alike.

In the case of the murder of Hubert Wilkes, what is certain is that the victim unwittingly devised and triggered the signal for the flash point, which was to precipitate his own demise.

Thirteenth December 1979 was the day before the eve of Bert Spencer's 40th birthday. The celebration was slightly premature because it was turkey time at the farm. There was almost a fortnight's hard work in the offing at Holloway House. The Spencers, Bert and Janet, were looking forward to sharing a celebration evening at the farm with Hubert Wilkes and his air hostess daughter, Jean, who was home on leave.

Bert arrived at his home in Kingsley Road, Kingswinford, at teatime after his afternoon shift at Corbett Hospital. He had hardly put the kettle on before he was followed in by Janet and then by their teenage daughter, Janell, and her close friend, Christine Bridgewater, cousin of the murdered paperboy. The time was 5.30 pm.

Janet poured a gin and tonic for herself and a large whisky for Bert. The atmosphere was happy and convivial. The girls were bubbling as they made themselves ready for a visit to the local youth club. The open fire exuded a cosy glow and the adults relaxed in front of the flames with topped-up glasses after they had changed their clothes for the evening out. Janet realised that she was out of cigarettes and asked Bert to walk down to the nearby Mount Pleasant pub to buy some for her. It was now 7.00 pm.

At the Mount Pleasant Bert found that there was a relief landlord in charge, an acquaintance from schooldays. Already merry, Bert ordered a large whisky and a drink for the temporary landlord. He was disappointed to find that the bar-stock had no Canada Dry ginger to mix with his whisky, only American. Knowing that that brand would inevitably give him heart-burn, with the logic of a merry man, he bought another whisky to dilute the mixer. Feeling vaguely unwell and unsteady due to the alcohol, Bert strolled back home with Janet's cigarettes in his pocket.

Shortly afterwards they set off for Holloway House Farm. Janet had drunk relatively little and it was she who drove their white Cortina the two and a half miles or so to the farmhouse.

'We'd arranged an early Christmas celebratory meal at the farm on the eve of my 40th birthday. Wilkes' daughter, Jean, was there, too. I wasn't a regular drinker, but I'd had a few whiskies,' confirms Spencer, adding, 'Wilkes was very hospitable. He could be an unsettling host and, perhaps due to the early stages of dementia, often displayed strange mood swings.'

As the car passed over the rubber signal pad across the drive, a warning bell was activated inside the house. In response, the pitch-black farmyard was suddenly flooded with light. Hubert Wilkes came bustling out to greet them. He was in state of some agitation. Janet had come prepared for some work on the farm accounts, an unvarying feature of a visit to Holloway House, regardless of occasion. She was carrying her adding machine and stepping gingerly as she walked forward, not wishing to step within chain-reach of the farm's watch dog, a vicious Welsh Collie which bit without barking. It made no exception for even familiar legs.

'It's all right. I've put the bugger in the shed,' huffed Hubert Wilkes. He went on to explain that he had just been visited by the police. Shortly before the arrival of the Spencers, a woman customer had called to buy some potatoes. Unaware of the presence of the guard dog, she had stepped within chain reach of the silent attacker. The dog had sunk its teeth into the woman's leg and her screams had brought Hubert Wilkes puffing to the rescue. After pulling the dog away he had locked it in its shed. The wound was a nasty one and the police had been called. Now Hubert Wilkes was perturbed about possible repercussions.

As he told the tale he led the way through the farmhouse to the front office. Already there were his daughter, Jean, and a friend of Hubert's, Alec Blount, the local National Farmers Union representative, a pleasant, rubicund-faced character. Drinks were poured. Bert, Alec and Jean retired to the lounge, leaving Janet and Hubert Wilkes in the office to work on the farm accounts. After chatting for about an hour, Alec took his leave and Jean accompanied him to the door. Normally it would have meant an accompanied protective walk across the yard to his car. But on this night, as previously mentioned, the dog was securely locked in its shed where Hubert Wilkes had earlier taken it in a *stable-door* reaction. The time was 9.15 pm.

While Bert and Jean had been chatting, waiting for the others to finish their work in the office, Jean had played the efficient hostess as usual, topping Bert's whisky glass at intervals. It was about 10.30 pm when they were joined by Hubert and Janet. Jean shared one settee with her father. Bert was seated in an armchair and Janet had the other settee to herself. By now, in the typically unwise manner of an infrequent drinker, Bert had consumed, at a conservative estimate, half a bottle of whisky. *Relaxed* was a euphemistic description of his condition as he sat enjoying the friendly atmosphere, half dozing.

Suddenly he was jerked from reverie as he heard Hubert Wilkes' conversation with Jean as she helped him to pour drinks. The man was always loud. The television was invariably switched on, even in company. And it was Hubert Wilkes' habit to talk over the background soundtrack. Now his voice was loud enough to penetrate Bert Spencer's alcoholic daze. Bert's rate of consumption had slowed down. He was not keeping pace with the others. After all, he had had more than a head start. It had registered with him only vaguely that Hubert Wilkes had been pouring heavy-handedly for the women. But, where the farmer himself normally drank from a large whisky tumbler, he was tonight using one the size of a medicine dispenser and that remained on the floor beside him mostly untouched. Later medical evidence was to suggest that for most of the evening it did not even contain an alcoholic drink.

Jean and her father were standing at the large dresser pouring drinks. Bert, who normally had the freedom of the drinks cabinet at the farm, as Hubert Wilkes had at the Spencer's home, heard Jean say, 'It's all right, dad, Bert already has a drink.'

Bert was startled to hear Wilkes snap angrily, 'The cheeky bugger!'

He looked up to see if his host was joking. Hubert Wilkes was not and he was glaring angrily. For once Bert felt distinctly uncomfortable in what for him were normally pleasantly familiar surroundings and congenial company. But the feeling was only fleeting. The irascible farmer was given to strange moods, regardless of time or place. It was easy to dismiss the unusual slight as the whisky was working its alchemy, suffusing Bert with a rosy glow. However, he was partly drawn out of his euphoric haze by an increasing awareness that Hubert Wilkes was continuing to act in a peculiar manner. The farmer was exceeding the limits of hospitality; pestering the two women to drink ever faster, topping their glasses prematurely and without asking, in what was becoming almost an urgent frenzy.

Suddenly the reality of the situation pierced the cloud cover of Bert's befuddled brain. The past utterances and sick boasts of the old farmer leapt back into his mind. Hubert Wilkes was actually trying to recreate the situation that he claimed, he so used to enjoy. The man was attempting to live out his own much re-told tales of sexual orgy and his particularly unpleasant, recurrent fantasy. But that could not really be happening, thought Bert, not with his wife and Hubert's own daughter as intended victims.

It took only two trigger words to dispel any lingering doubts. Hubert Wilkes turned from the dresser where he was pouring two fresh drinks.

With a theatrical wink at Bert, the old farmer said, 'Janet, I've made a *special cocktail* for you.'

'Wilkes regularly boasted about earlier sexual orgies with his close farmer friends when he previously farmed in Bromsgrove,' explained Bert. 'I'd never taken much notice and assumed they were just unpleasant flights of fancy. He often blatantly announced, in his usual highly pitched amplified voice, his intentions to relive his past when he thought the time was right. All other farm staff had heard him boasting that way. He would always give a lecherous wink adding, "I always made the women *special cocktails* and then the fun began."'

From his own past telling, it was all too clear that Hubert Wilkes was envisaging a repeat performance of his Rabelaisian delights of yesteryears. Perhaps it was that repeated indications of this dark aspect of the farm-er's peculiar personality, constantly rearing its ugly head, primed the tense undercurrents in the troubled Wilkes family.

Bert Spencer was in no state to allow analytical thought. If he had been feeling drunk before, he now felt sick and miserable. It was time to go. It was the finish of Holloway House Farm as part of his life, he mused, depress-ingly. Jean had already left the room and had gone upstairs to search for a book to lend to Janet, totally unaware of her father's present preoccupation. Bert stood up from his armchair and staggered across the lounge, heading for the toilet in the downstairs utility room. He made it to the lounge door, which he shut behind him. As he stepped into the unlit hallway he stumbled into the ever-present clutter of boots, Wellingtons and outdoor clothing, now with the addition of some DIY materials. It was now around 11.30 pm.

Life was about to take on a nightmare quality for the Spencers and their hosts. Bert Spencer was stepping into a shadowy world of unreality. He heard a sound as of rolling thunder. He saw a flash like a close-range strike of lightning.

Later, blood and hair were to be found on the skirting board. How long he lay he had no means of knowing. When he climbed to his feet he was no longer reacting to normal impulses from his brain. In the bizarre and weird half-world which he had now entered, his senses were functioning partially and selectively. He was in a state of mental limbo, in a condition today both well documented and medically recognised – if not yet fully understood.

Spencer was following a course of action uncharted by himself and impossible later to recall or comprehend. He cannot and does not dispute his actions between his fall and his re-entering the farmhouse or account for the horrific few seconds or minutes which followed. Others have part of that story. Bert has none.

Jean Wilkes was still upstairs when Bert stepped out of the house and into the farmyard. Some sight or sound, the outside floodlight being turned on or the squelch of feet on gravel perhaps, caused her to look out of the bedroom window. All she saw was the familiar and friendly figure of Bert Spencer walking across the yard to his car beyond the low wall. As she watched, Bert lifted the tailgate of the white Cortina estate and rummaged in his tool bag. Jean returned to her hunt for the book. She had seen nothing to disturb her. That was singularly unfortunate, for Bert was carrying a shotgun; a single-barrelled 12-bore. The gun was part of Hubert Wilkes' house armoury. Bert had picked it up in the hallway as he had left the farmhouse.

By now he was devoid of conscious thought, moving as in a dream, or nightmare, his actions dictated by some irresistible and incomprehensible inner compulsion. From the tool bag in his car he took a mini hacksaw and crossed the yard to a lean-to building to the side of the house. On a rickety workbench he began to saw off the barrel of the shotgun. For a drunken man using a thin, six-inch saw blade and working with no vice in a dark corner it must have been no easy operation. Under quite different conditions it later was to take a sober policeman nearly three minutes to replicate the task. It is surprising that such noisy and prolonged work was heard by no one in the house, despite the carrying effect of sounds at night in the countryside. Even Jean, still upstairs, away from the noise of the television and the vociferous Hubert, heard nothing.

It was now approaching midnight. The time span between Bert leaving the lounge and his delayed return had begun to worry Janet. No one knows if Bert had been lying unconscious for a long while or if the time had been occupied by his wrestling with the strange and unnecessary problem of truncating a shotgun barrel in the near dark. As Bert re-entered the farmhouse carrying the loaded sawn-off weapon, Janet was on her feet and moving across the lounge to the door. The door opened before she reached it. The Bert Spencer who stood there was like some unfamiliar doppelganger. His normally deep-set eyes were exophthalmic, bulging, with the iris totally visible. He stepped into the room, saying nothing. 'Are you all right?' Janet queried, only slightly anxious. 'Quite all right. Just feeling a bit sick,' answered her husband. Janet had no time to spot the gun

'I walked back into the sitting room carrying the weapon,' confirmed, Bert, adding, 'I strode across to where Wilkes was watching TV, raised the gun towards his temple and pulled the trigger. Then I stood still, staring around at what was to me an empty room. There was no dead body, no wife staring at me in a terrified state, no sound. Even the Edwardian wall clock seemed to have stopped ticking.' Strangely, the farmer remained seated in death.

Briefly, Janet stood transfixed by shock and fear. Her husband stood in a daze. He had made no attempt to reload the gun.

'I was unaware of Jean entering the room and screaming, I just stood feebly, rooted to the spot,' says Bert.

Janet launched herself at him, fighting to take the weapon from a somewhat deranged husband. It should have been no contest – a nine stone woman attempting to wrestle a shotgun from the grip of a fourteen stone man, a man skilled in judo and unarmed combat, a weightlifter and bodybuilder. However, Bert Spencer was aware of no struggle. He stood half-heartedly waving the shotgun up and down. One downward movement, not a deliberate blow, as Janet later was to readily agree, caught and split her above the eyebrow. Suddenly the gun broke into three sections, the barrel, the stock and the butt. Janet still had the stock gripped in her hands.

Bert Spencer was still seeing and hearing nothing – almost like being under murky water. The room was still empty according to the messages his brain was transmitting.

Surprisingly, Jean Wilkes was able to pick herself up and the two women fled from the room with Bert stumbling after them. Despite all that was not registering with him, he did recall seeing a smear of blood on the lounge door. It was hardly a chase. The women had the fleetness of foot born of terror. Bert Spencer was moving as in a foot-dragging dream sequence as if wearing lead boots. When he made contact with one or other of the women, in the hallway, it was to clumsily push or shove. Beyond the confines of the lounge, reality had returned to his sense of sight – vision without under-standing. At some time in the strange pursuit he had picked up another of the guns, which were scattered so liberally about the house. At one stage Janet had snatched up the telephone to ring for help and been struck some glancing blows from the gun about her head and back. Just one blow from the barrel or butt of a shotgun wielded by a strong and determined man is enough to incapacitate, maim or kill. Such a blow, wielded by a man with the strength of Bert Spencer could fell an Ox, but Janet Spencer was still able to think, move and evade her husband. So was Jean who made it to the front door to dash out into the night. Janet took the other route and fled out of the kitchen door to hide behind a tree.

'The women fled, I stood there alone in the house, stone deaf, with the body of my friend sitting dead on the settee in the lounge,' remembers Spencer. 'I was totally bewildered and disorientated, wondering how I'd managed to damage my hand. It was then I remember crying out, like a lost child, "Janet! Janet! Where are you?"'

Ever since that night of tragedy, Bert has had the episode on constant playback; fragmented, disjointed, compounded of his own limited mem-ory, statements made in court and later conversations with his wife during prison visits. But time has failed to inject any element of reason into the persistent nightmare.

Unfortunately for Bert Spencer, it would seem that at the time of his trial his counsel was not familiar with the work and writings of C.J. Jung; in particular his thesis on 'The Interpretation of Nature and the Psyche'. In Jung's concluding chapter he states that, '... Contrary to all expectations, a severe head injury is not always followed by a corresponding loss of consciousness. To the observer the wounded man seems apathetic, in a trance, and not conscious of anything. Subjectively, however, consciousness is by no means extinguished. Sensory communication with the outside world is, in a large measure, restricted, but not always completely cut off, although the noise of battle, for instance, may suddenly give way to a "solemn" silence … In a few cases the wounded think they are making swimming movements with their arms …' Bert had shown all the classic symptoms.

Spencer had fallen full length across the hallway and smashed his head against the skirting board – 14 stone falling against a solid wall, impacting just behind the temple. The medical world has little by way of explanation but there is profuse documentation on the subject of sudden head trauma being followed immediately by uncharacteristic and extreme violent behaviour, even in the normally most passive and even-natured of individuals, which Bert Spencer undoubtedly and evidentially was, with such behaviour being followed by a speedy return to normality.

Added to the possible psychiatrically regressive effects of a blow to the head, Bert was a walking time bomb for other reasons. He was taking tablets prescribed to combat depression and he had imbibed, in some six hours, over half a bottle of whisky – more than his average monthly consumption. For about five months, in his quest for physical excellence, he had been regularly ingesting anabolic steroids in the form of Dianabol. In the sixties and seventies little was known about possible side effects resulting from the intake of steroids. What was certain was that they produced the desired effects of increasing athletic performance and improving body shape and appearance. It was only beginning to be suspected by grass roots observers, competitors and coaches that there might be a price to pay in terms of altered behavioural patterns as well as the earlier suspicion of a decline in sexual potency. At that time scientific authorities were dismissive in their attitudes to the possibility of the muscle building steroids having any other detrimental potential. It was to take another seven years before *The Lancet* published an article describing 'Bodybuilders' Psychosis', a proven and recognised association between the intake of steroids and unexpected and extreme violent actions. It was a further two years before the American researcher, David Katz, published the results of his research into the phenomenon. He documented many cases of steroid users displaying violent criminal activity, ranging from assault to murder. In many instances the provocation, which sparked the rapid personality change was as insignificant as a jostled elbow or an imagined glance.

In 1979 such information was not generally known nor was the principle accepted. Currently, such frenzies are known as 'Roid Rage' – a term coined in the mid-eighties.

Shortly after 11.30 pm, just under half an hour before the eve of his 40th birthday, Bert Spencer had indeed become steeped in explosive potential. He himself provided the charge. The mix of alcohol, tranquillisers and anabolic steroids acted as the primer. His blow to the head was to be the detonator and the fuse was the embarrassing situation, from which he had fully intended to take his leave. Hubert Wilkes had lit the fuse unwittingly with a wink and two words; 'special cocktail'.

By the time alcohol and chemicals had finished working their alchemy that night on Bert Spencer, juggling with his conscious and subconscious minds and playing games with his sensory perception, the fit, quick-thinking athlete had been reduced to a robotic state. Interaction between his brain and his body was teetering on the very edge of chaos. As he stepped into the hallway he was hurled one step beyond. As he climbed to his feet he was in the grip of all of the classic symptoms of automatism – an irresistible impulse.

There was a fine Greek irony about his unthinking choice of weapon. It was the shotgun, which had originally belonged to Jack Poole of Yew Tree Farm, the gun that Bert had tried unsuccessfully to buy from him two years before. Hubert Wilkes, however, had heard of Bert's approach to Mr Poole and his spiteful dog-in-a-manger attitude had led to his negotiating the purchase for himself, yet another addition to his considerable armoury. Without telling Bert, Hubert Wilkes had had the weapon completely refurbished, the working parts re-blued and the woodwork resurfaced. Even if Bert had seen the weapon beforehand it was, by then, quite unrecognisable. Alas this old heavy12-bore shotgun was the weapon that Bert was blindly to pick up and the gun with which Hubert Wilkes was to be shot dead. This particular gun was the reason Bert's address was found in the address book at Yew Tree Farm and was the catalyst, which underlined him as an original early suspect.

For the two terrified women who had fled from Holloway House Farm it was the worst of nightmares. Spencer, usually a person representing protection and security, had metamorphosised into a demonic monster. Despite the almost overwhelming fear and shock, the women had been galvanised into survival action. While Janet concealed herself behind a tree, Jean ran, as she naturally thought, for her life. Bert had stumbled into the farmyard, still calling forlornly for his wife, Janet. He took a large torch from the open tailgate of his Cortina and then slammed it shut. This he did with such force that the penned army of turkeys squealed their protests into the night in a thousand banshee wails.

In her terror, Jean Wilkes thought that she had heard the shotgun discharged for a second time. In a frenzy of hysteria she hammered at the door of the first dwelling she came to. There was no answer. She ran on, stumbling and falling along an overgrown footpath, and then cut across the fields to the A449, towards some houses. She shouted and banged on the first door. It was opened, but the house had no telephone. Next door had and the 999 call was made, summoning the police and the ambulance service.

Meanwhile, Janet crouched behind a tree in the farmhouse garden watched as Bert swept the torch around, still shouting for her. She crawled across the garden and into the adjacent field. Still crawling, she gathered her flagging resources and made it to the main road. The ambulance which Jean's frantic call had summoned was on its way to Holloway House and approaching the spot where Janet had breached the boundary hedge. Hysterical, bloodied and at the very end of her tether, Janet Spencer flagged it down, climbed in and sobbed out her story. The driver, Arthur O'Nions and

the attendant driver, Barry Thomas, were both colleagues of Bert Spencer –
but they did not know Janet. In her state of high emotion the words tumbled
out confusingly.

Barry Thomas understood only that a man had been shot at Holloway
House, that his patient had seen the incident and that a gunman was on
the loose. As the driver turned off the A449 into Ashwood Lower Lane,
about three hundred yards from the farm, Janet became hysterical and
screamed at the ambulance men to go no further. Barrie Thomas stepped
out of the vehicle, intending to check on the situation at the farmhouse
himself. In view of the circumstances, a winter's night, a dead man in an
isolated farmhouse and a deranged killer roaming the area with a shotgun
and ammunition, Mr Thomas' intention was somewhat above and beyond
the call of duty. However, his walk into a possible life-threatening situation
was aborted.

Bert Spencer had, by now, partially re-entered the real world, as quickly
and as inexplicably as he had been removed from it. Still bewildered, he had
driven his car around the lanes and returned to the approach lane to the
farm. Seeing the ambulance and Barrie Thomas, he stopped and wound
down his window. If Bert Spencer was bemused, Barrie Thomas was amazed
to see his friend and colleague sitting there. He had no knowledge of the fact
that the injured and distressed woman in the ambulance was Bert's wife.

He bent forward to give Bert a warning, 'Don't go down the lane, Bert.
There's a gunman about.'

'I think it's me, Barrie,' Bert replied to his astonished colleague. He
leaned over to pick up the shotgun from the passenger floor pan. 'You'd
better have this,' he said, handing it to Barrie, adding, 'Be careful, it might
be loaded.'

'After 30 odd years of playing back fragments of the incident in my
head I still can't find any reason for what happened,' explains Bert today.
'The destruction and harm I caused on that night to Mr Wilkes' family and
friends is something that will never leave me. I've offered them my sympathy, but the guilt is far worse than any prison sentence. Hopefully, the 14

years I spent in some of Britain's most brutal prisons gave them some sense of justice and closure ... I still deeply and sincerely regret what I did and that will never change.'

A police car drew up and Barrie Thomas passed the shotgun to a police constable. Then began an almost carnival episode which would have been amusing in any other circumstances. Arthur O'Nions drove away to deliver Janet Spencer to Corbett Hospital. Barrie Thomas climbed into the passenger seat of Bert's Cortina and Bert drove slowly down to the turning to the farm with the police car following. On the short journey Barrie asked if Bert had any more guns.

'No,' answered Bert, fishing in his pocket. 'Just this cartridge.' So saying, he threw it out of the window. An insignificant action in the circumstances but one that was later seized upon by the campaigners and treated to an undeserved process of magnification.

The bizarre nature of the two-car convoy seemed to be lost on the participants; a killer chauffeuring an ambulance man and guiding the police to the scene of his crime in a night-time drive down a dark lane. Perhaps it reflects to a degree Bert Spencer's standing with his co-workers. But the drive was to turn to farce. Bert turned the Cortina into the driveway, which led to the rear of the farm, but the police car went sailing blithely on into the night, leaving the lone ambulance man in the company of a very disturbed and recent killer. The two men entered the farmhouse where the victim was lying. A farmhouse with several shotguns scattered about and ammunition by the handful.

Barrie Thomas examined the body of Hubert Wilkes, but realised immediately there was nothing he could do. Bert Spencer, the enormity of his actions only slowly impacting upon him, had reached for the whisky bottle and was drinking from the neck.

Eventually both men strolled outside into the lane when the police car driver finally found his way back to the farm. Quite peacefully, Bert Spencer returned with the others to the farmhouse, there to await the arrival of the police team.

The factors that categorise the bizarre murder of Hubert Wilkes are almost too obvious to state. As causative aspects – pleasure, profit and expedience were all absent. There was no premeditation and no motive. Bert Spencer readily, even helpfully, gave himself up. Had he been able and willing to give an account of the various contributions made to his final, temporary mental unbalancing there would have been no room left for mystery and speculation. As it was, both his silence about his knowledge of Hubert Wilkes coupled with the universal ignorance at the time of the chemico-medical facets of his and similar crimes left a clear and fertile field for both.

Pernicious rumour had a disappointing run, finding no sexual geometry to exercise the ready tongues. Instead, Paul Foot has to lead the band of campaigners down a quite different road. With a leap of imagination of Olympian proportions, he was to propound the theory that Hubert Wilkes had, that night, accused Bert of involvement in the murder of Carl Bridgewater. His contention was that Bert had then shot the farmer in front of witnesses to avoid detection.

Even if this scenario was accepted as the truth – there were more options open to Bert than this obvious explosive and violent action. As previously mentioned there were guns lying around the farm and enough ammunition to start a small revolution. It would have been a very simple exercise, when the two women were out of the room, to select a loaded shotgun and simply shoot Hubert Wilkes, and explain the gun had gone off accidentally. Guns were a familiar subject and the handling of them in company was commonplace. Spencer at the very worst would have been convicted of involuntary manslaughter, which could have carried a suspended sentence.

A lot has been made of the fact that Spencer shot Hubert Wilkes just four weeks after the Bridgewater Four were sentenced. It was the campaigners' theory that on the night of the shooting of Hubert Wilkes he had somehow challenged Bert and confronted him about the murder of the paperboy, saying Spencer was responsible and Bert simply silenced his accuser. If Bert had been responsible for the slaying of Carl Bridgewater, he was in fact in the safest position possible. There had just been an in-depth month long trial and four members of the Birmingham underworld had been convicted, which included a signed confession from one of its members in the shape of Irishman Pat Molloy. Unless Wilkes had a signed confession or film footage of Spencer carrying out the act – it is unlikely the police would have taken little or no notice of a third party. In fact the opposite was true. Following the shooting of farmer Wilkes the police did apparently swing into action and re-traced their steps surrounding their early suspect. Spencer was back under the microscope and every aspect of his life was scrutinised. Statements were re-examined and witnesses interviewed.

With no motive on which to hang a case, the prosecution was to be hard put to show premeditation. To bridge that gap they were to bring on, at the dying hours of the trial, Anthony Wilkes, Hubert's son, to introduce the 'dog factor'. Bert had befriended the vicious farm dog in order to get close enough to Hubert Wilkes to shoot him dead. The campaigners were to build on even that piece of misinformation in order to make a case for a copycat link, as a dog was present at Yew Tree Farm. No one heard it bark, let alone the noise of a shotgun, when the farm was plundered and Carl Bridgewater murdered. Had Spencer, Foot echoed, befriended the noisy dog by visiting Yew Tree Farm?

It was to be seven months before Bert Spencer was put on trial. After his conviction and sentence of life imprisonment, the Bridgewater Four campaigners were to have a long clear path to openly attack Spencer, who was somewhat silenced by his incarceration at Her Majesty's pleasure.

7.

The Silent Defendant

....

Bert Spencer was taken to Wombourne police station and in the early hours of 14 December, 1979, he was interviewed by Detective Chief Superintendent Robert Stewart and Detective Chief Inspector Weslea Watson. DCI Watson had already interviewed Bert in the early days of the Carl Bridgewater murder. Bert was, naturally, in a state of extreme shock. His recall of any of the preceding few hours was limited and of the killing itself quite non-existent. He was told just what he had done and he had to accept the facts, but it was impossible for him to come to terms with the enormity of his behaviour. His work with the ambulance service had for years meant that he was dedicated to care and life-saving. However, now he had to take on board the fact that he had committed an act of ultimate violence and for whatever reason, had taken another man's life. This was something Bert had to live with to this day even if it was due to an apparent mental collapse.

The shock was overwhelming. The total inability to understand his own actions added to the after-effects of his heavy drinking, his consumption of powerful steroid concoctions and a heavy blow to the head. This latter injury was to be the subject of two X-rays. He was in no state to indulge in any verbal sparring; nor did he wish to. He offered only a few answers, one that was not the absolute truth. That answer was very much to his disadvantage. When asked if he had any history of suffering from blackouts or fits, he correctly answered in the negative. DCS Stewart went on to ask if he was having any treatment for any disorder or depression. Again he answered *no*. That was his only lie.

In fact, he had suffered an understandable lowering of spirits since being questioned about the murder of Carl Bridgewater. It had seemed that his own innocent involvement with Yew Tree Farm and his own pastimes and interests had combined to wrap around him in a web of suspicion. After all, the initial enquiries surrounding Spencer as a suspect in the Bridgewater murder had come from an anonymous phone call – who could have done such a thing thought Bert? Was it a work colleague, a family member or even a close friend? It was as if all of his honest efforts had turned in on him, funnelling him down the years into the darkest of corners. Sometimes he felt people were discussing the case, talking about him personally. In fairness nearly 10,000 people had been interviewed and a percentage of those were initially suspects. He had sought the advice of Dr Wallington at Corbett Hospital who had prescribed some sleeping tablets. Perhaps Bert Spencer had a more precise definition of disorder or depression, maybe it was because he had only partly emerged from his terrifying mental fog, but he failed to make the point then, or later, that he was daily ingesting substances whose effect in combination was then quite unknown and unpredictable. Added to that was an overload of both stress and work, all topped off with a severe head injury.

The senior officers delved deep in their attempts to establish a motive, but Bert could only answer that he had none. His last recall of events prior to the killing was of Hubert Wilkes making his disgusting, if veiled, suggestion. He remembered feeling ill and starting to make his way to the downstairs toilet, before getting his wife to drive him home. After that, other factors had taken control and he had been moving on some strange and automatic pilot, in the grip of forces beyond anyone's understanding. There was no motive or rational explanation for what had happened at Holloway House Farm. No one, least of all Bert Spencer, was aware of the causative factors. He could only make the truthful answer that *no*, he had no motive and even worse, he had no recall.

Bert Spencer spent seven months on remand at HM Winson Green prison, Birmingham, before his trial. In line with the normal routine for prisoners awaiting trial on a charge of murder, he spent the first six months in the hospital ward under constant surveillance. In the ward were thirteen beds. The lights were permanently kept on and prison officers shared a

24-hour vigil – in case any of the accused men might prefer not to have their day in court. It was here that Bert came across Prison Officer Robert James Graham, unaware, of course, that the man was to feature in his life, years later, in a particularly malevolent way.

Knowing that he was experiencing a sample of just what life was to have on offer for many years' ahead, Bert's normal, happy go lucky manner, which had started to spiral downwards during the Bridgewater enquiry, descended into morose and despairing introspection. His behaviour was subdued and his attitude became one of increasing insularity. The days were filled with an endless round of ritual cleaning and inspection. Every prisoner action, or unusual turn of conversation was recorded by the supervising officer in the daily report book – an important detail in view of later events. The remand prisoners were not even permitted to look out of the windows into the yard below where the police dogs were trained. Five minutes were allowed for slopping out. Invariably, the next men in the queue for the lavatory leaned over the half-door, encouraging speed of function with self-defeating kicks and curses.

In the final month before his trial, Bert was moved to a three-man cell. It measured the standard six feet by twelve. Also shared was the sole toilet facility, one small plastic bucket. In those cramped conditions, in order to alleviate the inevitable foetid atmosphere, some men elect, to defecate on newspaper and to 'fly a pigeon', that is to wrap the faeces into a parcel and throw it through the small window opening. Some land in the yard below, but most catch on the rolls of razor wire beneath the windows. There they are left to hang, long after the contents have been weathered into bio-degradation, leaving a grotesque washing-line advertisement of 20th century prison conditions outside a jail, which was built in 1849.

Ann Whelan, mother of Michael Hickey who was detained at Her Majesty's Pleasure only four weeks before the killing of Hubert Wilkes, had sprung into action immediately after Bert Spencer's arrest. She wrote a letter to DCS Stewart in which she protested the innocence of the gang of four. She made the suggestion that DCS Stewart was party to such knowledge and voiced her hope that Bert Spencer would be 'questioned very deeply' about the murder of Carl Bridgewater. Then, a few weeks later, Mrs Whelan wrote to Paul Foot of the *Daily Mirror*, to enlist his help in establishing the innocence of four convicted men, using the accusation of Bert Spencer as a lever. Mr Foot left it until after Bert's trial and conviction before applying the pressure, which his investigative journalistic position allowed. The dark clouds were gathering over the convicted man, Spencer, and he would forever be linked to the murder of Carl Bridgewater.

The trial of Bert Spencer for the murder of Hubert Wilkes opened on 23 June, 1980. It was no surprise that Ann Whelan was present in court, or that DCS Stewart was in attendance.

As Bert entered the courtroom, DCS Stewart, together with DCI Watson, made a point of leaning over and asking solicitously, 'Are you all right, lad?' apparently feeling some sort of empathy with the lonely and still bewildered ambulance liaison officer.

Paul Foot records his own somewhat different version of that moment. He claims that DCS Stewart and DCI Watson failed to make an appearance in court that day, referring to them as 'two absent friends'. Mistakenly or otherwise, Mr Foot makes claim that because neither DCS Stewart or DCI Watson were called to give evidence, there was no mention in court of a conversation which he alleges Jean Wilkes was party to. This somewhat damning conversation, earlier on the night of the murder, between Hubert Wilkes and Bert Spencer, in which the murder of Carl Bridgewater had been discussed in detail. Indeed, there was no such mention because the conversation did not take place, nor had Jean Wilkes ever said that it had. Mr Foot deduces that this was a deliberate ploy to prevent references to the murder of Carl Bridgewater.

In his book on the murder at Yew Tree Farm, Paul Foot himself states, 'Certainly, Jean Wilkes, in *her* statement made at Holloway House between three and four o'clock in the morning to Stewart, Watson and WPC Rawlings, nowhere referred to Carl Bridgewater.' The value of this mythical conversation to the campaigners would have been the concoction of a feeble motive for the killing of Hubert Wilkes – that Wilkes had some special knowledge and had accused Bert Spencer of that murder and that Bert had then shot him to keep him quiet. In the absence of any such evidence, Paul Foot refers to the wild speculation of one Michael Howard, a one-time friend of Hubert Wilkes, who, at the time of the murder was presumably at home in Droitwich, some twenty miles away.

If the presence of Michael Hickey's mother was no surprise at the Spencer trial, the curious selection of one of the jurors was. The coincidence factor had struck at Bert Spencer once again. Called for jury service was a Miss Julia Hickey. After an immediate challenge she promptly joined Ann Whelan in the public gallery where they were seen exchanging notes. Of course, before her presence was challenged, Miss Hickey had already spent time with the body of jurors: time in which points of influence could possibly have been put across.

There was little ammunition for Bert's counsel to produce, in his defence, against the charge of murder and in favour of the reduced charge of manslaughter. Bert, in keeping his silence about the circumstances of that evening by not taking the stand, had denied himself the opportunity to argue his lack of premeditation. He had assumed that the events would have made that all-important point for him and that his own temporary mental state would have been self-evident.

Bert claims that, according to her murdered father, Jean Wilkes had a history of mental problems. This, of course, may have been just another part of his strange fantasising. But Bert Spencer had believed it. Twice, according to Hubert Wilkes, Jean had tried to take her own life. Bert felt that should he be forced, under cross examination, to repeat the old farmer's claims of past orgies and continuing incest in open court, ridiculous fantasies though they no doubt were, then the inevitable media attention could have driven Jean Wilkes to further extreme measures of self-hurt.

His wife, Janet, was also living on nerves stretched to the limit and he was fearful of her reaction as well. At such revelations, had Bert made them about Hubert Wilkes, the speculators of the media would have been dancing in the taprooms of Fleet Street and in the studios of the television companies. The pressures on the two women, speculated Bert, would have been insufferable, as their characters would inevitably have been dragged through the gutters of suggestion, innuendo and gossip. Untold misery and possibly dramatic consequences were meant to have been avoided by Bert's silence. However, the vacuum so created was to be almost as damaging. Much local speculation, groundless but colourful, was to follow in the years ahead.

Bert Spencer's hitherto untold version of the night's events was partly supported by the inquest report on Hubert Wilkes. On the night in question, Mr Wilkes, a known heavy drinker, had, in the comfortable surroundings of his own home, consumed only enough alcohol to register a mere nine milligrams per 100 millilitres of blood – little more than the proverbial sniff of a barmaid's apron. A fact that strongly backs up Bert Spencer's account of Hubert Wilkes' stated pattern of his orgiastic evenings.

On the other hand, there is some mystery about the amount of alcohol that the police claimed was present in Bert Spencer's sample. It was stated that it showed 185 milligram's per100 millilitres of blood. This suggested that perhaps Bert was not terribly drunk and that he had consumed only the equivalent of some four, maybe five, double whiskies. And yet he had been drinking at home, in the pub, at the farm, and from the whisky bottle on his return to the farm. At a conservative estimate this would have amounted to more than half a bottle of whisky – at least a month's intake for the fitness conscious body-builder. A minor mystery perhaps, but a damning factor in the argument for murder against manslaughter.

In a fair trial, hampered largely by Bert's stubbornness in his refusal to take the stand, the prosecuting counsel, Philip Cox, QC, perhaps sensing that all was not quite sound in the charge of murder, but having only instinct born of experience to substitute for hard evidence, leaned so far towards the defence as to break in on the summing up of Mr Justice Glidewell. He offered the suggestion that Bert Spencer could be acquitted of murder if his mind was indeed confused by drink. Had the defence counsel weighed in heavily enough with the initially provable evidence of the chemical mix in

Bert's body at the time of the killing, and contested the doubt raised that the hair and blood on the skirting board belonged to Bert Spencer, then perhaps the charge of murder would not have been allowed. Had medical evidence been available in the detail known and accepted today, then Bert Spencer would have possibly been found guilty of a reduced charge of involuntary manslaughter. Alas, it was not to be. The evidence given by Jean Wilkes and her brother, Philip, was shot through with hurt and surprise, but devoid of acid and venom directed towards Bert, despite the horrific turn of events at Holloway House. Anthony Wilkes, however, was to add weight to the wafer-thin argument favouring premeditation and intent. He claimed that Bert Spencer had made 'special friends' with the vicious guard dog in order to get safely past it on the night to shoot old man Wilkes.

Had Bert Spencer planned the killing of Hubert Wilkes, he could have done so without his ever having to leave the house. Guns and ammunition were available in several places. In planning a murder scenario, would any-one include the act of sawing off the barrel of the murder weapon prior to the act and at the scene of the crime? Not counting the fact that there were two witnesses, Jean Wilkes and Janet Spencer.

Mr Justice Glidewell was detailed in his summing up about the irrele-vance of the murder of Carl Bridgewater to this case. He emphasised that the interviewing of Bert Spencer during the Bridgewater enquiry was purely a matter of routine, as with thousands of others.

Hubert Vincent Spencer was found guilty of murder and sentenced to life imprisonment; a sentence which was in fact to run for more than fourteen years, some five years in excess of the normal tariff for what was classed as a motiveless, drunken, domestic murder. In recent years, similar cases, even multiple killings, committed while under the influence of men-tally destabilising substances, have been seen to attract sentences as light as three years' probation.

Perhaps the saddest postscript to the tragic death of Hubert Wilkes was revealed by the post mortem. Hubert Wilkes, in the normal course of events, was a man looking at death only months away.

Bert Spencer was sent to Shrewsbury prison for a short time. There he met artist Ken Leech, an ex-paratrooper medic, who, in earlier days, had practised his medical skills on offshore oil rigs. This talented prisoner was later to demolish one of the many hurdles that were to be strewn in Bert's increasingly stony path. In the usual routine of prisoner shuffling, necessitated by many reasons, such as avoiding contact between antagonistic inmates, Bert was returned after three weeks to Winson Green prison in Birmingham. After two weeks he was transferred to the equally primitive and infamously named prison, Wormwood Scrubs, in London. This was to be his home for the next six and a half years.

He arrived at the Scrubs just days after a major riot, the result of which was the implementation of a 24-hour 'Bang-up' regime, which was to last for three months. But, by now, the short, sharp culture shocks had had much of their stings pulled. Claustrophobic desperation had been replaced by a compound of resignation and despair.

The harshness of his induction to a Wormwood Scrubs reacting in rage to the recent inmate violence had little impact upon Bert himself. Following the usual pattern of the aftermath of a prison riot, the ringleaders and main participants had been shipped out, leaving the other inmates to take the brunt of the backlash attitudes of the understandably edgy staff. Already, Bert Spencer had decided upon and adopted a survival strategy, which he hoped would take him through the long years ahead. He was to reduce his radius of social contact to the very minimum necessary for continued sanity and to live a self-contained existence within a shrunken perimeter - as far as was practical inside the all-encapsulating shuffle of prison routine.

It would be easy to summarily disregard the years he spent in Wormwood Scrubs. They could be dismissively summed up by saying that for three years Bert Spencer worked in the tailor's shop sewing donkey-jackets, hospital and kitchen whites. For one year after that he served the sparse Scrubs' rations from that most dangerous of prison locations, the kitchen hot plate. For the remainder of his three plus years there he was employed as the principle cleaner on Number three landing in the notorious lifers D Wing.

To leave it at that would be to sidestep the aspects of prison life which the general public would be hard-pressed or flatly unwilling to believe. Facts of life are generally obscured by the 'wall-to-wall-carpet', 'make it tougher' and 'hang 'em high' brigades. Prison life is degrading, conditions are often Dickensian and situations arise which can be successfully life-threatening. Prisoner behaviour is sometimes barbaric in the extreme and staff responses can be geared to meet the level of threat. The grim bricks of Her Majesty's Prison, Wormwood Scrubs have seen it all. Kangaroo courts with inmates as judge and jury have carried out sentences of death. Prisoners, terrified beyond endurance, have found their own exit routes from unbearable situations. Gang male rape is not uncommon. Men have been murdered in their sleep by a cellmate. In a 'bang-up' situation, violence perpetrated by prison officers upon inmates is un-witnessed and the guilty staff are unidentifiable, except as members of the 'mufti squad', clad as they are in riot gear and black-visor helmets.

In any maximum security prison there is no hiding place from the constant threat of violence; not even in a segregation unit, which is designed to provide sanctuary for identifiable targets. There were no tears when a notorious paedophile was murdered in just that situation in the October of 1993, but still, the law of the land was broken and possibly the breach was aided by, at the best, official negligence, or, at the worst, by the turning of an official Nelson eye.

Fights and woundings, often unprovoked, are common occurrences. The improvised weapons that are used can be lethal. These can include the square and heavy PP9 radio batteries, swung in sock containers as a cosh, the detached iron bed-leg as a club, a razor blade melted into a tooth brush handle makes a fearsome edged weapon, craft knives and kitchen utensils – from carving knives to meat cleavers – are available to a determined inmate. The kitchen also provides boiling fat and the addition of sugar to boiling water is used to give the sticking effect of napalm. Stainless steel serving trays can be ground to a cutting edge. The list goes on, as do the eruptions of violence often fuelled by anything from heroin to hooch (illicitly distilled spirits), linking with the threat of staff reprisals to form an endless belt of tension.

In the inmate sub-culture the strong prey on the weak as gangland patterns are formed on similar structural bases to those of the more deprived inner-city areas. In D Wing, Wormwood Scrubs, are confined some 250 of some of the most dangerous men in the world. These are Category A prisoners – serial killers, IRA or Loyalist terrorists, sadists, rapists and armed robbers, the 'cream' of the underworld – many with the outside contacts to apply pressure through prisoners' families. Some are career prisoners, men who know that they will never be released and who have no particular wish to be. Such men have ambition only to be king of the concrete and steel jungle and work hard towards that end. Men who are nothing on the outside, often through their own self-importance, are deemed feared and respected. Their presence in a prison wing is to make the simplest and most basic of human traffic movement into a potential survival course – queuing for a meal, slopping out or taking a shower. The weak and vulnerable who opt for a life of segregation on Rule 43, find that they have continuing problems; their food and drink is often contaminated in unspeakable ways and their relative inaccessibility serves only to increase prisoner ingenuity against such shielded targets.

This was the nature of the world into which Bert Spencer, one-time respected ambulance liaison officer, now inhabited. It is a world in which George Orwell's basic tenet of life holds good – all convicts are equal, but some are far more equal than others. The pecking order of the inmate class structure is determined by many factors, the main one being the nature of the crime and sentence. Other factors include the prisoner's ability to bring outside influence to bear, either through access to money or through his notoriety. Also the traditional rules and values of the prisoners themselves, which are operated in the twilight world of prison life like a *Lord of the Flies'* regime and, finally, an inmate's own personality and ability to withstand and counter the mental and physical pressures which are as much a part of prison life as the bricks and bars. At the bottom of the prison caste system are the sex-offenders and child-killers.

Bert Spencer in the normal course of prison life was neither weak nor vulnerable. Having said that he had experienced a negative mood swing with inmates at Wormwood Scrubs, after only a matter of weeks, when the pro-Bridgewater campaigners, through their standard-bearer, Paul Foot, fired their first public salvo in their efforts to brand him as the killer of Carl Bridgewater. The real persecution had started. It was October 1980. The *Daily Mirror* published Paul Foot's first article on the Bridgewater case, and the campaign was to be continued through all the years' of Bert Spencer's long sentence. Each renewed burst of anti-Spencer propaganda was to create added stress and more problems for Bert. The campaigners were to use many forms of attack over the years and the resulting problems, which were unloaded upon him were just as varied, in nature and in degree.

The four men convicted of the murder of Carl Bridgewater had a head start, some many months, ahead of Bert Spencer in the prison system, enough time to use the efficient inter-prison grapevine to prepare the ground to the campaigners' requirements in anticipation of Bert's arrival at any of Britain's penal institutions. The prison system contains its proportionate population percentage of unbalanced mavericks, anxious to curry favour with their more notorious peers and some of these men were not slow to pick up on an opportunity to leave their mark on Bert Spencer. After all he was a new target, a loner with no criminal connections, a victim of the urban legend syndrome, condemned by misinformation and delivered with unimpeachable authority from an unidentifiable source.

Bert Spencer has been spat on, attacked with scalding liquids and a variety of weapons. He has dealt with all of these situations with the skills in which he is so proficient, without straying from his role as a model prisoner. He kept these violent attacks to himself and never made any complaint to the authority or sought the dubious security of being segregated on 'Rule 43'.

Michael Hickey, less physically capable and far more vulnerable, experienced similar problems during his prison years, but his problems were not manufactured by Bert Spencer. Michael Hickey, although mentally fragile, has shown human endurance beyond belief, has always been active in taking up the chants of the campaigners and accusing Bert, a man he has never met and about whom he has no direct knowledge, of the murder for which he and his three associates were convicted. On at least two occasions the Hickey cousins, Michael and Vincent, have daubed those claims for the world to see in giant lettering on prison roofs as part of the campaign strategy. Other campaign tools were the frequent articles by Paul Foot published in the *Daily Mirror*. Then he followed it up by his bestselling book, *Murder at the Farm*, published in 1986. Also the Thames Television programme of the same title, which was broadcast on 25 March, 1987. Added to this was the accusatory letters that Mr Foot was wont to write to Bert Spencer and, in the May of 1993, BBC2's showing of Don Shaw's film production, *Bad Company*. There were also the sophisticated techniques of the well-timed pieces of false evidence of confessions supposed to have been made by Bert Spencer himself, when he allegedly admitted shooting Carl Bridgwater. All these supposed confessions are dealt with in detail in *Chapter 9 – The Prison 'Confessions'*.

In all, it was a strategy that would equate to attacking a tethered goat with a machine gun. Although there were other markers to signpost the passing of the prison years, few were heart lifting and most were miserable in the extreme. On several occasions Bert was able to use the specialist knowledge, which he had acquired and practised during his years with the ambulance service.

He was fortunately nearby when a prisoner was subjected to a murderous attack. The assailant, a long-term no-hoper, had been trying to effect a transfer from the Scrubs to a less demanding institution. The victim was standing in a toilet recess, stripped to the waist, ironing his kitchen whites. As he turned to leave he was hit in the stomach. The punching hand held a large pair of tailor's shears. The attacker struck and fled while his victim slumped to the ground, lying on his back, with the shears projecting from his side. Bert Spencer was close enough to hear the screams of agony and he ran to help. As he attended to the victim, Terry, the shears popped out of the man's side. Bert staunched the fountain of blood with the clean kitchen whites while help was summoned – this undoubtedly saved the prisoner's life.

Bert's immediate reward was simply to be allowed to take an unscheduled shower. After some time on a life-support machine, Terry regained his health and fitness. Five months later, Bert was called to the governor's office where a commendation from the Home Office was brusquely read out to him. After which, he was summarily marched out again back to his cell. Some prisoners may have expected and received a royal pardon.

He was again able to render immediate assistance when a prison officer collapsed on Number three landing, suffering with a heart attack. This time there was no blood and therefore no extra shower on offer. But, once again, in the course of time, he received the summons to the governor's office to listen to a reading of a Home Office commendation. He was more pleased when, two years later, he was visited by the man's son, also a prison officer, who thanked him profusely for the assistance that he had rendered to his father. He also informed Bert that the man had since suffered a second attack from which he had died.

Unfortunately, when his good friend, fellow prisoner John Glynn, a diabetic, died in grotesque circumstances, Bert was not at hand. Unaccompanied, he collapsed in the shower, but the diabetic coma did not kill him. He actually drowned in the inches of back-fed sewer effluent, which had long been a polluting presence in the shower area. Doubtless, 'death by drowning' did not appear on the death certificate.

One of the few lighter moments happened at Wormwood Scrubs when Bert Spencer had his first of two meetings with Prince Charles. As they shook hands, the prince, hard-pressed for a conversational bridge over the yawning divide asked, sincerely enough, what conditions were like in the prison? Direct, as ever, Bert replied, 'Bloody awful'. And they were.

I have personally spent time, while researching a fictional prison novel I was writing, at Wormwood Scrubs at the beginning of the millennium. I also spent a few days on the infamous lifers' D wing, housing category A prisoners. Although the archaic building was depressing and claustrophobic, standards had obviously improved since Bert's time there. In the 80's the old building was a cockroach-ridden playground for vermin, although mice are often encouraged as inmate pets. The food was often quite unpalatable, served by inmates with severe respiratory infections and rationed to minimal quantities. Once, for a demonstration to a naïve and unworldly prison visitor, Bert had gathered up the breakfast bacon ration from six inmates and had fitted the pieces into one small matchbox. But the prince wouldn't have wanted such detail, *bloody awful* probably summarised his own opinion anyway.

Every few months the prison tedium would be brought to a peak. The staff would create a major alert by finding, or alleging to have found, a gas canister, a gun or a cache of edged weapons. The prisoners would then endure a close-down situation during which there would be no work, no visits, no exercise, association or recreation. In those periods time would hang interminably and tension would tighten and the very air would seem to crackle with electrical discharge. During one such close-down a close friend of Bert's came close to death – not only was Bert in constant danger, but anyone he was friendly with. However much a prison is said to be in a close-down situation, the inmates still require feeding, although in twenty-first century Britain the regime is far more relaxed. Back then it meant that cell doors had to be opened and that prisoner movement had to be permitted from the cell, along the landing and onto the stairs and to the food servery and back. A man making the return journey with his hands holding a tray of food, requiring a degree of balance, and probably with his mind on anything other than violence, is particularly vulnerable. A particularly difficult form of attack to defend against is the 'trap-door spider lunge'. The assailant, for reasons of his own, monitors the approach of his intended victim, watches with his door ajar and then springs out to strike with his chosen weapon, usually edged, before slamming his door protectively shut to await removal by prison officers from his cell and from the prison.

In the case of Bert's friend, the weapon was a jagged broken sauce bottle. It was still sticking from his neck when he crashed to the bottom of a flight of stairs. He did survive but it was a close call from a quite unprovoked attack. Due largely to the campaigners' relentless programme of accusation and vilification, Bert Spencer was never free of the possibility that some madman would launch a frenzied attack against him, spurred on by the implanted suggestion that he would be ridding the world of a child-killer. Bert learned to walk with caution, to watch his own back, to choose where he sat or stood and who he would allow to share his near space. Initially nerve-racking, this type of prison-survival behaviour quickly became second nature. Apart from writing the occasional protest letter, there was little else that Bert Spencer could do to exercise control over his life. He was a caged animal, constantly being prodded between the bars of his cage, with keepers unable to prevent the torment; even had they felt such inclination. The Bridgewater campaign was growing and the rooftop protests fuelled the press and media frenzy. Every time an article or news clip was printed or broadcast Bert was often linked and mentioned as the one who had 'got away with murder!'

All that was left for Spencer was to get on with the hard business of seeing out the prison years and to hope for the impossible – that some dramatic intervention would see him removed from the pillory where Ann Whelan and Paul Foot had had him placed. Despite their attentions, he turned from soul-destroying introspection to an expansion and development of his own talents and interests.

His good friend, Ken Leech, had also been transferred to the Scrubs and the company helped to rekindle Bert's interest in art. Another inmate, Reg Dudley, was a feared member of London's underworld but an artist of considerable talent who helped Bert to develop his skills. Despite having to improvise and scavenge for materials, using old bed-sheets for canvases, wood glue for size and brushes, which were whittled-down shaving brushes. Bert was a natural and was able to gain an A level in art, win awards in the annual Koestler competition, and, eventually gain recognition in gallery exhibitions. Of course, as a prisoner, he could not enjoy the financial benefits his work could have drawn. He also sculpted in clay and made grandfather clocks to a professional standard from the most unlikely of waste materials and with tools, which were the products of ingenuity.

In the gymnasium he continued with his weightlifting and bodybuilding and honed his self-defence skills, both from choice and as a sensible survival precaution. He worked his way through shelves of library books and absorbed what he read – his main areas of study being chiropody and psychology. He learned bookbinding, joined the Open University and became an expert horticulturist. The latter became a labour of love and would lead to a prestigious first prize win in a national gardening competition award, organised by the magazine, *Gardening News*.

'The award was covered by the national press and in the media,' explains a proud Spencer.

It was an amazing feat as there was no plumbed water to the beautiful blooming garden creation Bert had worked so hard on. Also the prison was the somewhat undesirable, and at the time often violent, HMP Wayland, Norfolk.

All this he achieved as he negotiated the obstacles of the labyrinthine 'de-catting' procedure whereby prisoners are regularly assessed with a view to decisions being made concerning their risk factor. Despite a flawless prison record, it took six and a half years for Bert to be granted Category 'B' status and to be transferred to Kingston prison, Portsmouth, where 150 other lifers were housed. There the regime was more relaxed and the environment cleaner. Theoretically it was a place where a lifer should have been able to live out his years of punishment without an added overload of stress. But it was not to be. There was to be no respite from the grimly unflagging attentions of the Bridgewater campaigners as constant repetition lent an unreal weight to their often-invented scenarios. Their minds were rigid. They believed the four convicted men, The Bridgewater Four, were innocent and so they were never at Yew Tree Farm. Added to this they also believed Bert Spencer was not at work at Corbett Hospital and, therefore, he was at Yew Tree Farm, and it was he who murdered Carl. It is very difficult, even if Bert had the opportunity and the time, to argue with either a closed or a made up mind.

Such inversion of the facts was delivered in many forms to a massive audience over a period of many years, always blighting any occasion of small uplift, which may have otherwise tended to lighten Bert Spencer's almost intolerable burden. Each new attack left him feeling like a crustacean without a shell as time and again Paul Foot regurgitated timeworn and groundless claims of 'new evidence' in his efforts to sway public opinion against him. It was the easier of the roads which the campaigners took – defaming a lone and isolated target, rather than concentrating their efforts on infinitely more daunting task of providing proof positive of the innocence of the convicted four.

I was a freelance journalist at the time and as the campaign grew to a crescendo in the mid 90s I too was swept along – although my interests lay in the possible innocence of the four and not the guilt of Mr Spencer. I had read Paul Foot's book and had watched the film about the case, *Bad Company*. I had read Foot's articles in the *Daily Mirror*. I saw the rooftop demonstrations, including Michael Hickey's incredible feat towards the end of November 1983.

Twenty-one-year-old Michael Hickey scaled the roof of Gartree prison, Leicestershire, and began a protest against his conviction for murder. Incredibly, Hickey's rooftop protest was to last 89 days – a world record. Remarkable if only for the conditions he endured. There is little in the way of buffers between that area of the east Midlands and the Russian steppes to counter the cold winter winds blowing westwards. Also throughout the protest, Hickey was sustained by provisions sent up on lines by his fellow prisoners. I must admit I was impressed and often thought to myself – would a guilty man do that? Although again, the incredible media attention this achievement of endurance would attract, inevitably the press and media would always use these as a means to place Bert Spencer as suspect number one. There were a lot of armchair detectives who naïvely believed everything they read, although it was germinated from a very small source, mainly Foot and Ann Whelan, it reached millions. I personally feel there was no malicious intent on the part of either the award winning journalist, Foot, or

Michael Hickey's mother, Mrs Whelan. Foot was doing what he thought was right and what he believed in. Ann was a devoted mother trying to free her son from a murderous crime she believed he was totally innocent of.

After three and a half years at Kingston, Portsmouth, Bert was given an unintended retrograde push by the prison authorities. From the progressive and constructive atmosphere of Kingston he was projected into comparative chaos. His new jail was HMP Wayland, in Norfolk. It was difficult to adjust. Wayland was noisy, aggressive and unpredictable. Drug abuse and violence were part of the daily pattern of life. Vandalism and small-time arson were the norm. Organised theft and muggings were the commonplace activities of the roaming gangs whose 'membership cards' were ethnically distributed. The subway leading to and from the canteen shop – the prison equivalent of the company store – was just one of several regular ambush points. One of Bert's few pleasures at Wayland was to accompany the more vulnerable inmates on their weekly journey to the canteen, just to deny the gangs a few prospective victims.

There was, however, one major benefit to be enjoyed at Wayland. After nine years, Bert finally had access to in-cell sanitation in his single-cell accommodation.

Three more years on he was finally graded Category D and was despatched to experience the reverse culture shock of open prison on the edge of the Wash in Lincolnshire. His new home was North Sea Camp. There were no dogs, no perimeter fence, few locked doors and work in the open air. The near future held the promise of work in the community, in the nearby villages and in the town of Boston. There was also the opportunity for some limited decision-making and the hope of release in the foreseeable future.

While at Wayland he had met and enjoyed the visits of an unusual lady. His move to North Sea Camp had brought him almost to her doorstep and the knowledge immeasurably improved what previously had been a distinct bleakness of future prospects. Although he was still not free from the overshadowing spectre of the campaigners.

While Bert was at Kingston and Wayland the propaganda campaign had peaked with the release of Paul Foot's book in 1986 and the Thames Television programme in 1987, followed by the Appeal Hearing of the Bridgewater case in late 1988 and early 1989. It could be that despite the failure of the Hickeys, Robinson and Molloy appeal, Paul Foot and the campaigners had achieved some measure of success. The normal tariff for a drunken, domestic murder is nine years. When Bert Spencer was finally released he had served over fourteen years for just such a crime. Despite a record of exemplary conduct while in prison, something had delayed his release for over five years beyond all reasonable expectations.

'Perhaps the band of campaigners can take full credit for inflicting fourteen years of added torment to a man's punishment and stealing five years of his freedom, in excess of the normal retributive demands of the law,' commented Bert as he neared his release date.

Despite the crushing blow to the campaigners' hopes, which the failure of the Appeal Hearing had dealt them, the campaign bandwagon rolled on, following Bert Spencer to North Sea Camp and beyond. Yet again, prisoners were to give false evidence against him, as *Chapter 9* describes in detail. And on television, BBC 2 was to devote three hours to a somewhat slanted dramatised made-for-TV film entitled, *Bad Company*. The film intended to show the Bridgewater Four were innocent and Hubert Spencer was the actual 'prime suspect' and always had been.

During all the years of mental flagellation, which Bert Spencer endured at the hands of media people, there was one small voice of support. The situation was summed up in an editorial comment that appeared in the *Portsmouth News* on 12 April, 1989.

'... In an unsuccessful attempt to clear Carl's murderers, campaigners have pointed the finger of guilt at Spencer. One of the people who suggested Spencer could have been Carl's killer was *Daily Mirror* columnist, Paul Foot.

'Spencer says he and his family have suffered ten years of persecution. He points out that a child-killer is regarded as the lowest of the low...'

There is no doubt that fellow prisoners can make life very unpleasant for prisoners who have offended against children.

The article went on, 'Just because he has committed one very serious crime and is an easy target, Spencer should not be accused of an even more heinous offence, in order to get others off the hook.

'*A journalist of Paul Foot's standing should realise that better than most people.*' (italics are those of the original article).

However, it takes more than mild censure in a local newspaper to deter Mr Foot. Indeed, it takes more than supported fact, the conclusions of several high level police investigations and the results of the deliberations of learned members of the judiciary to sway Mr Foot from his chosen stance. He was that sort of investigative journalist and I have no doubt that everything he wrote he believed – although he appeared to show little regard of the trouble and stress he was causing Spencer on a daily basis. After all the Bridgewater Four had gone through a detailed four-week trial and subsequent Appeals – and in the eyes of the law they were guilty as charged. Bert had been interviewed and cleared and after all, he had a cast iron alibi.

Expedient propaganda is an age-old tool, which has sent many an innocent to the scaffold or the stake, but today, the application of 21st century technology can spread misinformation faster than any medieval plague. The pro-Bridgewater and anti-Spencer campaigners have used both to the full to overload Bert Spencer with added stress and torment.

To quote a report on prisons, crime and punishment; 'The pains of imprisonment should not exceed what is required for the deprivation of freedom. Persons are sent to prison as a punishment – and not for punishment – both propositions are refuted by the daily experience of prisoners within the prison system.'

In Bert Spencer's case, the added problems that were piled on top of his own deprivation of freedom were created not by the prison authorities, but from an outside agency, which was allowed a free hand to test this prisoner's endurance and survival capabilities to the full.

Whether deliberately or consequently, the campaigners had placed Spencer in grave danger – almost placing a bounty upon his head. A man with a lower breaking point might have sought his own way out of a supremely testing situation. Or maybe one of his many attackers would have hit their target and that would have been the end of Mr Spencer. Had these scenarios happened, of course, the campaigners could have considered their point made and written Q.E.D. after their efforts.

Although each attack upon him brought a natural lowering of spirit in its wake, Bert Spencer managed to cope with the overload of stress and frustration, which the unrelenting campaign against him superimposed upon the considerable pressures of normal prison life. At times when the pressures peaked, and remedy other than the opiate of the prison tea-urn was needed, he would turn to the gymnasium and heave weights to the point of exhaustion. Alternatively, he would take up pen and paper and write an angry letter of protest, knowing that, at best, it was nothing but an ineffectual, token gesture.

However, when Bert's daughter, Janell, contacted him in a state of distress as a result of a ploy by a Bridgewater Four supporter, Bert was to take up the pen to a more positive effect.

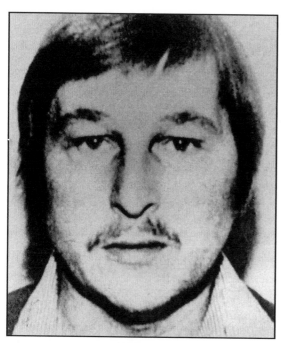

*Bert Spencer, aged
40, at the time of the
shooting of his friend
Hubert Wilkes in 1979*

*While in prison for murder Spencer turned to art
– this a Dutch Canal scene*

*Bert Spencer painted landscapes, people and also animals
– this a stunning example of a tiger*

*Religion was often reflected in Bert's art
– this a Quaker Meeting House*

THE INSTITUTE OF AMBULANCE OFFICERS
LIMITED

Incorporated 1961

This is to Certify that

Hubert Vincent Spencer

is a _____Graduate_____ of

THE INSTITUTE OF AMBULANCE OFFICERS
LIMITED,

an Association established to promote, encourage, and improve
the theory and practice of Ambulance Service Organisation and
Administration and all operations and expedients connected
therewith, and to give an impulse to ideas likely to be useful in
connection with or in relation to such theory and practice to the
members of the Institute and to the community at large.

WITNESS our hands and Seal at

this **28th** day of **July** *1971*

_____ Chairman

_____ Honorary Secretary

Bert Spencer became a graduate of The Institute of Ambulance Officers Ltd on 28th July 1971

Bad Company, released in 1993, was a stunning movie with a great cast including Hollywood star, Jonny Lee Miller. However, this dramatised film would prove to be very damning for Bert Spencer

Top: Grieving parents' Janet and Brian Bridgwater entering court in 1979 (BPM Media)

Below: A dilapidated Yew Tree Farm shortly before it was pulled down – a photo of Carl Bridgewater can be seen below (BPM Media)

Yew Tree Farm with its traditional frontage facing farm land
(BPM Media)

A later crumbling Yew Tree Farm
– a side view looking towards the A449 (BPM Media)

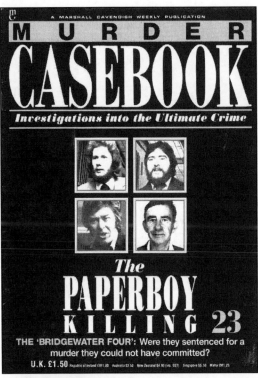

Top: Murder Casebook, published in1990, one of many magazines dedicated to the murder of Carl Bridgewater (Marshall Cavendish Ltd)

Bottom: A typical insert pointing the finger of suspicion at Bert Spencer as the real murderer of the paperboy - Murder Casebook, published in1990 (Marshall Cavendish Ltd)

Top: *Real-Life Crimes Magazine, published in 1994, covers the possible miscarriage of justice in the case of the Bridgewater Four (Midsummer Books Ltd)*

Bottom: *Real-Life Crimes Magazine, published in 2004, supporting the case of the Bridgewater Four - if you look closely you can make out part of Bert Spencer's face on the cover (Eaglemoss Publications Ltd)*

Top: Another insert suggesting Bert Spencer as the real murderer of Carl Bridgewater - Real-Life Crimes Magazine, published in 2004 (Eaglemoss Publications Ltd)

Bottom: A powerful campaign booklet, The Wrong Men, written Jill Morrel. The male in the photo is Pat Molloy's son Nick (photographer Tim Page) at a vigil outside the Home Office June 1993 (published by Bridgewater Four Support Group)

Top: The Bridgewater Four campaign attracted many celebrities – here we see actor Richard Wilson at the June 1993 vigil outside the Home Office

Bottom: Patrick Molloy, one of the Bridgewater Four, who received a 12-year prison sentence for manslaughter at the original trial. Molloy died of a heart attack in prison in 1981 aged 51 (Newsteam)

Freedom at last as the case against the Bridgewater Four is quashed in 1997 (front row from left to right) Anne Whelan, next to her son Michael Hickey, Ann Hickey, next to her son Vincent Hickey and Jimmy Robinson (BPM Media)

A jubilant Michael Hickey celebrates being free after spending 18 years in prison (BPM Media)

Emotions are running high as the first taste of freedom for the three men sink in. An emotional Michael Hickey (far left) hugs his mother, Ann Whelan, who lead the campaign from the start (BPM Media)

Outside the court of appeal as a joke is shared between the two mothers Ann Whelan and Ann Hickey (BPM Media)

170

Top: An iconic image as Michael Hickey kisses the ground outside the steps of the Court of Appeal in 1997 (BPM Media)

Left: Vincent Hickey today – we spent many hours chatting about the case and how it had affected his life over the years (BPM Media)

*Bert Spencer today, aged 76, at his local Dojo club
(author's collection)*

*Left: Bert Spencer today, aged 76, wearing his judo outfit (author's
collection). Right: Bert Spencer today, aged 76, with his partner,
Christine (author's collection)*

The top criminologist and presenter; Professor David Wilson
(photo taken by the author)

Professor David Wilson interviewing an emotional Bert Spencer
for the Channel 4 documentary about the book, being made by ITN
Productions. (photo taken by the author)

8.

An Inspector Calls

....

Bert Spencer had been in prison for almost five years when the harassment of his family was suddenly escalated. Through the years the hate mail had been directed at Bert in a constant stream with his family receiving it in sporadic bursts. Occasionally the spray-can artists would attack the home of Bert's brother, Don. And always the vile letters and the graffiti would refer to the murder of Carl Bridgewater – never to the crime that Bert was convicted for.

It was 19 November 1984 and another family anniversary, namely Bert's daughter Janell's seventeenth birthday, with him incarcerated in Wormwood Scrubs. Janet answered a knock at the door expecting to see a neighbour standing on the step of her Kingswinford home. Instead it was a stranger, tall and well dressed and sporting an overlarge tiepin. Janell was vaguely aware of something peculiar about his appearance, but just what it was failed to register. Janet had her mind on other things. What should have been celebratory days were always overshadowed by past events and the present situation. She and her daughter were alone in the house.

The stranger introduced himself as Detective Inspector Curry of the West Midlands Serious Crime Squad and produced what appeared to be an official warrant card. Once inside the house he took out a letter, written on prison headed paper, in Bert's unmistakable copperplate hand. He refused to let Janet read or handle it, claiming that it was vital evidence. To whom that letter was originally written has never been established, nor are its contents known. The 'inspector' appeared to find the situation somehow amusing. He grinned as he told Janet Spencer that the letter contained Bert's full and frank confession to the murder of Carl Bridgewater. He added that he was due to visit Wormwood Scrubs the next day to take a formal statement from her ex-husband, as Bert and Janet were, by now, divorced. It was time, said the 'inspector', for Janet to stop covering for Bert and to tell him the truth. The visitor played his part so well that Janet collapsed in distress, huddled and weeping on the floor. 'Detective Inspector Curry' remained seated while Janell rushed to kneel by her mother, calming and comforting her. To her amazement, when she looked up, the 'inspector' was staring at the pathetic tableau in evident amusement.

'I'll bet that's spoiled your birthday,' he said with a smile of satisfaction. There were no birthday cards in that room and the event had not been mentioned. The teenager's thoughts whirled as she realised with a shock that the man's peculiar appearance was due to the fact that he was wearing stage make-up. As she struggled unaided to get her mother into a chair, the words on the fateful piece of cardboard flashed into mind, 'THAT CHAP WHO DISGUISES ISSELF WAS SEEN AT THE FARM WHERE CARL BRIDGEWATER WAS SHOT...'

With that in mind, it was stomach-churning for the girl to be in the same room as a man who saw fit to disguise himself with make-up and who obviously found amusement in her mother's hysterical collapse. Could he really be a policeman? Had she known at the time the history of their sinister visitor she would have had even more cause for alarm. Ignoring Janet's distress, the 'Detective Inspector' continued with his interview in a line of questioning which suggested that he was attempting to manufacture a bizarre conspiracy, comprising Bert Spencer and some of his friends and acquaintances. Presumably as replacement candidates for the Hickeys, Robinson and Molloy quartet. Both Janet and Janell noticed that the visitor made a habit of speaking with his head noticeably inclined towards his over-sized tiepin. Later, they were to discover that the tiepin was indeed a microphone, that the interview had been recorded on tape and that the tape had been made available to the campaigners.

Eventually the surreal episode was ended when a neighbour called at the house and 'Inspector Curry' made a hasty departure from the stage. It was with relief that the two women watched him go, but that was not the last they were to see of the bogus police inspector. On his next visit he was to bring with him a minder of man-mountain proportions.

Still believing that their strange visitor was a high-ranking police officer, Janet felt that she had nowhere to turn apart from to Bert. Through the good offices of the Probation Service she was able to relay the disturbing birthday events to him at Wormwood Scrubs. Bert's reaction was predictable. Full of anger and frustration at the psychological assault on his unprotected daughter and ex-wife, he vowed to them that he would identify the impostor and lead the police to him. In view of Bert's situation at the time, as a Category A prisoner in the high security D Wing at the Scrubs, it must have seemed a forlornly reactive promise to make. But his daughter believed it. She was well aware of Bert's personality traits, a wide streak of stubbornness and a sharply competitive edge.

Unknown to Bert, the man whom he was to hunt was a potentially dangerous member of Birmingham's underworld, a man known to the police and to the security forces in England and Ireland. From the restricting confines of his prison situation, finding the impostor had the look of a mission impossible, but Bert set about his task with logic and determination. The only real lead he had was that the man had announced the brand of ground bait that would attract him. He had been seeking a confession to the murder of Carl Bridgewater, a confession by proxy from Janet. Bert had to find a means of dangling the even better prospect of such a confession – by himself – as a way to bring the impostor out into the open, and so identify him and deliver him into the hands of the police.

Bert was intrigued, beneath his anger, about the man's interest in him and his possible connection with the events at Yew Tree Farm or with the campaign group – there had to be some reason behind his sudden appearance on the scene. Bert's lines of communication were limited by his prison situation and his field of play was severely restricted. But, only a few days after the impostor's visit to his one-time home, he was unexpectedly thrown a lifeline when yet another player entered the curious game. He received a letter, dated just two days after the bogus police inspector's visit, from a

Janet Cotter at the very address which had been written on the reverse of the mysterious piece of card six years before – 107, Stony Lane, Smethwick. The card actually had printed on the opposite side, '...HE SCARED DON'S MISSUS, 107 OR 108 STONEY LANE. UWP 751R.'

Initially, Bert had only the timing of the visit and the letter to suggest a connection between the two happenings. Janet Cotter's letter seemed innocuous enough, if a little strange in the circumstances. Although the address was enough to set alarm bells ringing. He began to wonder just what forces were now working against him and why? Was there some connection with the ever-growing campaign group? Was the bogus police inspector just some publicity-seeking crank, or had he some more personal and sinister interest underlying his sudden appearance on the scene, six years after the murder at Yew Tree Farm?

Bert wondered too about the significance of some sort of gathering and ominous storm. Shortly before the 'inspector's' visit to his ex-wife and daughter, Bert had been made aware of a statement made by a former part-time work colleague and ex-special constable, a statement which currently was the subject of yet another police investigation (see *Chapter 9, The Fitzpatrick statement*). And now there was what seemed to be a sequel to the visit, the letter from Janet Cotter written from an address, which had appeared on the famous piece of card, an address in the lane where he had spent his childhood and the early years of his marriage.

It was as if unknown forces were massing against him and sending in their front-runners to harass and perplex him. In the claustrophobic confines of a prison cell, quite cut off from basic communication facilities, the feelings of distress and frustration were almost overwhelming when each incident seemed to be part of a structured plot designed to link him to the murder of a 13-year-old boy.

Rightly or wrongly, it seemed to Bert that Janet Cotter had to be more than an inactive spectator. Somehow, somewhere, it seemed that she had to fit into the tangled pattern of events surrounding the origin and finding of the piece of card and maybe even to have some link with the mystery visitor. Her first letter, although in no way unfriendly, still contained indications that it was purely a range-finding shot and that a more substantial barrage would follow. She wrote asking if Bert would like to strike up a pen pal friendship with her and listed her various interests. The subjects listed suggested that she had done some homework on Bert as her stated interests coincided neatly with Bert's own, which had been mentioned in several newspaper articles. These included art, writing, psychology and sport. Curiously, for an aspiring pen-pal, she asked what Bert thought of Michael Hickey and volunteered the information that her former boyfriend, Harry Rushton, lived at Vicarage Road, the other address mentioned on the card. The card had stated, '... TED SAYS HE LIVES IN VICARAGE ROAD ...'

It was around this time that Bert also began to receive a resurgence of the hate mail with which he had for so long been afflicted, again all of it pertaining to the murder of Carl Bridgewater and none referring to the shooting of Hubert Wilkes. This hate mail however had changed in its format. The letters took the form of 'greetings' cards containing hand printed obscenities and sick references to the murdered boy. The majority of the letters bore the postmarks of Birmingham, Warley, Aston and Handsworth.

There followed a frequent exchange of letters between Janet Cotter and Bert Spencer with Bert passing on Ms Cotter's letters and the hate mail to Staffordshire police for expert comparison. He was prompted in this by the fact that, for reasons, which can only be guessed at, Janet Cotter's letters indicated that she harboured some kind of obsession relating to the piece of card. Bert kept the correspondence going because he felt instinctively that it could lead him in the direction of 'Detective Inspector Curry'. The coincidence of the inspector's visit and the timing of Ms Cotter's first letter, together with its content, made him sure.

After an eight-week exchange of correspondence, Bert put an idea into practice, which he hoped would bring the impostor into the open and also establish if there was indeed any connection between 'Inspector Curry' and his new pen pal. After all, Cotter had appeared out of the blue and writing from so significant an address. If his suspicions were correct, he felt that it would be a poetic touch if he could enlist the help of Ms Cotter to contact, identify and have apprehended the bogus police inspector who had so distressed his daughter and ex-wife.

As told in *Chapter 5 – The Piece of Card*, he asked Ms Cotter to have an advertisement inserted in the *Express & Star,* the evening paper covering Wolverhampton and the Black Country. Wording the advertisement carefully, Bert aimed it at the mystery caller, hinting that should he make contact as Bert had an important secret to reveal. He was already keeping the Staffordshire police informed of his intentions and sending Janet Cotter's original letters and copies of his own, with explanations of his responses, to them.

Janet Cotter replied to this request saying that she could not get the advertisement inserted immediately. Having no access to local newspapers, Bert never did find out if it ever appeared. There was, however, no need.

The following day, 'Detective Inspector Curry' himself wrote to Bert. It was the first move in what was to prove to be a strange and protracted correspondence. In this letter, the writer admitted to being the bogus police officer and signed himself, 'Alan Johnson'. This was to prove to be yet another alias. Although he did give an address: 375, Washwood Heath Road, Birmingham. At least Bert now had something concrete to work on. This, and future 'Johnson' letters, he also passed on to the Staffordshire police force.

It was to be a peculiar cat-and-mouse game. 'Inspector' Curry, now transformed into Mr Johnson, who also seemed to have in mind the objective of extracting from Bert Spencer a confession to a crime he had not committed. Maybe he thought Bert was going stir-crazy? After all, long-term prisoners often acquire strange psychological twists. With long-term incarceration behind and ahead of them, irrational fantasies can overtake men: schizophrenic voices sometimes dictate their behaviour. In D Wing, Wormwood Scrubs, at least one prisoner has killed himself after complaining of nightly torment from an incessantly whispering ghost. Perhaps 'Alan Johnson' was hoping that Bert Spencer had broken down enough to take on board implanted suggestion. As it transpired, 'Johnson' himself had first-hand knowledge of the effects of long-term imprisonment on the minds of men.

Bert's only objective was to identify 'Johnson' and to deliver him into the hands of the police. In this, his resources were limited. His only communication with the outside world was by censored letter. His prison wages would equate, in 1993, to about £4 a week. He was allowed one prison-issue sheet of writing paper and an envelope a week. Anything else, apart from food and basic toilet requisites, he had to purchase from the prison canteen. Armed only with writing materials and his own inner belief and determinedness, he was entering the lists against an opponent who enjoyed the benefits of freedom, an apparently affluent lifestyle, underworld associates and, as Bert and the police were to discover, a cunning practised over years of operating with the IRA. He was a demonstrably callous man and, as Bert was later to discover, a prison escapee from Mountjoy Prison in Dublin, Ireland, who had been sentenced to fifteen years for armed bank robbery. Such was the bogus police inspector who had so frightened the Spencer women.

The duel by correspondence became a mind game, one that Bert had initiated and necessarily shared with the Staffordshire police. This passing of information to the police served a dual purpose. Not only did it keep them informed of his intentions and planned moves, and generate their interest in 'Alan Johnson', but it served as a hedge against future misinterpretation of Bert's writings. This was wise, as Bert Spencer's planned strategy was to write to 'Johnson' feigning mental deterioration and to imply that he was contemplating the taking of his own life, and that, before so doing, he had a secret which he wanted to share with him. Bert hoped that taking this tack would have the effect of galvanising 'Johnson' into a face-to-face meeting inside Wormwood Scrubs where the man would be apprehended on a serious charge of impersonating a police officer. The urgency that this ploy was intended to generate would, hopefully, spring from 'Johnson's' fear that Bert might commit suicide and take his 'secret' with him to the grave.

It was indeed a convoluted plan, but necessarily so. Bert himself was being attacked in many ways. No touch of prison paranoia was needed to convince Bert that he was the target of a complicated plot, or to dictate the need to match the deviousness of the other side's gambits.

At an early stage in the exchange of letters, 'Johnson' stated that he had made a visit to Philip Wilkes – the son of the old murdered farmer, Hubert. What he hoped to gain from that is difficult to imagine. Indeed, 'Johnson's' arrival on the scene and his interest in the Bridgewater affair leaves questions unanswered to this day. Was he employed to insert himself into the anti-Spencer campaign? Or was he acting as some sort of self-employed bounty hunter, seeing some form of financial return awaiting his successful efforts? Or did he have some far more sinister connection with the tragic event at Yew Tree Farm?

Bert was still not sure if 'Johnson' had contact with Janet Cotter, or was it all some bizarre coincidence? He was not going to mention it to either party, but did devise a plan of action. Bert drew upon his artistic ability in an attempt to identify the man. Working on the principle that most people receive the offer of being immortalised in oil paint as a well-deserved compliment, he offered to paint a portrait of 'Johnson' – if he would send in a clear photograph of himself and an indication of the background preferred.

'Johnson' was not to be taken in by any such overt ruse. Instead, he suggested that Bert could paint a self-portrait, which he, 'Johnson', would buy. In the meantime, the police, and, separately, a friend of Bert, had investigated the address which 'Johnson' was using: 375, Washwood Heath Road, which turned out to be an accommodation address, a seedy snooker hall in a shopping arcade, where no one would admit to knowing an 'Alan Johnson'. The letters from Bert, however, continued to be collected from there and answered, often by return.

Bert already had a finished self-portrait and made arrangements for 'Johnson' to collect it from Bert's daughter, Janell, at her Kingsley Road home in Kingswinford. He also arranged for the police to be waiting. The bait he dangled was that he would affix to the back of the painting an envelope, containing, as he put it, 'a tiny piece of a particular jigsaw puzzle'. 'Johnson', obviously balancing curiosity against caution, rang Bert's one-time home and changed the collection arrangements. He arranged to meet with Bert's daughter at 8.00 pm on following Sunday evening in a pub at Kingswinford. Then he pre-empted that meeting. On the Sunday morning, Janet Spencer opened her front door to see a massive figure almost filling the doorway. He had, he said, come to collect the picture as, 'Alan Johnson' could not make the evening meeting. As Bert's daughter spoke to the caller who had the look of a nightclub bouncer, Janet was making her way round the back of the house in order to catch sight of the car or anyone in it. Her curiosity was rewarded as she saw a figure in the driving seat. While her daughter was refusing to hand over the painting, the car driver and Janet Spencer were briefly face to face. Before he sped off Janet had time to recognise, at the wheel, 'Detective Inspector Curry' – AKA 'Alan Johnson'. Janet, angry and frightened at the same time, turned her attentions to the man-mountain, now stranded on her doorstep. Janet bravely challenged him, demanding to know his name and that of the car-driver. Visually shaken, he gave his own name as Paul Campion and that of the driver (truthfully as it transpired) as Keith, but withheld the surname. So 'DI Curry', who became 'Alan Johnson' was now Keith! With little choice, Keith returned to pick up his massive companion and parked outside the house.

This time both Janet and Janell had plenty of time in which to make a positive identification. Sheepish at his sudden retreat from an angry woman, but still glib, Keith 'X' explained that he was Bert's only chance and that his sole aim was to help him. He had, he said, already proved that Bert had no connection with the events at Yew Tree Farm – so could he have the painting?

In no uncertain terms, Janet told him that he was a pathological liar, that the police already knew that Bert had no connection with the murder, and no, he could not have the painting. After watching Janet Spencer crumple on his first visit, the angry tirade left him shocked and surprised. As he drove off, the women noted the make and registration number of his car, a Fiat, TWP 462R. That night, Keith X rang the Spencer home. It was 11.20

pm. He apologised for upsetting the Spencer women and offered to pay £100 for the painting – he also claimed to have already paid a lot of money for it already to Bert. His offer was refused.

The next day he rang again, at 5.30 pm asking if Bert's daughter would meet him to discuss the matter of the painting. Arrangements were made for him to come to the house in Kingsley Road, at 8.00 pm that evening. The police were informed immediately and kept a vigil at the Spencer home from 5.00 pm until 11.00 pm. Keith X did not show up and the police took the women to a friend's house to spend the night. By then they had checked out the Fiat car with the DVLC at Swansea. It was owned by a Miss Small-wood who lived in Moseley, Birmingham. The man who was living at the same address was named, Hodgekiss. They also told the mother and daughter how they had checked out the snooker hall in Washwood Heath Road. No one, of course, at the snooker hall knew an 'Alan Johnson', and the person who collected the 'Johnson' mail did not match the description of Keith X, nor did the description of the owner of the snooker hall. Again, as Bert already knew, it was no surprise that the police should comment that the snooker hall clients were less than co-operative when it came to answering questions.

Some months later, Tuesday 2 July 1985, Bert's ex-wife and daughter received a telephone call from the police at Wombourne to say that the Fiat car had been sold at auction and that the owner had given a false name and address. Shortly after receiving this information, Keith X rang again. He wanted to meet Bert's daughter in her lunch hour and asked where she worked. Janell refused that piece of information, but the brave teenager agreed to meet him in a pub near to her workplace. The meeting was fixed for 1.00 pm the next day. The police were once again informed and they immediately arranged to send a policewoman to pick her up and take her to the pub meeting. As arranged, the policewoman arrived at 12.15 pm. In the pub she told Janell that the bar was sprinkled with police officers and that Keith X would be arrested on arrival.

Keith X, warned perhaps by some insider intelligence or the instinct born of long experience, failed to turn up. However, he rang the pub and spoke to Janell. The police listened in to the conversation in which Keith X said that he had been warned not to attend the meeting, as there was a possibility of his being arrested. He went on to say that he was going, accompanied by his solicitor, at 5.00 pm that evening to Wombourne police station to discuss his impersonation of a police officer.

Surprisingly, he did just that, admitting that he was in fact, Keith Littlejohn. The police then rang Bert's ex-wife and daughter to warn them to have no further contact with him – describing him as a 'nutter' and a 'glory boy' who enjoyed putting pressure on vulnerable people.

After the police call Keith Littlejohn rang Janell again, asking once more for a meeting to discuss the painting, still hopeful of obtaining the mythical message in the envelope attached to the back. When told that it was in the possession of the police, Littlejohn tried to turn on the pressure with the teenage girl. He told her to get it back. When asked what he did for a living, Littlejohn asked if she had ever read *Harry's Game,* Gerald Seymour's novel. Apparently he saw himself as the lead character, Harry, the undercover operative who took on the IRA, a killer with government sanction. Remarkably, this may have been close to the truth.

✳   ✳   ✳

Keith Littlejohn and his older brother Kenneth share well documented and controversial lives. Kenneth Littlejohn had been dishonourably discharged from the Parachute Regiment and served three years for robbery before being released from prison in 1968. In 1970 the Midland Motor Cylinder Company in Smethwick, Birmingham, was robbed of £38,000. The wages clerk, Brian Perks, claimed to have been overpowered by an 'Indian man' who then took the money. Perks was Littlejohn's brother-in-law and the police suspected a staged incident involving the two men. A warrant was issued for his immediate arrest. Kenneth went on the run to Dublin, together with his brother, Keith.

The brothers had already proved they were not without power and influence. Both had a chequered past, that was interwoven with what appears to be civilian acts for their own personal profit, together with alleged British intelligence operations, mainly in conjunction with MI6, in a fight against IRA terrorism. To add to this their acquaintances were peppered with the aristocracy. Keith had spent time in Borstal and was known to Lady Onslow, a divorcee, who was closely associated with the ex-Borstal organisation, Teamwork Associates, in London. Lady Onslow was introduced to his older brother, Kenneth. Onslow became aware of sensitive information in the brothers possession and contacted her friend, Lord Carrington. Subsequently, on 22 November 1971, a meeting was arranged at Onslow's London flat between Kenneth, Keith and British minister, Geoffrey Johnson Smith. It was at this time that the official 'Wanted' status for Kenneth Littlejohn, in respect of the Smethwick robbery, was downgraded to a trifling 'Desired to Interview'.

More controversy surrounded the brothers when Edmund Woolsey, 32, a Catholic civilian, had his car stolen. The police informed Woolsey that the car had been found abandoned in County Armagh. On 18 September 1972, as he was retrieving the vehicle, a bomb attached to his car exploded, killing him instantly. While not a member of the Official IRA, Woolsey socialised in similar circles and was known to both Keith and Kenneth Littlejohn. The Official IRA claimed that Woolsey had been lured to his death by the British Army who had set up the booby trap based on information supplied by the Littlejohns.

The brothers did not finish there. In October 1972 they turned over the Allied Irish Banks branch in Grafton Street, Dublin, robbing them of £67,000; at the time the largest haul in Ireland. Kenneth and Keith were arrested in London and served an extradition warrant from Dublin. At this point, with both looking at lengthy prison sentences, the brothers broke their silence and explained they were officially working for the British government as both Secret Intelligence Service officers and the Official IRA – as double agents. They claimed they were used by the British authorities to spy on the IRA, together with robbing banks in Ireland in order to discredit the terrorist group. Following an instruction from the Attorney General, the extradition proceedings were held in-camera on the grounds of national security. At the extradition proceedings the brothers tried but failed to prevent a prosecution by the Special Criminal Court under the Offences against the State Acts 1939. The Irish Attorney General had given assurances that they would not be charged with political offences under the Act.

It would appear the British government turned their back on the brothers, after the brothers kept all the money they were 'instructed' to steal and were becoming an embarrassment to the authorities.

Tim Carey, bestselling author of *Mountjoy: The Story of a Prison*, stated, 'I think the British authorities just wanted to cut their ties with these people (the Littlejohns). They realised they had made a really bad mistake by getting them involved and basically they wanted nothing more to do with them.'

In 1973 the two violent armed robbers were given a combined prison sentence of 35 years. They were sent to the infamous Mountjoy prison, built in 1850, it was the last stop for convicts bound for Australia. It was tough and squalid – one of Ireland's hardest prisons to do time in. Mountjoy prison, known as The Joy, housed 500 of the country's most dangerous criminals. Among them were leaders and fighters of the Irish Republican Army – the notorious IRA.

Prison officer Mick Kelly, who was stationed there at the time the Littlejohns moved in, commented, 'Conditions at that time were very poor. Just the very basics.'

As suspected double agents, sending them to The Joy, was more or less signing their death warrants. But, as usual, the Littlejohn brothers had other plans. Their daring and brazen escape attempt was covered in the Sky Television documentary *'Real Prison Breaks'*, narrated by Sean Bean.

On reaching The Joy, and abandoned by their government, Keith and Kenneth were, as expected, constantly attacked, as all suspected MI6 operatives were, by the very people they allegedly were spying on – the IRA. Eventually after one brutal attack on the landing stairs, by several IRA convicts, the brothers were isolated and moved to an abandoned basement cell. They were now left to rot, but the brothers had a plan.

After constant badgering they got themselves a boxing bag to train with – but that was the last thing on their mind. Next they acquired a briefcase, which they used to keep documents in for their appeal. The briefcase was basically a courier service, helping the brothers to smuggle stuff in from the outside. It was their 'get out of jail free' card. Hidden in the briefcase was a hacksaw blade and Ken began the daily process to saw through the bars of their isolation cell as Keith noisily punched the bag to drown out the sound. They hid each day's saw cuts in the cream coloured bars by covering them with toothpaste. But when they finally cut the hole both men realised they were too big to get through the aperture – being over six foot each. Time was running out, as they knew they were being moved back into the main prison. They need to lose weight rapidly. Knowing that a prisoner losing weight would look suspicious, the two brothers go on hunger strike, like many of the IRA prisoners had done. They say it is to protest against being held as political prisoners. In just two weeks both men each lost over two stone in weight.

After they are down to the sufficient weight and can get out of their cell, they have one more obstacle in the shape of a looming 25-foot perimeter wall. To combat this, the Littlejohn brothers had been tearing up bed sheets for months and painstakingly weaving them into a rope to hopefully hold their somewhat lessened weight. The grappling iron was made up of scraps of iron from the sawn bars. All escape equipment was hidden in the punch bag – making a useful locker in front of the noses of the screws.

Monday 11 March 1974, as the rest of the prison was having their supper, Kenneth cuts through the last window bar. One of the guards, Prison Officer Mick Kelly, said how small the hole was the men escaped through. They then had a simple drop of eight feet to the empty yard. However, freedom was hard to come by as Keith tried and tried to get the grappling hook to fix on the 25-foot wall. 10 frustrating minutes passed without success. By now the guard was checking the isolation cell and realised the men had escaped. It appeared after months of planning their bid for escape is over. What happened next was beyond the dreams of the escapees.

Author Tim Carey takes up the story, 'When the Littlejohns got to the south-east corner of the prison, by D Wing exercise yard, they found four planks, nearly the height of the wall.' Smiling he added, 'For a maximum security prison that is a bit of a no-no.'

Building contractors had finished work that day and left some lumber behind. Hardly believing their good fortune, Keith and Kenneth make a ramp. They get up to the top of the wall quite easily, getting down is another matter. Keith once again tries his grappling hook, but fumbles and drops it 25 feet to the floor, as the wailing prison sirens announce their attempted escape. The brothers risk all and using Keith's jacket, older brother, Kenneth, climbs down and makes it. Having slightly further to drop, Keith hits the floor, the impact breaking his ankle. It is a desperate situation with the worst possible outcome. In a supreme show of brotherly love Keith begs Kenneth to run from the wall and to try and save himself. He finally acquiesces and reluctantly leaves his brother. Within minutes Keith is recaptured. With all the publicity surrounding the men, speculation is rife as to who actually sprung them from the maximum security prison.

'The Littlejohns had to have had assistance in this escape,' comments Carey. 'I just can't see them being able to do it without. Where did they get the hacksaw blades? Why were there no prison officers around and why were those planks against the wall? And why was Kenneth Littlejohn not captured shortly after his escape?'

Kenneth Littlejohn, during a BBC interview while on the run, was asked if the British security services had helped them escape.

Smiling riley, Kenneth replied, 'Oh not at all. I think they would like to see us dead, not out. I mean we must be an embarrassment to them.'

Towards the end of the interview he was asked about Keith and himself being used as a pawn for MI6.

Looking into camera, smoking a cigarette, he replied, 'I was a mug, a crook, a fall guy, a patsy, I was used and abused.'

Kenneth was eventually spotted and caught in London after 20 months on the run. He was extradited to Ireland to join his brother, Keith, to serve out the rest of his sentence. The brothers were finally released in 1981 – on condition they never returned to Ireland. Since their release little is known of the whereabouts of Kenneth, although just over three years later Keith Littlejohn had injected himself into the Carl Bridgewater murder enquiry – with Bert Spencer now firmly set in his sights.

*   *   *

When Keith Littlejohn walked into the police station with his solicitor to admit his impersonation of police officer 'Detective Inspector Curry', the police could take no action – the statute of limitations on that particular offence, wipes the slate clean after six months, when he made his admission, it was some eight months after the original offence. It appeared that both Littlejohns had nine lives, at the very least.

Not realising that by now his real name was known to the Spencer family, Keith Littlejohn wrote again to Bert on 17 July, 1985. He still gave his address as 375, Washwood Heath Road, and was still using the alias, 'Alan Johnson'. He went on to complain that Wombourne police had taken the painting to pieces and that there was no secret message. How Keith Littlejohn obtained that piece of information is a mystery. He then, in his letter, mentioned that he had been listening once more to the tape recording he had made on his first visit to the Spencer women.

He commented that the police would not act against him, '... Because what I would have to say in court is a serious indictment of their conduct in this matter ...'

After that curious written comment, Littlejohn continues by casting doubt upon Bert's alibi, having obviously investigated, or been told about, the layout of the working area which Bert Spencer used to occupy with Mrs Riebold. Since Carl's murder, the open-plan layout had been altered and partitions now divided up the working area. Littlejohn or his informant researcher had been less than thorough. Littlejohn next tried to distance himself from Paul Foot.

The letter continued, '... this matter is not common knowledge now, except through the columns of the *Daily Mirror* with whom I have no contact whatsoever. It is obvious that Foot is well down the road too, Bert, and I would not like that left wing arsehole to beat me to the post...'

About Janet Cotter, Littlejohn was equally scathing. He wrote, '... she seemed to be a little nuts. An animal rights activist who likes drawing names everywhere evidently...'

Curiously, Littlejohn went on to claim that he had hired a private detective to investigate Ms Cotter and that he had never met her, spoken to her, or knew of her – apart from the address on the card.

However much Littlejohn denied his associations, it is a fact that the tape he made, using his tiepin microphone at the Spencer's house, was made available to the campaign group and that an extract from Bert Spencer's written reply to Littlejohn – an extract 170 words in length – was published in Paul Foot's column in the *Daily Mirror* of 5 September, 1985. The piece was headlined, 'DEATH OF AN ALIBI'.

With the identity of 'Inspector Curry' and 'Alan Johnson' destroyed and now revealed to the police, Littlejohn ceased his more obvious activities in the direction of the Spencer family. Information filtered back to Bert Spencer to the effect that the affair had renewed police interest in Keith Littlejohn's day-to-day activities and, as a result, he had been arrested in London and charged with credit-card fraud, being subsequently convicted and jailed. It was fitting that events had taken that particular turn; it meant that Bert Spencer, from the restriction of a prison cell, had reached out incredibly far and evened the score for a serious affront to the family he no longer could physically protect.

After the police investigation into Littlejohn's impersonation of a police officer and his subsequent actions, papers were prepared and forwarded to the director of Public Prosecutions. However, it was decided that no further action should be taken – as the following letter shows;

Official communications to be addressed: The Chief Constable (address as below)

STAFFORDSHIRE POLICE

Telephone: Stafford 57717

Telex: 36107

ED

Our Ref. CID. 79/3306

> **Chief Constables Office,**
> **Cannock Road,**
> **Stafford**
> **ST17 0QG**

Your Ref.

23rd September, 1985

Dear Sir,

<u>Keith LITTLEJOHN and others</u>

In reply to your letters dated 25th June and 12th July, 1985, regarding the above-named, I have to inform you that enquiries have been made and the result forwarded to the Director of Public Prosecutions, but no action is being taken.

Yours faithfully,

(C.H. Kelly)
Chief Constable
No. C21543 H.V. Spencer,
H.M. Prison,
Wormwood Scrubs,
Du Cane Road,
LONDON, W12 0AC.

9.

The Prison 'Confessions'

....

Each penal complex in the British prison system has its own unique atmosphere, which seems to pervade the very bricks. It is almost as if inmate and staff attitudes are, in part, conditioned by the architecture itself. There is something about penal institutions, which ensures a continuity of each one's own particular and idiosyncratic customs and practices; making them almost tribal in their survival despite the constant population drift. There are, however, across the whole prison spectrum, threads of commonality in inmate behaviour. Perhaps the wearing of prison garb creates a personality vacuum into which old-established and different codes of ethics can seep. Whatever the reason, many prisoners are only too ready to swap previously held standards for those of a new sub-culture.

Peer pressure can account for some behavioural patterns, which form a ready common denominator for those seeking the approval of their fellow inmates. These usually take the form of attempts to manipulate the prison system in small games played for low returns, 'little victories' as Fletcher, Ronnie Barker's famous character in *Porridge*, calls them. From malingering through to smuggling, little harm is done, but the games become more serious and the returns improve when prisoners begin to co-operate with authority for personal gain.

'Grassing' – spying on other inmates and informing the authorities, is regularly rewarded with the granting of extra privileges or goods from the stock of confiscated property resulting from cell 'spins' which are often made on the recommendation of the informer.

All of which is part of the familiar pattern of everyday prison life. The spread of personality types contained within the British prison system varies little from a cross sectional sample of any community – the percentages

still remain; psychotics, sycophants, the hooligans, the gregarious, the lon-
ers, the harmless side-liners and the positively evil are all there, as they
are at any social gathering, from the Shire Hall cocktail party to the local
PTA gathering. Although prison does seem to breed a peculiarity of nature
– the prisoner who blatantly fabricates information to lay against a fellow
prisoner for no apparent reason. Certainly in such an act there is no profit
unless bribery is the spur. The censure of their fellows can mean a life of
protective segregation on Rule 43, which, in prison, is the road to nowhere
but misery. That leaves pleasure or expedience as the driving force behind
the twisted mind.

When the victim of false evidence is a lifer, the harm can be of major
proportions and damage limitation almost impossible to effect. Sometimes
it is clear that the publicity motive has been present; sometimes the false
informant sees his action as opening the door to a possible prison transfer
and sometimes it is apparent that outside pressures have been brought to
bear. On occasion the act of betrayal springs from the workings of a deranged
mind, but often the motive remains forever inscrutably abstruse.

Five times during his prison years, Bert Spencer has been accused of
confessing to the murder of Carl Bridgewater. At first glance the motives
underlying these several slanderous allegations give the impression of a
mixed and random bag. Further inspection shows in each case a definite
pattern of significant timings involved –positive enough to give a strong indication of some outside agency at work to the detriment of Spencer.

The consequences for a prisoner with an accusation of child murder
hanging over him can be grimly Orwellian. Such men, some innocent, have
been scalded, semi-starved, battered, maimed and even murdered after
being judged by a kangaroo court. It is a prospect to make many men run
for the dubious cover of Rule 43. Bert Spencer never did.

To know Bert Spencer is to dismiss the fabrications out of hand. Policemen make no such subjective judgements. They deal in facts and evidence.
Five times allegations of confession to the murder of Carl Bridgewater
have been made and five times the subsequent police investigations have

revealed the accusations to be lies. Such allegations are invariably retro-spective – some with a gap of many years between the alleged happening and the actual accusation, a fact that while casting doubt upon the veracity of the informant also complicates the job of the police investigators. Unfor-tunately, the negative result of the investigation invariably fails to receive the same strength of media exposure as the offending accusation.

In reverse of the personality picture painted by his false accusers – that of a weak and tormented soul, pouring out his heart in a prison-cell confes-sion – Bert Spencer, from his first days in prison, had decided to show the gregarious side of his nature and to live a self-contained life, and to project the image of existing within a defended perimeter. He sought the company of no one, joined no group or faction and generally made a brusque response to unsolicited approaches. The friendships he did make were few but firm and based upon shared interests if not values. He has a zest and enthusiasm for life, which in prison, he kept well cloaked for much of the time, viewing as he did his immediate world and its denizens with a suspicious and jaun-diced eye.

Each fabrication against him was painstakingly and clinically dissected by the police and each investigation exonerated Bert Spencer. Although no official vindication is sufficient to totally sweep away the wisps of suspicion so tenaciously clung to by sensation-starved prison inmates – the ones who live in the permanent hope that something will occur to fill the vacuum of their days. Some mud sticks and this fed the believers of, 'there is no smoke without fire', mentality.

The pattern of false accusation probably began with a letter written by a prisoner, George Wells-Johnson, to Mr Michael Shersby, the Conserva-tive MP for Uxbridge. At the time, Wells-Johnson was working with Michael Hickey in the laundry at Long Lartin prison, near Evesham. This rambling, nonsense letter was written in December, 1982. Paul Foot, with an enthu-siasm which must have caused raised eyebrows and ripples of wry amuse-ment, declared it to be, '... good news and a substantial movement in the case.' He went on to describe the missive as, 'This powerful letter ...', and claimed that when Roy Hattersley received a copy from Ann Whelan he was, 'immediately impressed'. So too, claims Mr Foot, was Mr Tom Sargent of Justice, a criminal reform organisation specialising in cases of miscarriages of justice, when, in due course, he received his copy. One wonders just what impressed such intellects when perusing the letter from Mr Wells-Johnson.

In essence, George Wells-Johnson had read Michael Hickey's copy of the trial transcript, and stated;

> '...*honestly could not believe somebody could be found guilty on the evidence presented. Thinking deeply about what I had read, I made up my mind I would find out if he was guilty ... I asked him things the police would never have thought of ... He is not guilty of murder ...*
>
> *In Wormwood Scrubs prison is a man who has confessed to his solicitor of CARL BRIDGEWATER's murder. I have found out via the grapevine that this man will not or cannot say anything because of pressure by the police "concerned in both their cases" not to say anything, it has been said that if he keeps quiet he will only serve eight years of his life sentence ... You will say that the legal minds of this country know much more than me about this, I agree with that ... I am an out and out TORY, all my family are. We are beginning to wonder though if we have made the right party choice. Willie Whitelaw sits on a fence ... He is not the right man for the job ... Give the lad a retrial to prove once and for all his guilt or not ... There is such a lot being covered up by certain people because of the scandal it will cause if it came out ...*'

Despite the fact that it may be thought that such a piece of writing had all the persuasive power of half an ounce of cheap Old Holborn tobacco; Paul Foot saw it as the first green shoot in a previously barren field, and, surprisingly, it may have had an effect. Certainly, Mr Hattersley was subsequently to request a public enquiry into the case and Mr Sargent was prompted to make a visit to George Wells-Johnson at Long Lartin. This meeting resulted in Tom Sargent being steered to visit another prisoner, a Michael Ishmael, then at Gartree Prison.

The Ishmael 'confession'

It was April, 1983. Michael and Vincent Hickey had ended a 22-day roof-top protest at Long Lartin only two weeks previously. While on the roof the Hickey cousins had displayed an inked banner made from a sheet. It read, 'SPENCER KILLED CARL. WE ARE INNOCENT'. Later on into their protest the same message was painted in large letters of white on the roof itself, there to be photographed for the newspapers and to be featured in television news bulletins. Despite the massive wave of publicity, the protest failed to elicit any Home Office action. More pressure was needed. With Wells-Johnson and Ishmael being used as tools to dupe the representative of Justice, the scene was set.

The contention of Michael Ishmael was two-fold. He claimed that Bert Spencer had visited him in his cell at Wormwood Scrubs and had confessed there to the killing of Carl Bridgewater. Michael Ishmael also made claim that Bert had told him that he had deposited a sealed envelope with his solicitor containing a written confession with instructions that it should be opened only in the event of his death – presumably in the hope and expectation of some posthumous absolution, had he been guilty.

In 1981, Michael Ishmael was a Category A prisoner in D Wing, Wormwood Scrubs, with a cell on landing No. 2. Bert Spencer's cell in that same wing was on landing No. 3 in D Wing. There was no cross-fertilisation between prisoners on different landings. Their recreation hours are staggered to ensure this: candidates for showers are carefully monitored and all inmate movements are observed by prison staff. All traffic of Category A prisoners are accompanied by prison officers with a dog handler and the journey logged, however short.

Michael Ishmael was a gangling six footer with a bullying, arrogant attitude on landing No. 2 where he judged the competition to be feeble. He walked with a John Wayne swagger, sported a large, gold medallion around his neck and bragged incessantly about his life and contacts in London's underworld. He ate an exclusively kosher diet – an important point for those tasked with assessing his story.

The strict daily routine in D Wing would make it impossible for Bert Spencer to have spent time in Ishmael's cell on another landing. To those who know Spencer, the idea of his taking tit-bits to another man's cell is laughable, but this was part of Ishmael's allegation. The availability of surplus kosher food being obtainable from a prison kitchen also stretches credulity beyond its elastic limit – certainly in the early 80's.

The day after making his statement to the prison authorities, Michael Ishmael opted to be placed in the segregation unit, protected under Rule 43 against the inevitable reprisals of his fellow inmates against a 'grass'. He was duly transferred to Parkhurst prison on the Isle of Wight. But, as events were later to prove, removal from the Scrubs was not the sole motivating factor behind Michael Ishmael's actions.

In due course, Bert had his mandatory interview with the police. Detective Chief Superintendent Frank Ridgway of the Manchester force was in charge of the investigation into Ishmael's allegations. Bert offered to help put the matter to rest by penning an instruction to his solicitor for him to hand over to the police any and all paperwork which he might be holding on Bert's behalf. The offer was unnecessary. DCS Ridgway had already explored that avenue and put that particular untruth about any written confession to bed. The senior policeman was also aware of the improbabilities and impossibilities contained in the rest of the Ishmael's tale. Satisfied that it was a total fabrication, DCS Ridgway made his report to that effect on 26 June, 1983. In November of that year, the Home Office declared that there were no grounds to justify further action.

Although, of course, damage had already been done – some mud sticks and, for some, there is no smoke without fire. On 21 April, 1983, the *Daily Mirror* had published Bert Spencer's alleged confession. Subsequently,

Ishmael had refused to say anything about the matter to DCS Ridgway. For once Bert was to be allowed a small measure of reply. His vehement denial was published in the *Express & Star*, the newspaper local to his Kingswinford home. This rare right of reply appeared to cause some annoyance to Paul Foot, to judge from his indignant comment in his book. After all, why should a prison inmate be allowed even a suggestion of a rebuke, even if he is only returning the odd ball kicked up field by his detractors?

A common denominator in the game of manufactured prison 'confessions' is the time gap between the supposed incident and the revelation. It took two years in the case of Ishmael. It took a further two years for Ishmael to make a written retraction. On 6 February, 1985, inmate B13088, Ishmael, Michael, wrote from HMP Frankland, Durham, to Reg Dudley, a former associate of Ishmael in the London underworld, now a prisoner at Wormwood Scrubs, a fellow artist and an associate of Bert Spencer. All communications to and from Category A prisoners are routinely monitored by prison staff, and, between prisoners, are routinely coded, as this one was.

The original letter was given to Bert Spencer by Reg Dudley, Bert made a copy and passed the original to Detective Sergeant Powell of CID administration at Cannock Road station, Stafford. The letter makes interesting, if difficult reading, revealing, as it does, just how some examples of false evidence come to fruition. Some text has been translated by Mark Roman (Bert's friend at North Sea Camp) – the extract reads;

'*Look, I saw Arthur,* (a visitor to Ishmael in prison), *and what he told me knocked me bandy. Bert Spencer and what he told you is a hundred percent genuine and I have never seen him in my life and have never spoke to him.*

One of the Hickey's told me that they had been in touch with Spencer … gave him some money and knowing the score he then agreed to tell that story to his prison governor as long as I backed it.

I was reluctant to anyhow but did so for reason stated and "NO WAY" at all would I have done so "if" what he is now saying is true, so all I can now feel is that I've been taken for an idiot and I'm not very happy.

   I'll personally see the Hickey's but will you in the meantime sincerely apologise on my behalf next time you are in communication with Spencer. If you are right, Reg, I'm sick as a pig. I'm home next year so I'll get in touch with Bert Spencer and apologise in person and try to rectify a wrong that I swear I was a duped innocent party to. It's a catch 22, isn't it!

   Anyhow, please apologise strongly to Spencer as like me he has been really fucked in more ways than one: and thanks for marking my card as, until Arthur told me, I never even thought anything was wrong. Please remember to tell Bert that I will definitely make some arrangements to see him next year and meanwhile I hope to see some of those who set me up ...'

The unfortunate Ishmael's Catch 22 situation was possibly created by what he saw as the slimness of his future prospects on his release from prison. Here was a professional villain, his head full of information concerning currently operational major criminals and past crimes, about to be freed to roam his old haunts, stigmatised as a 'grass'. He had lost all street credibility and was fearful of losing much more if he attempted to rejoin the unrelenting and ruthless company, which he once kept. Now he needed to re-establish himself with his peers 'on the out' and in order to do that it was necessary to put right his offence against both prison traditions and the law of the land. An open and public retraction would have left him prey to charges of wasting police time and conspiracy to pervert the course of justice. Such a retraction would also lead to a possible problem within members of the Birmingham underworld whose code is as unforgiving as that of London villains.

   Perhaps Michael Ishmael did manage to square his particularly difficult circle. To Bert Spencer it is a matter of no concern. The Ishmael affair was just a foretaste of things to come.

In the September of 1986, the next bearer of false witness against Bert Spencer made his bid for the limelight. This time the problem came from an unlikely source, just ten days after the publication of Paul Foot's book, *Murder at the Farm*, surrounding the killing of Carl Bridgewater.

The Mbatha 'confession'

Vermet Mbatha was a Nigerian serving a life sentence. He was grossly over-weight, of a highly nervous disposition and quite unstable. At Wormwood Scrubs he worked in the Braille room with Ken Leech, the artist who had first recognised and encouraged Bert's abilities in that field. By 1986, Bert and Ken Leech had been transferred to HMP Kingston at Portsmouth.

Ken Leech was surprised to receive a letter from James Nichol, solicitor to Michael Hickey and Ann Whelan. The letter was dated 29 September, 1986. It read;

> *'Dear Mr Leech,*
>
> RE: VERMET MBATHA
> *I have recently interviewed Mr Vermet Mbatha, with whom you spent some time on the same Wing whilst you were serving part of your sentence at H.M. Prison, Wormwood Scrubs.*
> *Mr Mbatha has given me certain information, which he said can be corroborated by yourself.*
> *I would be most grateful if you would agree to see me, in order that I can discuss the matter with you. I am prepared to travel to Portsmouth.*
> *I thank you for your anticipated corroboration.'*

Ken Leech wrote back by return, agreeing to a meeting. Mr Nichol journeyed to Portsmouth and inmate Leech learned that Vermet Mbatha had made a statement to the effect that Bert Spencer had confessed to the

murder of Carl Bridgewater in the presence of himself and Ken Leech. Mr
Nichol must have been disappointed to hear Ken Leech's emphatic denial
that such an incident had ever occurred and to receive Ken's written statement to that effect.

It is not known what prompted Vermet Mbatha to make his allegation. Perhaps the answer is implicit in the fact that Mbatha was later to be
diagnosed as suffering from a mental disorder and transferred to a mental
institution; Park Lane top security hospital, Merseyside.

Only five months later, Bert Spencer was to learn of yet another spuri-
ous allegation being made against him. Once more he was being accused of
making yet another confession to the murder of Carl Bridgewater.

The Gibson 'confession'

Paul Gibson and Paul Long were lifers, jointly convicted of murder, serving
part of their sentences at Wormwood Scrubs during the period that Bert
Spencer was there. A letter to Bert from Paul Long, dated 18 February,
1987, reads as follows;

'Dear Bert,

*I am writing to inform you about certain events that have been tak-
ing place in recent months. I received a letter, completely out of the
blue, from a Mrs A. Whelan of 23, Laburnum Trees, May Farm Close,
Hollywood, Birmingham, 47 5DN. In it she requested a VO (Visiting
Order) to come and see me about something that I might be able to
help about certain enquiries. She also requested that I should add
the name of L. Godridge (uncle to the Hickey cousins) on the VO, as
he would be supplying her with transport.*

*Instead of writing back or sending the VO, I took the letter to
Miss Kater, my prison probation officer, who immediately wrote a
letter to the lady asking her for further information. A few days later,*

Mrs Whelan telephoned Miss Kater and it was arranged for me to speak to that lady on the phone. In the conversation that followed, Mrs Whelan read out to me a statement made by Paul Gibson, my co-defendant, that implied that whilst he was visiting your cell, and in my presence, you broke down in tears and confessed to the murder of Carl Bridgewater. Gibson went on to say that as a result, you and I had conspired and manoeuvred to have him (Paul Gibson) removed off the wing. He went off the wing four times to my knowledge.

I immediately denied over the telephone to this lady that any such event had taken place and I went on to warn this lady that Gibson had made allegations of this nature about prisoners before and that he had a history of concocting evidence against not only his fellow prisoners but against prison officers as well.

Eventually I sent Mrs Whelan a VO within a letter telling her to let Miss Kater of the prison probation service know when she intended visiting me. The 28 day period for the VO has now run out and I have heard nothing from her since.

Bert, if as a result of all this, anything comes of it, rest assured, I am willing to make a statement that would be favourable to you. But only on your say so.

Paul Gibson is now at Gartree after causing more havoc at Wakefield, where he got transferred to from here. I think he's spent more time on Rule 43 over ripping people off, than anywhere. And with his many attempts at suicide and attention seeking episodes, I wouldn't be surprised, if sometime in the future, they end up certifying him. I wish you all the best for the future, just let me know through a solicitor or otherwise if there is anything I can do to help you.

Regards
Paul.'

For Bert Spencer, the knowledge that yet another allegation had been made against him was, of course, disturbing, although its effect was lessened by the nature of the source and the fact that it did not become the basis of an official enquiry. Such enquiries were always tedious and draining, even though the results inevitably vindicated him in the eyes of the authority.

Of far more concern was the timing and the source of the next and strangest of the 'confession' allegations.

The Graham 'confession'

The allegations made by Ishmael, Mbatha and Gibson are run of the mill behaviour, part and parcel of prison life, as are subsequent retractions and apologies. Such lies, so facilely manufactured, create quite disproportionate problems for the victim, the prison authorities and for the police. The in-depth and mandatory investigations that follow as a matter of course are only the beginning of the stress and distress which are heaped upon the target prisoner. All of which indicates the size of the question mark raised by the actions of Prison Officer Robert James Graham.

In the December of 1988, Prison Officer Graham made the allegation that, while on remand at Winson Green Prison, Birmingham, Bert Spencer had made a confession to him that he had murdered Carl Bridgewater. It had taken nine years for Robert Graham to recall this not insignificant alleged incident. Had it ever happened, of course, it would have been a star entry in the prison diary and would have been reported at the time and referred to the prison psychiatrist, Dr Richard Washbrook. Apart from maligning Bert Spencer, Robert Graham was stating that he, himself, had been guilty of gross dereliction of duty in not reporting such a serious happening. Mr Graham further compounded his strange behaviour by including in his statement the fact that he passed his supposed information on to Michael Hickey!

The timing of Mr Graham's startling statement was particularly significant. Once again, Bert was awaiting the decision of his Local Review

Committee – the body which is, in effect, the parole board, responsible for assessing a prisoner's suitability for release and making its recommendation known to the Home Office. Of perhaps even greater importance was the fact that the Court of Appeal was in the process of hearing the appeal by the surviving trio of the four men (Patrick Molloy had died in prison in 1981), cousins Michael and Vincent Hickey, and Jimmy Robinson – all convicted of the murder at Yew Tree Farm. Their main thrust was not only that they were innocent of child-murder, but that Bert Spencer was guilty of the said crime.

The moment of such timing needs no underlining, particularly when considered in conjunction with the gap of nine years.

On 26 January 1989, while the Court of Appeal was still in session, Bert Spencer was interviewed about his alleged confession to Prison Officer Graham by Detective Sergeants Stokes and Williams of the Hampshire Constabulary. These experienced officers must have been as mystified as Bert himself, knowing, as they did, the tight-knit procedures, which were operated in the case of prisoners remanded on a charge of murder.

There was a strange sequel to the affair. Prison Officer Graham attended the appeal hearing, expecting to be called to repeat his allegation. Before he could bask in his anticipated fifteen minutes of fame, he was joined by two large, well-dressed, official-looking men who spoke to him briefly, quietly and very seriously. Several eyewitnesses attested later to the incident. Flanked by his visitors, Prison Officer Graham stood up and left with them. Whoever the men were and whatever they said to the prison officer, they obviously carried considerable official weight. Robert Graham's name was removed from the witness list.

In 1991, Bert Spencer was in transit from Wayland prison in Norfolk to North Sea Camp in Lincolnshire. In the twisty manner of many prison transfer journeys, Bert Spencer had to spend four nights while en route at Winson Green prison. There he encountered Prison Officer Robert James Graham, coming out of the hospital wing with which Bert was so familiar. Their mutual recognition was acknowledged with curt nods as their paths crossed. Prison Officer Graham was wearing the insignia of increased rank on his epaulettes. Only he has the full explanation of such promotion and Bert could find out no more official information.

The Hickeys and Robinson appeal failed. Bert Spencer was now at an open prison and the possibility of a finite release date was now a reality. But the catalogue of false accusation had not yet ended, nor had the campaigners finished their programme of persecution.

During the two years that Bert was to spend at North Sea Camp, he was to endure the spin-off results of yet another showing on television of the documentary, *Murder at the Farm* – this time on New Year's Eve, 31 December, 1992. The programme pulled no punches and followed the theme of Paul Foot's bestseller. It placed Spencer as suspect number one, for the murder of the 13-year-old paperboy. This broadcast was shortly after fresh allegations were made by two other inmates that Bert had allegedly once again made confessions in their presence.

Then, just when it seemed that the campaigners had no more bullets left to shoot, yet another television production on the subject of the two farmhouse murders was produced. This documentary style film dealt not only with the shooting of Carl Bridgewater but also Bert's murder of Hubert Wilkes. The three-hour movie was shown over two nights, it was entitled, *Bad Company*. This was a dramatised production but delivered as fact. It starred Angus Deayton as journalist Paul Foot with Michael Hickey played by Johnny Lee Miller, who became a huge Hollywood star.

Surprisingly, this time, the TV critics were themselves more damaging to Bert than the programme itself.

The allegations of confession were no less difficult to understand than were the several previous incidents of false witnesses.

The Charlie/Fitzgerald 'confession'

It was fortunate for Bert Spencer that the two prisoners at North Sea Camp who dreamed up the last of the prison 'confessions' lacked the intellect to underpin their fabrication with some solid groundwork. Tommy Fitzgerald and his friend, Charlie (his second name is unknown), lived at the camp hospital, a favoured berth where inmates could enjoy privileges unknown anywhere else on the prison site. At the hospital they had their own television and video set, and as many video tapes as they required. Lights-out did not apply. A free supply of tea and coffee, treasured commodities in the prison environment, and early access to the dining room at meal times, all combined to create quite a relaxed setting in a working prison.

As hospital orderly, Charlie had very little to do in the way of work and spent his days in an armchair in front of the television. Tommy Fitzgerald was an old lag, a career inmate who was a skilled tailor. He worked as a storeman where his expertise with the needle earned him small but regular perks. At the time of his impending release, Fitzgerald begged the then prison governor to let him stay on.

Both men had been prison friends of Jimmy Robinson at other establishments and proudly boasted of their relationship with him. At North Sea Camp they were not popular and had the reputations of being both grasses and pathological liars.

Bert had been at North Sea Camp for over a year, once again his Local Review Committee parole assessment was due in a few weeks. And then the bombshell fell. Fitzgerald, with Charlie in the background, had joined the queue of alleged confessors. Their story was palpably weak and their local reputations added no colour or strength. But, nevertheless, it was another hurdle strewn in Bert Spencer's path.

In fact the two men plotted to devise two separate stories. Charlie, a large man who, on his release, returned to run his family business of driving JCB's on the mud flats of Lincolnshire, made up the incredible story. It surrounded Bert having confessed to him that he had murdered Carl Bridgewater, and that this confession had been made in the prison chapel in the presence of a Quaker minister. Not content with that, Charlie and his friend, Tommy Fitzgerald, alleged that Bert had repeated his confession in the presence of them both in his room in North Wing, 211/212, a room to which, so they claimed, they were regular visitors.

The subsequent police investigation did not take long. The Quaker minister quickly put the one story to rest and denied all knowledge of any confession. When the police tested the accusers on their second story they asked them if there was anything unusual that they could remember about Bert's room. They unanimously said that there was nothing in the room that was out of the ordinary. Apparently, they had failed to notice in that small, two-man room, an oil painting which occupied twenty square feet of one wall, a bright picture of a cheetah hunting down a Thompson's gazelle. There were other paintings too, large, but not as big as that one.

Once again the police investigation had exposed a tissue of blatant lies. As to the motive, it would seem that the only possible one could be a desire to ingratiate themselves with the criminal fraternity – a strong possibility in the case of Tommy Fitzgerald, a hopeless recidivist for whom a life as a permanent member of the prison system held more preferable vistas than the prospect of life on the outside.

When last heard of, Tommy Fitzgerald was serving yet another sentence for shoplifting. Charlie was still working on the bleak, grey and windy mud-flats and maybe listening to a nagging conscience.

Quite often it was not always a false confession that would bring unwanted attention on Bert Spencer.

The Fitzpatrick statement

In 1984, an ex-bar worker and latterly a special constable, Mrs Fitzpatrick, volunteered the information to Staffordshire police that she had been shown a shotgun in Bert Spencer's car. Had it ever happened, the incident would have been quite irrelevant anyway. Bert Spencer's last contact, he alleges, with the lady had been in 1975 – three years before the death of Carl Bridgewater, four years before the death of Hubert Wilkes and nine years before her statement was made.

Paul Foot, in his book, claims Mrs Fitzpatrick, a special constable, told the police she had seen the gun in the car boot in 1978, the important murder year, and had worked with Spencer several times during that year. Her information had created a secret Home Office inquiry under DCS Ridgway of the Manchester police.

As mystified today as he was on first hearing of Mrs Fitzpatrick's communication with the police, Bert Spencer, stretching his memory to bring her into focus, describes her as, '... one of a very quiet, inoffensive and pleasant family trio'.

In fact, so quiet and unassuming were the three people that they were known to fellow workers only as, 'the Merediths'. Two of the trio were a married couple, Mr and Mrs Meredith, and the third member of the group, the woman in question, was sister to one or other of the married couple. Bert assumes that this sister was, or became, Mrs Fitzpatrick.

This was to be the one piece of questionable information, which was to be laid against Bert that did not stem from within the prison system. Somehow, the fact that it was not sourced from the lips of some self-seeking old lag made the event even more hurtful to Bert. Bert had always enjoyed working with the Merediths and it had seemed that the arrangement was mutually satisfactory.

In the seventies Bert's wife, Janet, was the company secretary of Licensee Refreshments who provided an outside catering service at major functions. The managing director, now retired, was Mr Reg Morgan of Tipton. Part of Janet's function was to liaise with and coordinate the sixty or so part-time bar staff – which work-force included Bert himself and the Meredith trio. Bert was one of several part-time bar managers. Bar staff were encouraged to state their preference for the bar manager with whom they wished to work. The Merediths usually opted to work with Bert with whom they had a harmonious working relationship.

With the Merediths as his bar staff, Bert worked at many venues such as Brierley Hill Civic Hall, Dudley and Stourbridge Town Hall, Dudley Technical College and various hospital functions. The major events for the company were the days at Uttoxeter racecourse where, about four times a year, Licensee Refreshments would be engaged to set up five or six bars on site.

Bert twice attended the racecourse days where he managed 'Tatt's Bar'. On those occasions he was not working with the Meredith/Fitzpatrick team. His bar-help consisted of a washing-up lady and a serving CID officer.

The company headquarters were at The Tipton Arms pub, with offices upstairs and the use of the yards and outbuildings. The practice was for Janet to leave her Datsun car at The Tipton Arms. Bert would then drive to the venue in Reg Morgan's Granada with Reg and Janet as passengers. On arrival, the car would be unloaded of general trade items, cash floats and paperwork. The car would be locked and Janet would retain the key.

Mrs Fitzpatrick's statement included the fact that Bert had shown her a shotgun he had in the boot of Reg's Granada. Bert had told her, she alleged, he carried it for protection against the possibility of being mugged and he used to make everyone aware of the fact. Again, the allegation produced yet another police enquiry, which resulted in no action being taken. But still this piece of information was repeated by Mrs Fitzpatrick at the Court of Appeal hearing which began in the December of 1988. Questioning of the staff of Licensed Refreshments revealed no one to back up Mrs Fitzpatrick's story. No one had ever heard Bert Spencer either boast of carrying a shotgun in the car or had anyone ever seen such a gun – not even Reg Morgan who owned the vehicle. Mrs Fitzpatrick's statement was dismissed by the judges and she was described as an 'impressionable witness'. Impressionable? Easily influenced? By what or by whom?

In Foot's book the statement made by Mrs Fitzpatrick differs from Bert's recollection. Apart from the alleged discrepancy with regards the year being 1978, she told the Bridgewater Four's solicitor, Jim Nichol, some startling information. She alleges on one occasion, at Brierley Hill, she had been helping Bert unload stocks from the back of his blue Vauxhall Viva. In the boot was 'something that was not very wide, but was about 18 inches long, wrapped in a sheet'. She claimed Spencer had said, 'that is just my gun I keep in the car.'

At the 1988 Court of Appeal hearing, after listening to all of Elaine Fitzpatrick's evidence, it was said that after 'extensive' police inquiries, there appeared to be no evidence that Spencer carried a gun in the boot of his car.

10.

A Case to Answer

••

Long before Paul Foot was to start his *Daily Mirror* campaign and Ann Whelan's crusade was in its infancy – a powerful article appeared in the *Guardian* on Tuesday 7 October 1980. The author was Eileen Ballantyne and she was one of the first journalists to cast doubt about the convictions of the Bridgewater Four, less than 12 months after their conviction and sentencing.

I contacted Ms Ballantyne and spoke to her about the article. An obviously highly intelligent woman, she was certainly an early frontrunner, if not the first, to cast doubt on the convictions of the Bridgewater Four. I absorbed her words with great interest and she makes some strong points – as one would expect from a respected *Guardian* journalist. It was a huge feature and a brave early move for the broadsheet.

The article centred on fresh evidence released by the Director of Public Prosecutions (12 June 1980) following the sentence of the Bridgewater Four on 12 November 1979. Amongst the 50 pages of statements, which were not made available to the defence at the trial, was one that revealed the questioning of Hubert 'Bert' Spencer as a possible suspect in the case. Although the article picked up on the coincidences, and a few inconsistencies – easily made at this early stage, it made a case for not only the innocence of the Bridgewater Four, but the guilt of the Spencer One.

The article also intelligently viewed the signed confession of Pat Molloy. He was known to police as a, '… neat, methodical burglar who never left a mess behind him'. Although one has to question the fact that Malloy alleged that the drawers in the main bedroom, which he was supposed to have been rifling when he heard the shooting downstairs, had been stacked in neat piles. This was actually how they were found, which was in contrast to the rest of the rooms searched. Had the police put words into the mouth of Molloy or was he actually there? Ballantyne also points out, quite rightly, that Molloy specialised in, '... school, house and office break-ins, with more than a 150 convictions in all', he had no record of violence.

The majority of allegations made against Bert Spencer by the campaigners have, over the years, developed into what is almost a mini industry, founded mostly upon speculation and baseless claims. Shoring up the hypotheses have been several forms of media propaganda, which have been remarkably effective. The reaction of even some case-hardened television viewers have served to demonstrate that even experienced professionals can confuse a well presented TV drama with documentary reality and, as a result, to see that to which they are directed.

In the postscript to *Murder at the Farm*, Paul Foot states that after the showing of the Thames TV programme, of the same title, based on the book, he was, '... struck once again by the power of television to shift the public mind ...'. He was quite right, of course, but he omitted to add that without the benefit of a sound information base, the public mind easily falls prey to the traffic in misinformation.

Regarding the television presentation of, *Murder at the Farm*, Tony Judge, spokesman for the Police Federation, made the comment that it was, '... a clever and insidious way of making a point ... if Dr Goebbels had had that weapon at his disposal, there is no knowing what he could have done with the minds of the Germans. It is power without responsibility...'.

Adolph Hitler espoused the philosophy of reiterative misinformation and used it too well to shift the mind of his German public. In *Mein Kampf*, he wrote that, 'The broad mass of a nation will more easily fall victim to a big lie than to a small one ...'. Often experience provides no argument to this dictum.

In the case of Bert Spencer, many of the allegations had been dismissed by the police and the judiciary at an early stage, but they were to be continually resurrected. It was often the case of public accusation followed by a less well advertised rebuttal; then, instead of a public retraction there would be a period of dormancy before the allegation was made again. Bert Spencer was no simple sitting target; he was bound and gagged as well.

As early as 1980, Sir Norman Skelhorn, Director of Public Prosecutions, had issued a statement saying that, 'Hubert Spencer was one of a substantial number of men seen by the police in the early stages of the investigation of the murder of Carl Bridgewater and eliminated from the inquiries'.

Nine years later, during the Appeal Hearing, Lord Justice Russell, had stated that, 'we are satisfied without doubt that Spencer had played no part in the events at Yew Tree Farm'.

Five police inquiries had reached the same conclusion, but the persecution of Bert Spencer has been continued unrelentingly through the intervening years, and beyond, right up to the present day.

While the Bridgewater affair itself has all the complexity of the Gordian knot, the case that the campaigners make against Bert Spencer is essentially simplistic. They would have it that, on 19 September, he left his workstation at Corbett Hospital in Stourbridge and drove to Yew Tree Farm one or more times for the purpose of burglary – at least once wearing full ambulance service uniform, apart from the cap. That he was there at 2.50 pm and again at 4.20 pm, at which time he shot Carl Bridgewater, a one-time neighbour, in order to prevent his identifying him. In the meantime, in their contention, he had spent time searching the massive property, leaving it in a state of chaos, having forced entry to the farmhouse at TWO points – via a window and by the back door – and had removed numerous antique household items of quite low value and had taken time to conceal others around various parts of the farm. All this, Bert Spencer, is alleged to have accomplished while coordinating the flow of patients and transport at Corbett Hospital without his absence being noticed.

The allegations, of course, need some under-pinning in order to project them out of the realm of mere conjecture. In the case of Bert Spencer, this amounted only to background circumstance – factors which have rarely weighed heavily since Llewellyn slew his faithful hound, Gelbert. It was

Bert's misfortune that his work and interests over many years had provided ready-made and convenient links to connect him, albeit superficially, to the tragedy and its location. Superimposed upon this situation were later factors; one – a proven but credibility-stretching coincidence, and the other which suggested more than a hint of manipulative interference by a human agency, i.e., the episode of the piece of card and the disappearance of the ambulance service records.

The Allegations

The *main* contentions of the anti-Spencer campaigners have been that;

    i.   **The Roger Edwards Sighting:** The sighting made by Roger Edwards of a uniformed man driving a light blue Vauxhall Viva saloon car into the footpath leading past Yew Tree Farm at 2.50 pm on the day of the murder. This was Bert Spencer who had left his post at Corbett Hospital – either for one extended period of time or more than once during that afternoon.

    ii.   **The Gladys Jones Sighting:** Because Mrs Gladys Jones saw no vehicle in the driveway of the farm at 4.30 pm, it is implicit that the killer or killers had left the immediate vicinity by that time. Having sightings around or after this crucial time of 4.30 pm, conveniently contradicted sightings of other vehicles etc. –which were favourable to Bert Spencer.

    iii.   **The Piece of Card:** Bert Spencer had himself written a strange message on the piece of card and planted it where it was found – in order to divert suspicion from himself and to implicate a man who was a stranger to him.

iv. **The Connections With Yew Tree Farm:** He was familiar with the residents of Yew Tree Farm and was a frequent guest there with an intimate knowledge of the farmhouse and its contents.

v. **The Murder Weapon:** At the time of the murder Spencer owned a shotgun.

vi. **The Antiques:** He coveted the antique contents of the farmhouse.

vii. **The Dog Factor:** He had cultivated a friendly relationship with the dogs at both Yew Tree Farm and Holloway House. This would enable him to more easily break into Yew Tree Farm, without the dog barking, raising the alarm. Regarding Holloway House, it would make easier access to the yard at night in order to break into the outside office (where shotgun ammunition was kept). It would also help Spencer to saw off the shotgun barrel unencumbered.

viii. **The Irrelevant Cartridge Case:** A pattern of post-crime behaviour was established by the fact that Bert Spencer threw a live shotgun cartridge from the window of his car when he was driving ambulance man, Barry Thomas, down the lane to Holloway house. This neatly tied into the fact that 15 months before, two days after the murder of Carl, an empty cartridge case was found in the road about half a mile from Yew Tree Farm.

ix. **Copycat Murders:** The killing of Hubert Wilkes showed copycat similarities to the murder of Carl Bridgewater.

x. **The Motive:** The motive for the killing of Hubert Wilkes was rage, induced by Mr Wilkes having accused Bert Spencer of having murdered the 13-year-old paperboy.

xi.   **The Spencer Alibi:** Bert Spencer had no cast-iron alibi for the afternoon of the murder at Yew Tree Farm.

xii. **The Missing Records:** In order to cover his tracks, Bert Spencer removed the relevant movement records from two locations, Corbett Hospital and Warley control centre.

xiii. **The Identification Factor:** As a onetime neighbour of the Bridgewater family, Bert Spencer would have been recognized by Carl who had interrupted the robbery at the farm. To avoid identification, Bert had shot and killed the boy.

It is around at these points that the anti-Spencer/pro-Bridgewater Four campaigners structured its attack.

Examination and Conclusions

It is interesting to examine the main points of the anti-Spencer campaign, not least, because there are few hidden facts to weigh against the well-publicized accusations. But the facts are there, and mostly have been since the day of the murder of Carl Bridgewater. They have simply been ignored by those who have chosen to speculate or even manufacturer a case against Bert Spencer.

In the paragraphs following, bare facts are considered in a fresh and impartial light. The main problem is to understand how simple matters of fact came to be reshaped. Often these facts were delivered by a cynical hand, presented to form a picture of a man, which is a total distortion of the truth. The secondary puzzle is to comprehend how otherwise rational and thinking people could be persuaded to embrace such a warped version of events – a version that has no basis in logic or reality.

i. The Roger Edwards Sighting

As previously described, at 2.50 pm Mr Edwards, a company director, turned off the A449 into Lawnswood Road. The turning is just 30 yards away from the opening to the footpath leading past Yew Tree Farm. Ahead, a light blue Viva was making a left turn onto the pathway. As Mr Edwards drew nearer he had clear sight both of the driver and a car.

The factual residue of Roger Edwards' sighting leaves us with a Vauxhall Viva saloon, light blue in colour and a driver wearing a dark blue uniform tunic with one-pip on his epaulette. The driver, whose age Mr Edwards estimated to be about 55, had dark, greying, wavy hair. The car also had a newish appearance.

Paul Foot was to describe the Edwards sighting as, 'definite and damning in every way of Hubert Spencer'. However, when, on 1 December, 1981 – the day of the Bridgewater four's application for leave to make a full appeal – Patrick Bennett, QC, opening for Vincent Hickey, sought to bring up the subject of the Edwards sighting and relate it to Bert Spencer.

Lord Chief Justice Lane interjected, 'He looks nothing like him, does he?'

Mr Bennett's withdrawal was immediate and comprehensive and he assured the court that it was not his intention to suggest that Hubert Spencer had committed the murder. Why then did he raise the matter?

At the time, Bert Spencer was 38 years of age; his hair was short, light brown and very straight. His tunic bore *two* pips on each epaulette. As his work colleagues knew, although it could carry no evidential weight, it was always Bert's habit not to drive wearing his jacket. He would fold it and place it on the passenger seat. Similarly, it is a fact that at the first hint of sunshine, Bert's eye condition necessitated his wearing glasses with Reactolite lenses. 19 September, 1978, was a bright, sunny day.

Neither could Bert's Vauxhall Viva be described as 'newish'. Two months later its condition caused it to realise a sale price of only £175.

Although Paul Foot was happy to embrace the Edwards identification of the Viva saloon, after his own highly contrived one-pip/two-pip theory (as explained in Chapter 4), he was to suggest that Mr Edwards' recollection of seeing only one shoulder pip was enough to lessen the credibility of the description of the driver.

The timing of the Edwards sighting was one and a half hours before the time of the murder of Carl Bridgewater. The only other sighting which could possibly have been that of a Viva saloon was quite vague and took place at 2.55 pm, just five minutes afterwards. With the time gap between these sightings and the known time of the killing of Carl, added to a description which even the counsel for Vincent Hickey agreed bore no resemblance whatever to Bert Spencer, it is difficult to follow Mr Foot's reasoning behind his assertion that the Edwards sighting was, 'definite and damning in every respect of Hubert Spencer'.

ii. The Gladys Jones Sighting

The essence of the first sighting reported by Mrs Gladys Jones of Yew Tree Cottage is that she saw a blue *estate* car backed into the driveway of the farm with its tailgate raised. The back door of the farm appeared to be shut.

Mrs Jones viewpoint was from the bottom of her garden on a rise above the farm and some 225 yards away. Looking downhill, there is a clear view into the driveway of the farm and on the main entrance, the back door to the farm. She was almost certain that the vehicle was a Ford Cortina, and most positive that it was an estate. That the vehicle was blue, a Ford, and that it was an estate was positively supported by the sighting made, at a few yards range, by Mr Anthony Cross, a highways inspector. Not only was Mr Cross familiar with different makes of vehicle, but he was also in a position to be positive about the time, 3.50 pm. Some 10 minutes before Mrs Jones walked to the bottom of her garden, Anthony Cross had actually turned off Lawnswood Road and onto the footpath leading past the farm. He had parked only a few yards from the rear end of an estate car, the back of which was projecting from the driveway of the farm – presumably just before manoeuvring into the position reported by Mrs Jones. Mr Cross had no doubt that the estate was either a Ford Cortina or a Granada, blue in colour.

To get a clearer view, Mrs Jones had stepped from her garden into the adjacent field. Although she stood there for some five minutes she saw no sign of human activity. Still curious about the identity of the visitors to the farm, Mrs Jones checked again about half an hour later, somewhere around 4.30 pm. From her vantage point the blue Ford estate was no longer visible. From that, it has been deduced that the killer or killers had fled the scene. However, had the blue estate simply been moved from the driveway and parked on the footpath – either on the 30 yard stretch between the driveway and Lawnswood Road or further down the path away from the farm – then it would *not* have been visible to Mrs Jones.

Witness statements would seem to confirm that that is exactly what had happened. There were sightings of a blue vehicle, or vehicles, on the footpath only minutes after Mrs Jones' confirmation that the driveway of the farm was empty. Mrs Geraldine Waldron stated that at about 4.45 pm she saw a medium or dark blue vehicle parked on the pathway, near the hedge at the bottom of the track (some 70 yards from Lawnswood Road and about 30 yards further down the path from the driveway of the farm). On the track stood a tall man wearing light-coloured clothing (Bert Spencer is five foot eight inches tall and ambulance uniform is dark blue). At around the same time, a medium-ranged vehicle was seen on the pathway by Edward Dickens, obviously manoeuvring into the entrance to the driveway, facing towards the farmhouse and positioned diagonally across the path. Another report by Wendy Stagg, at approximately the same time, describes a blue estate car parked at the entrance to the footpath near a plumb-coloured Allegro. Standing in the road was a man talking to the driver of the estate car.

Another witness, Brian Clarke, stated that ten minutes later he saw a medium blue Austin/Morris J4 van, angled in the position previously occupied by the medium-sized vehicle. Several interpretations can be made of these sightings, which are less confusing than first glance suggests. However, at 5.00 pm the footpath was clear, except for a dark blue Ford estate containing two or three men, witnessed by Terence Phelps. The vehicle was stationary, near the road and looked as if the driver was waiting to join the flow of traffic. The driver was in his forties, had a head of thick, dark hair and was wearing a light shirt and tie.

Is it likely that this blue Ford estate was not the same vehicle that was seen by Gladys Jones? And is it likely that the occupants were not the killers of Carl Bridgewater? If the driver of the plum-coloured Allegro, another vehicle spotted by Wendy Stagg, was not connected with the killers, why has he never come forward with vital descriptions of the men in the blue Ford estate?

Most importantly, by no stretch of any reasonable person's imagination could Bert Spencer and his blue Viva saloon be fitted into the rash of sightings which were reported in the vicinity of Yew Tree Farm between the hours of 4.00 pm and 5.00 pm on the day of the murder.

iii. The Piece of Card

The whole story of the famous *piece of card* was detailed exclusively in *Chapter 5*. There is nothing in this whole convoluted affair has been so convincingly dismissed as having any connection with Bert Spencer as has the matter of the piece of card and its cryptic message. And yet that strange piece of jetsam has been dragged to the surface time and time again. As we have seen, the piece of card, originally found by a group of children in Oldbury Road, Smethwick (a road into which both Stony Lane and Vicarage Road lead), was picked up two days later in Telford Way by Bert Spencer's sister-in-law, Valerie Spencer. Coincidentally, this was the same day that Jimmy Robinson was released after being held on remand then tried for the Tamworth meat robbery. That same night the piece of card, significant for its mention of Carl Bridgewater, was handed into Smethwick police station by Bert Spencer.

However, police interest in the peculiar, but possibly weighty find, did not manifest itself until fifteen months later, five days after the killing of Hubert Wilkes. The enquiry kicked off when Bert's brother, Don, Valerie's husband, was interviewed by the police to see if he could throw any light upon the many questions posed by the finding of the card and the content of the message written upon it. The police record of the incident had obviously been filed under Bert's christened name of Hubert Vincent. The 'Bert' to whom the card was addressed was not a connection particularly obvious to any third party unaware of the name of which he was generally known.

After the killing of Hubert Wilkes, however, coincidence reared its head and a connection became an apparent possibility. The card was addressed to a 'Bert', the message mentioned Carl Bridgewater, and now Bert Spencer had killed his employer in a farmhouse not half a mile from Yew Tree Farm. Another killing, another 'Bert' and a member of Bert's family had found the card while in his company. In the years before the remarkable coincidence was proven, the episode survived as a frustrating and intriguing puzzle for everyone concerned. Don Spencer, of course, was as mystified himself.

Despite wide exposure in the press, no one else called forward with any enlightening information. The children who as adults were able to clear up part of the mystery were unaware of the media attention at the time. In the absence of any explanatory intelligence, the campaigners openly accused Bert Spencer, now remanded in Winson Green prison, of being the originator of the card and the architect of the incident. His motive, so they claimed, was to divert suspicion from himself and to incriminate Harry Rushton – a man he did not know – in the murder of the paperboy. This was all based on the fact that Rushton had access to ambulance service uniforms and its possible tie-in with the sighting made by Roger Edwards. Of course when the film, *Bad Company*, was released, this was reflected in such a damning way that it almost left no doubt in most viewers that Mr Spencer was totally responsible, as not only the author but also the culprit who placed the card that was found. Whether it was known that some children had already discovered the card and placed it quite innocently in a different location negates the fact that Bert had anything to do with it – certainly the placing of it.

Over four years later (10 February, 1984), Don Spencer was again being questioned about his recall of the incident, this time by Paul Foot. The time span of more than five years had done nothing to add any more salient facts to Don Spencer's memory bank – nor could it have done. And yet Paul Foot was to make his somewhat preposterous report on the interview as detailed in *Chapter 5 – the Piece of Card*.

For years afterwards, working on the 19th century English novelist, Arnold Bennett's concept, '... Journalists say a thing they know isn't true, in the hope that if they keep on saying it long enough it will be true ...', the campaigners kept their contention in high profile, insisting that Bert Spencer himself was at the hub of the mystery.

Seven years after the card was handed in to the police, Janet Cotter, who lived at the Stony Lane address, which was mentioned on the card, began her strange, delayed-action correspondence with Bert and prompted perhaps by her contacts with Paul Foot. Ms Cotter, originally purporting to be writing to Bert as a pen-friend, demonstrated in her letters that she had an all-consuming fixation about the piece of card. So much so, that Bert was driven to the conclusion that it was even possible that she had produced the card herself. Two years later, in the April of 1987, Janet Cotter was still writing about the piece of card. This time to the regional newspaper, the *Express & Star*, complaining that her address and details accusing her then boyfriend, Harry Rushton, were included on the card that had been found in a street, a few hundred yards from her home, nine years before. In her letter she complained that the incident of the card had severely troubled her family and had led to Rushton being interviewed by the police. Once again she alleged that Bert Spencer had written the card.

This time her renewed concern was certainly sparked by the Thames TV programme, *Murder at the Farm* (based on Paul Foot's bestselling book), which had been broadcast only days before, on 25 March, 1987. The question of the card was highlighted and some seven million people saw and heard Bert Spencer being accused of having written the card and engineered the incident.

Janet Cotter received acknowledgment of her 'help' in Mr Foot's book. A few weeks after Janet Cotter's letter to the *Express & Star*, Paul Foot wrote to Bert in Kingston prison on similar lines. He accused Bert of writing the card, called him a liar because of his denials and suggested that he was unbalanced. On 3 August, 1987, he was again busying himself with correspondence, with the piece of card at the forefront of his mind. Once again he wrote to Bert Spencer accusing him of being the author of the card and requesting that he be granted an interview with Bert in prison, claiming that he would be able to make the necessary arrangements with the Home Office. On that same day, Paul Foot wrote another letter in which the subject of the card was featured prominently. The addressee was the then Home Secretary, Douglas Hurd. After penning his request that the Bridgewater Four should have the benefit of a full Appeal Hearing, a public enquiry or a retrial by jury, the letter continued '... However hostile the Warwickshire (police) report, it cannot be disputed that at least two prosecution witnesses have changed their minds since the trial and that Bert Spencer *wrote the incriminating card* (author's italics). These alone, quite apart from the mountain of other questions, would seem to make the case for the appeal...'.

As we now know, the Appeal Hearing took place a year later, with devastatingly disappointing results for the campaigners. Of single significance was the demolition, by Home Office experts, of the anti-Spencer allegations involving the piece of card and the confirmatory emergence of the truth of the placement of the card in its final location by the group of young people.

Even after this public rejection of his claims, Paul Foot was not inclined to leave Bert Spencer in peace.

He wrote to him again in May, 1989, and it was in no spirit of contrition, but affirming that, '... I stick by what I wrote about you in the book and said on television...'.

As the standard bearer of the anti-Spencer/pro-Bridgewater Four, Paul Foot has served the campaign faction well. He has proved to be quite unrelenting in his pursuit of a man, totally innocent in the eyes of the law, of the allegations made about him. The campaign marched on defiantly even when the cause was shredded and tattered and all that was left as an objective was the obliteration of any vestiges of peace of mind which may still be retained by Bert Spencer.

iv. The Connections With Yew Tree Farm

At the time of the murder of Carl Bridgewater, Bert Spencer had not worked for farmer Wilkes for many months and had neither worked nor shot on the land which Hubert Wilkes leased around Yew Tree Farm for the same period. The work for Holloway House Farm had always been seasonal and this had been a longer lay-off spell than was usual. As was his normal practice, Bert had filled the gap with other part-time jobs.

During Bert's absence from the scene there were no changes in the day-to-day routine at Yew Tree Farm. Fred Jones and Mary Poole continued to watch the world go by from their wicket gate and household essentials were routinely delivered on a regular basis. Paul Foot talks of someone keeping a lengthy, 'mysterious and macabre' surveillance on the farmhouse, 'someone who knew it', he also commented. Anyone as familiar with the location as was Bert Spencer would have known very well the general pattern of movement around Yew Tree Farm. Significantly, he would have been well acquainted with the delivery arrangements at the farmhouse and would have studiously avoided any possibility of a confrontation with a scheduled arrival.

Only strangers would have let themselves be caught in the farmhouse late in the afternoon, perhaps strangers who had previously made a door-knocking reconnaissance and had established the vulnerability of the residents. Only strangers would have expected a generous haul of easily transportable antiques. Whoever the robbers were, it is apparent that when the availability of cash-generating antiques prove to be disappointing, some of the gang, two at least, were prepared to lurk outside the farmhouse awaiting the return of the enfeebled residents. After the cold-blooded, or maybe panic-induced, killing of the young paperboy, it would seem that their intentions, after interrogating the old couple about the contents of the safe and the whereabouts of any cash, were only too horrifyingly obvious.

Faces familiar to the district would hardly have been prepared to keep such a vigil outside the farmhouse. But the facts strongly point to at least two people having done just that: two men, possibly three, sat waiting for the return of Fred Jones and Mary Poole. They waited in a blue Ford estate car, positioned on the footpath where they could quickly assess the situation when the farmhouse residents returned, ready to either follow the couple inside or to make their getaway if the old people were to return with any daunting company.

Maybe the watchers had just committed a chilling murder. The body of a young boy lay inside the farmhouse, just yards away. With the anticipation of a near certain further double murder in mind they sat, watching and waiting. If this was indeed the case, such behaviour suggests the presence of practiced and hardened criminals – not shocked and terrified, locally recognisable amateurs, for whom an opportunist burglary had escalated through panic into a nightmare of murder.

Fred Jones and Mary Poole were not the isolated old couple, living on the edge of nowhere – an image of them which has been projected. They had friends, contacts and visitors. While there was hardly a constant stream of callers to the farmhouse, there were many people locally who were more familiar with the interior of the farmhouse than was Bert Spencer. Not least, perhaps, were some members of the Albrighton Hunt who were occasionally given the hospitality of Yew Tree Farm. Bert's circumstantial connections with the farm and the crime, his knowledge of the surrounding area, his interest in antiques and his use of sporting guns, were common denominators among several locals, many of whom had much closer connections with the farm and its grounds. And they, like Bert Spencer, could in no way be connected with the murderer of the young paperboy.

Attempts have been made to associate Bert Spencer with the farmhouse and its residents in a much closer fashion than was true.

Paul Foot has remarked that Bert Spencer was known to have, '... led gangs of hospital and ambulance workers to Mr Wilkes farms (including Yew Tree) on summer evenings'.

In fact, Hubert Wilkes' elder son, Anthony, was responsible for organizing the gang labour on the farms. All that Bert Spencer did, at Hubert Wilkes' request, was to pass the word around when there was a requirement for part-time labour to work on Holloway House or Yew Tree land.

Paul Foot has also stated that Bert had, '... built up a close relationship with Yew Tree Farm and its tenants', and that he was, '... a frequent guest ...' and, '... used to borrow Jack Poole's gun to shoot rabbits on the farm ...'.

As recorded earlier, Bert Spencer was never a guest at Yew Tree Farm and had stepped over the threshold of the farmhouse only twice before (not counting the visit during the auction after the murder) – the only occasions on which he had had direct conversations with the residents. On one of those visits he had gone to ask Jack Poole about buying the shotgun. The gun, as we are aware, was not at the farmhouse. Mr Poole kept it at Yew Tree Cottage. Bert never did see it or knowingly handle it – even when it became the property of Hubert Wilkes. The only time he came in contact with the weapon was when he unwittingly picked it up, on that fateful night when he blasted the old farmer.

To residents of Yew Tree Farm, Bert Spencer was never more than an infrequently passing stranger, an employee of Hubert Wilkes.

v. The Murder Weapon

At the time of Carl's murder Bert Spencer allegedly did not own a shotgun (although Jimmy Robinson did). The fact that no spent cartridge was found at the scene of the killing at Yew Tree Farm renders those items of information quite irrelevant to the murder investigation. Without the possibility of being able to compare ammunition used with a suspect weapon, no conclusions can be reached. Regardless of this, the campaigners have made a great effort to show that Bert Spencer did, in fact, own a shotgun at the time.

When Spencer was interviewed by the police at Corbett Hospital on 16 November, 1978, he informed them that he had not owned a shotgun for some 12 months. He had previously owned a 12-bore, single-barrelled shotgun, which he had sold to a near neighbour, Robert Thompson of 52, Kingsley Road, Kingswinford. Mr Thompson, a builder, owned a country cottage near Bridgnorth where he kept the gun. Three days later, the police interviewed him. He confirmed Bert Spencer's account, the important part, at least; he had had the gun in his possession for about a year. The only discrepancy was that Mr Thompson had forgotten to obtain the necessary licence for the weapon and he claimed that the gun had been lent to him rather than sold. However, the timing of the transfer of possession was established and the weapon was not returned to Bert Spencer.

It was 7 December, three weeks later, that Jimmy Robinson led police to a patch of waste ground where they recovered his buried shotgun. It was a single barrelled 12-bore, the barrel sawn off and the stock shortened, giving it the silhouette of a highwayman's pistol. These modifications are common within the criminal fraternity, maybe to facilitate concealment and portability. All of which is totally irrelevant to the murder investigation. Without a tell-tale used cartridge case to match for marking with one fired from a suspect weapon, ownership of a shotgun told the investigators nothing – apart from adding background colour.

Paul Foot would seem to have missed the point.

In a letter to Bert Spencer in Kingston prison, dated 1 July, 1987, he declared, '... your statement in the *Express & Star* is a tissue of half-truths and downright lies. Why did you say you did not own a shotgun when you did? Indeed, you directed the police to the man who had it – the builder Thompson'.

Peculiarly, the whole issue of the weapons used in the murders at the two farms appears to be the subject of much confusion and muddled thinking. The facts are quite simple. Carl Bridgewater was killed with a shotgun blast fired from a weapon that took cartridges of the size and type of an Eley 5. The boy was shot from a range close enough to obscure the nature of the shotgun barrel. Close range wounds from a full length or sawn-off barrelled shotgun are impossible to distinguish with any certainty. Jimmy Robinson owned at least one shotgun, the one to which he directed the police: this gun had a sawn-down barrel. It is unlikely that this gun was the murder weapon. Had it been, it could have remained undetected in its burial place.

When Bert Spencer shot and killed Hubert Wilkes, in an inexplicable act he took a full length shotgun from the farmhouse and sawed the barrel down in the dark farmyard. This sawn-off shotgun was the gun with which Mr Wilkes was shot.

The gun used to kill Carl Bridgewater has never, and can never, be identified and neither can the barrel length be determined. And yet, from several quarters, there has been insistence that in both murders the weapon used was a sawn-off shotgun.

Even Lord Justice Russell, in the reading of the reserve judgment in the Court of Appeal on 17 March, 1989, made a misleading reference. In dismissing any suggestion of there being a copycat link between the two farmhouse murders he stated that, '... all the two killings had in common were the proximity of the two farms, the use of a sawn-off shotgun discharged at close range while the victim was seated on a sofa ....'

When writing in the *Observer* nine days later, Richard Ingrams too, made claim that both murders were committed with a sawn-off shotgun. It may be true, but only the killer or killers of Carl Bridgewater know for certain.

To Bert Spencer, shotguns, like antiques, were a trading commodity, a source of small profit. He was no target or clay-pigeon shooter, so interested in the sporting life that he relished the handling pleasure of his own touch-familiar weapon. He was quite content to buy and sell-on legally the odd shotgun, which he might happen across. For shooting vermin or the

odd rabbit, he was happy to ask permission to borrow a gun from Mr Wilkes'
armoury – even though that was not done on a casual basis: a formal request
had always to be made.

In order to distance Jimmy Robinson from the events at Yew Tree
Farm, Paul Foot would have it that Robinson took the police to where he
had buried his shotgun in both the knowledge of his own innocence and a
total ignorance of even the basics of forensic ballistics, i.e., that Robinson
was unaware of the fact that it would be impossible to identify the murder weapon without the correct spent cartridge. Such ignorance would, of
course, be shared by many people. But that such a lack of knowledge be
possessed by a man who frequented such haunts as the Dog and Partridge
pub Selly Oak or the California at Weoley Castle is difficult to conceive.

By Jimmy Robinson's own account, the California in particular was
a Fagin's den of criminal talent, a swap-shop of criminal expertise. It is
commonly held knowledge that pistols, revolvers and rifles have grooved
barrels while shotguns have smooth bores. The grooved barrel produces
individual and unique markings on a bullet fired through it. The smooth
bore of a shotgun produces no such markings on the small lead balls comprising a shotgun cartridge load, although both types of weapon leave
identifiable markings from the firing pin's impact on the projectile casing.
Remove the empty shotgun cartridge from the scene of a crime and all
that can be deduced from the lead shot and the wadding, which have been
discharged is the cartridge type and the bore size of the weapon. Later
production of the offending weapon is no help to the investigation; connection with the crime is not possible to prove. That such basic knowledge
of weaponry would be foreign to a member of Birmingham's underworld
and frequented known haunts of professional criminals is hard to believe.
For an investigative journalist to use as a point of argument is, at best,
incredibly naïve.

Certainly up to the point of the Bridgewater Four's successful appeal
in 1997, the campaigners were giving attention to attempt to prove that
Bert Spencer did own a shotgun some weeks before the Yew Tree Farm

murder. Certainly he was not the owner of a gun in the September of 1978; but even had he been, it would have been a matter of no determinable significance.

vi. The Antiques

Bert Spencer's lifelong and deeply ingrained interest in antiques seems to be a genetic trait, passed down from his father, Leonard, a general dealer whose shop window was his horse-drawn cart. From his early teens, Bert bought and sold household items, learning as he went, progressing from coronation mugs to Staffordshire figures and from Timex wristwatches to Ormolu mantel clocks.

Clocks became Bert's special interest and a subject of detailed knowledge. At his moment of greatest stress, immediately after shooting Mr Wilkes, with his senses almost completely malfunctioning, he was able to register that the Edwardian wall clock appeared to have stopped ticking. Even then, in the most grotesque of circumstances, a germ of antiquarian interest surfaced unconsciously through his mental haze.

Despite his expertise, Bert was never in a position to afford the luxury of becoming a collector. As he bought, so he had to sell to finance his latest acquisition. It seemed to be a step towards a desired situation, combining potential with opportunity when, in 1971, with a partner, Kenneth Farndon, he set up an antique business in rented shop premises at 90, High Street, Wordsley. The High Street proved to be anything but a prime site for an antiques shop and the business failed to take off. It lasted only a few months and was closed six years before the murder at Yew Tree Farm.

This interest of Bert's in antiques was recast by the campaigners into yet another fabricated millstone to hang about him. Like most early Victorian farmhouses, which remain untouched by time and DIY enthusiasts, almost every household article inside Yew Tree farmhouse could be described as 'antique'. And much of it was. It was Bert's misfortune that he had ever had cause to cross the threshold and have sight of the large display case containing its family of stuffed foxes. Taxidermy is not to everyone's taste, but, of its kind, the display was the work of unusual quality. Bert was taken with it, talked about it at Holloway House, and later went to bid for it at auction with Hubert Wilkes when the contents of Yew Tree Farm were placed on the market.

The auction took place five months after Carl's murder. Bert attended in the full expectation that the police would be there in plain clothed force, probably some whose acquaintance he had already made while being interviewed about the killing. It was hardly a confrontation, which a guilty man would readily chance in the cause of making a bid on long-dead foxes. In the event, DCI Robert Stewart was in attendance, together with a small team. Bert was outbid for the foxes, which fetched a price only a little short of the police estimation of the total value of the items that had been stolen from the farmhouse in the previous September.

Whoever had stolen the articles from the house had hardly been selective. The haul had consisted of almost anything that was portable and which looked to be saleable – hardly the likely choice of someone versed in the business of antiques and their value. On the day of the auction, the massive, rambling farmhouse was packed with people, shoulder to shoulder, most of them local and most of them interested in antiques. Had the ambulance liaison officer not existed, no doubt some of the more hard-lined campaigners would have had no problem in selecting another surrogate to victimise in the name of justice – but none perhaps so conveniently placed as Bert Spencer.

vii. The Dog Factor

Based on the unremarkable fact that both Yew Tree and Holloway House farms had a resident dog, the campaigners have drawn two conclusions, both designed to bolster their main allegation against Bert Spencer. One is that he had cultivated an easy familiarity with the vicious Collie at Holloway House in order to facilitate unimpeded access to the farmyard. The suggestion being that the killing of Hubert Wilkes had been cold-bloodedly premeditated and that, on the night of the shooting, it had been Bert, not Hubert Wilkes, who had taken the dog and locked it away in its shed. This of course, had it been true, would have conferred upon Bert Spencer the desired personality profile to fit the campaigners' requirements – that of a callous planner, cold-blood enough to shoot a child.

To support this contention, two reasons were compounded; firstly that he may have had to break into the outside office in order to acquire ammunition and that, for reasons impossible to fathom, he may have planned to take a shotgun from the house and saw off its barrel in the yard. Both suggestions are, of course, quite preposterous. There was an availability of shotgun and ammunition at several points around the house and the passenger parcel shelf in the Land Rover. The possibility that anyone would include the unnecessary truncating of a shotgun barrel, on site, as part of a planned murder is too ridiculous to consider. Unless of course this was the smoke screen, together with all the other factors Bert juggled in his defence. The scenario was more suitable for a fictional novel rather than true crime facts.

On that December night it was Hubert Wilkes himself who had locked the dog away, prior to the arrival of the Spencers. The outside office had not been broken into and the key was still in Wilkes' trouser pocket when his body was examined. Surely the sawing off of the barrel of the shotgun was the impromptu act of a man temporarily deranged.

The second conclusion drawn by the campaigners is based on the statement from Gladys Jones, the nearest neighbour who lived some 250 yards away, that the dog at Yew Tree Farm had not barked on the afternoon of the paperboy's murder.

From her statement, Paul Foot deduces that, '... Once again, the evidence suggested that whoever broke into Yew Tree Farm had some knowledge of the place, and was well enough known to the dog to move it without it barking ...'.

This, of course, serves to emphasize his contention that the break-in and killing was the work of someone local, not strangers. Bert Spencer was a local, the gang of four were not, ergo yet another small lever had been produced to ease Bert Spencer into the frame.

It would seem that the campaigners' conclusion is that Bert Spencer was capable of exerting some Svengali-like influence over dogs and that he brought it to bear in order to carry out his murderous intentions. Two farms and two dogs – and yet another factor was added to the suggested hypothesis of two copycat murders.

However, Bert Spencer had only encountered the Yew Tree Farm dog twice as it was not allowed the free run of the farmlands. It was no vicious Collie or slavering Rottweiler; it was a small terrier, a family pet, given to barking at any intrusion, familiar and regular visitors and strangers alike. To suggest that this dog failed to bark, or that someone was able to prevent its barking on that afternoon is quite impossible to believe. Whoever broke in through the front window of the farmhouse had first to run the gauntlet of the flock of geese which paraded constantly at the sides and front of the house. Their noise, the sound of breaking glass and the later smashing of the back door lock would certainly have been disturbed enough to set the dog barking. Gladys Jones herself affirmed that the animal barked even at her, the most frequent visitor to the farmhouse. Conclusion – the dog must have barked!

All that Gladys Jones' evidence confirmed was that she, inside her cottage, beside a busy road, screened from the farm by her garden trees and at a distance of 250 yards, failed to hear at the dog bark – just as she failed to hear the breaking in and the blast of a 12-bore shotgun.

In the case of the shooting of Hubert Wilkes, the dog factor was dredged up in an attempt to show premeditation. Encouraged by this, efforts have been made to build the issue of the dogs into a case that linked the farmhouse murders.

viii. The Irrelevant Cartridge Case

Three days after the murder of the paperboy, attention in the investigation was focused upon an incident so trivial that at any other time it would never have happened. About one mile from Yew Tree Farm a spent shotgun cartridge case was lying on a pile of gravel in a lane that leads off the A449. A sharp-eyed bread deliveryman spotted it and stopped to pick it up. Despite the distance from the scene of the crime, given the fever of public outrage at the time, it was a natural and even commendable action.

The cartridge case was an Eley 5, the same type of cartridge with which Carl had been shot. The manufacturers' had produced several million of the kind, a popular load used normally for birds, rabbits and vermin, but deadly when used at close range against a human being. The empty case was found in the Doctors Lane at Gorse Corner, a location that then was often used as a temporary campsite by travellers. The surrounding Ashwood, Prestwood and Kinver area is shotgun country, used by farmers, sportsmen and poachers alike. To comb the area would be to unearth spent shotgun cartridges by the hundred and many of them would be Eley 5's.

Local newspapers declared that the empty case could have been thrown from the killers' car as they fled the scene. And so it could have been. It could also have had a travel history as turbulent as that of Hans Christian Andersen's little tin soldier. One can assume, had it been thrown from the killers' car it was either hurled into Doctors Lane by a passenger as the car headed north towards Wolverhampton or by the driver himself after turning into the lane. Neither direction would be an expedient choice for anyone contending a panic-tight time schedule. A desperate need to be back, seated at a desk in Corbett Hospital, nearly three miles away in the opposite direction – which would be the situation if Spencer was responsible. Also an empty and possibly damning cartridge case hardly posed a disposal problem. With the possibility of the murder weapon coming to light there was perhaps, some potential value in hiding the case or certainly destroying beyond recognition. Certainly it had no use in that it was shown that that particular cartridge could not have been fired through the gun, which Robinson had produced – an almost inevitable and predictable conclusion. Even were it reversed, it would have served only to link Robinson to a location a mile away from the farm, possibly two days or more after the murder.

However, determined to leave no stone unturned, Paul Foot reached long and deep to create a connection between the murder of Carl Bridgewater and Bert Spencer, which he labelled, 'the mysterious cartridge case'. Some eight years after the finding of the empty cartridge case his postulation was that there was great significance in the fact that fifteen months after the murder of Carl, on the night that Bert Spencer shot Hubert Wilkes, a cartridge case played a trivial and inconspicuous part in the account of the aftermath of that tragedy.

As we know, minutes after the shooting Bert Spencer was driving ambulance man Barry Thomas back down Ashwood Lower Lane to the scene of the crime at Holloway House. The police car was following. Ambulance man, Thomas, asked if Bert had any more weapons in the car.

Bert answered, 'No. Just this cartridge.'

He produced a live cartridge from his pocket and threw it out of the car window.

Bert Spencer threw a live cartridge from his car window in Ashwood Lower Lane on 14 December, 1979. Ashwood Lower Lane joins Doctors Lane about half a mile from Holloway House. Fifteen months previously, an empty cartridge case had been found lying in the middle of Doctors Lane. From those disconnected and trivial facts Paul Foot seems to have taken the view that they showed some indication of forming part of a modus operandi. As he declared in his book, '... The coincidence seemed complete'.

ix. The Copycat Murders

The claim that the two farmhouse murders had a copycat link is an unsubtle tactic designed to override analytical thought and to dispense with rational thought processes. It is a glib method of avoiding pending facts.

The similarities between the two killings are obvious and few, and are of little or no significance. The differences are considerable and are equally as obvious.

The killing of Hubert Wilkes was a motiveless murder, induced by the combined effects of jealousy, drink, drugs and a severe blow to the head. The shooting of Carl was a cold-blooded murder committed in the course of an armed robbery, which Carl had unwittingly interrupted. There is some argument for it being an accident, a panicky gunman with a nervous trigger finger discharging the weapon unintentionally, although it tends to fall down when the circumstances are examined. Apart from that, it takes quite a few pounds of pressure to pull a shotgun trigger, although this mechanism can be altered, in skilled hands, to make it easier. With Carl seated, as he was on the sofa, the gun must have been held at waist height and aimed deliberately at his head. The fact that the murder weapon had been taken to the farm is itself proof of intention to use it to threaten and intimidate or, as it happened, worse.

Bert Spencer took no weapon to Holloway House. The tragedy occurred towards the end of what was intended to be a convivial evening, shared with friends. The murder weapon was leaning against the wall in the hallway. Had there been no guns lying about the house, it is open to question whether or not the tragedy would have occurred. In his temporarily chaotic mental state, it is quite likely that Bert may have just as easily opened the door and wandered off into the night.

Following some sightings it is possible to conjecture, after the murder of Carl, the killers waited in the vicinity, sitting coolly in their car outside the farmhouse. The only reason for this had to be that they were hoping for the return of the old residents; in which case, more robbery and yet more violence were their subsequent intentions.

Following his shooting of Hubert and his briefly continued aftermath of palsied frenzy, Bert Spencer drove round the rural block and was returning to the farmhouse when he encountered first the ambulance and its crew, and then the police car. With an ambulance man passenger and the police car following, he drove back to the farm and the scene of his crime. When the police car missed the turning, he waited quietly in the farmyard for its return. He neither resisted arrest nor sought to distance himself from blame.

Given small similarity and vast differences between the two murders the campaigners seized upon the dog factor, the discarded cartridges, Bert's working association with the Yew Tree area, his interest in antiques and his occasional shooting forays to point to a copycat syndrome.

In his book, Paul Foot states, '... The obvious links between the murder of Hubert Wilkes and the murder of Carl Bridgewater put Spencer much more firmly in the frame ...'

As we have seen, those similarities and their insignificance were summarised by Lord Justice Russell in the earlier Court of Appeal hearing. In the face of the constantly repeated attacks, which have been made on Bert Spencer the words of the reserve judgment, read on 17 March, 1989, bear repeating in turn.

The crime (the killing of Hubert Wilkes) had, said Lord Justice Russell, been labelled, '... a copycat murder of the Carl Bridgewater killing. It was, of course, nothing of the kind ...'

He went on to say that the similarities were merely, '... the proximity of the two farms, the use of a sawn-off shotgun discharged at close range while the victim was seated ...'. He concluded, '... but there, it seems to us, the similarities begin and end ... We entertain no doubt whatever that Hubert Spencer had nothing to do with the killing of Carl Bridgewater'.

And so it should seem to any reasonable person with an eye for facts and no ear or eye for unfounded and unsupportable allegations.

x. The Motive

In the absence of obvious motive for the murder of Hubert Wilkes, the campaigners have demonstrated their eagerness to provide one. A motive tailored to suit their requirement – that it should provide a connection between the shootings of both Mr Wilkes and Carl Bridgewater, and so implicate Spencer in the earlier killing of the young paperboy.

If it could be shown that on the night of his death, Hubert Wilkes, had driven Bert Spencer over the edge by accusing him of being the murderer of Carl, then Bert Spencer's violent reaction could be ascribed to a sudden impulse to eliminate a man who knew too much. Possibly a somewhat ridiculous scenario more suited to the pages of a 1930s whodunit – except that Hubert Wilkes was not murdered by stealth, carried out by a masked assassin. Even if this extraordinary hypothesis had been true, there are many ways that Spencer could have silenced Hubert Wilkes. As explored in *Chapter 6 – A Cocktail for Murder*, often shotguns were left in the hallway, sometimes loaded, it would have been very easy for Bert Spencer to be showing the old farmer a shotgun and simply saying it had gone off accidentally. In this, one of many possibilities, Spencer, at the very worst, would have been charged with manslaughter. Also if the police had not suspected foul play then Spencer would have probably received a suspended sentence.

There was no suggestion of any such turn of the conversation during the evening in the witness statements made by Mr Wilkes' daughter, Jean, and Bert's wife, Janet. Nor has anything appeared in the statement made by Hubert Wilkes' friend, Alec Blount, who was also present at the start of the celebrations. They all ate, drank and chatted in one another's company all night. Perhaps the idea of implanting, by wishful thinking and invocation, a particular strain of conversation into the actual events of the night in question, was germinated by a curiously phrased question directed at Bert Spencer by Chief Inspector Watson, in the immediate aftermath of the killing of Mr Wilkes. Not a time, perhaps, phraseology used to be measured in the colder light of later years.

Chief Inspector Watson asked Bert Spencer what would appear to be a quite hypothetical question, 'If Jean Wilkes says that among matters discussed (immediately prior to the killing of her father) was the Carl Bridgewater murder and that you talked about being interrogated and answering questions on a pro forma, a questionnaire, would that be the truth?'

Jean Wilkes had at no time made reference to any such conversation in her forthcoming statements. But the chief inspector was casting about, searching for a motive, a reason that could explain the bizarre murder of the farmer. Although it was a search in which even Bert Spencer could not assist. His recollections of the latter part of the evening, shortly before shooting Hubert Wilkes, are still a mystery to Bert.

And so a die was cast. An idea had been dropped into the melting pot. A link between the two murders could be established – if only it could be shown that a conversation had taken a particular turn. But it had not. It must therefore have been manna from Heaven to the campaigners when, six years after the event, farmer Michael Howard came blustering onto the public stage.

Michael Howard, friend and business acquaintance of Hubert Wilkes, was, at the time, chairman of the Hadzor and Oddingley Conservative party. After the murder of her father, Jean Wilkes had spent some time at Michael Howard's farm near Droitwich. But even during that period of close contact with the farmer she made no mention nor gave any indication that any such conversation had taken place to enrage Bert Spencer. In fact, Jean Wilkes could think of no reason at all why Bert Spencer could have shot and killed her father.

Undeterred by the wide evidential gap, Michael Howard decided to throw some small weight behind the anti-Spencer campaign. Howard, this pillar of the Establishment, wrote to Paul Foot – the somewhat radical journalist. In the letter he said he had read some reports about Spencer confessing to prison inmates that he had murdered Carl and that he was convinced that the murder of his friend, Hubert Wilkes, had been sparked by Mr Wilkes having accused Bert Spencer of that murder.

At a meeting with Paul Foot, Mr Howard elaborated on his speculation. He had, he said, already passed his unsupported opinions on to the police. He went further, expressing his detailed ideas of what had taken place at Holloway House on television. This was the Thames TV production, *Murder at the Farm*. The detail he supplied was quite outstanding, considering that at the time of the murder he, presumably, was at home at Upper Goosehill Farm, Hanbury, near Droitwich. It would appear his only knowledge of the events of that night was that which he had gleaned from newspaper reports. It also appears that Jean Wilkes herself has never added support to, or confirmed, his ideas.

Despite the fact that the farmer's theory had basis only in his imagination it did have a more serious effect than simply generating self-publicity. At the unsuccessful Court of Appeal hearing in the late November, 1988, Mr Benet Hytner, following the track of Michael Howard's fanciful embroidery of actual facts, told the court that Bert Spencer could have erupted in a murderous frenzy which resulted in his killing of Hubert Wilkes. A frenzy, he continued, induced by Bert's guilt over the murder of Carl Bridgewater and his being confronted with Hubert Wilkes' awareness of it.

This public exposition of Michael Howard's private and somewhat baseless theory led to such newspaper headlines as, 'TALK ABOUT CARL! – "MAY HAVE LED TO MURDER"'. The protective and declamatory exclamation marks failing to lessen the impact on most of the general readership, as it most certainly did on the prison population. To them, motive for the killing of Hubert Wilkes had been established; it did have a direct connection with the murder of Carl Bridgewater and Bert Spencer was the common factor.

By nebulous theorising, confidently predicted during his brief interlude in the spotlight of publicity, Michael Howard, unabashed by facts and his temporal and spatial distancing from the actual event had impressively filled an otherwise safe void for the campaigners. If he felt that he owed Bert Spencer a considerable disservice, he had paid out in full. Only a prison inmate can imagine the problems and anguish Michael Howard's actions inflicted upon Bert Spencer. Problems which were renewed by the repeat showing of *Murder at the Farm* on New Year's Eve, 1993.

xi. The Spencer Alibi

At the time of the murder of Carl Bridgewater, Bert Spencer's function was that of Ambulance Liaison Officer at Corbett Hospital, some three miles from Yew Tree Farm. His workstation was in an open-plan reception area of the hospital where he worked at his desk behind an unclosed counter. Adjacent to his own desk was another, which was occupied by a hospital secretary, Mrs Barbara Riebold, whose secretarial services were available to both the ambulance liaison officer and to some of the hospital's medical personnel. Similarly employed was a second secretary, Mrs Celia Johnson, who, on the day of the murder at Yew Tree Farm, was not at work at Corbett Hospital. This meant that Mrs Riebold had to spend even more time coping with the constant flow of ambulance liaison work and less with the not so immediate tasks required of her by the hospital consultants and administration staff.

Both Mrs Riebold and Bert Spencer sat at their open-plan workstation in full view of waiting patients, staff in the medical records office, anyone using the lifts to and from the ground floor and people visiting the WRVS refreshment area. There was an overpowering wealth of witness evidence available to confirm Bert's presence at his workplace on the afternoon of 19 September, 1978. Indeed, when Mrs Riebold was interviewed by the police at Corbett Hospital, just six days after the murder of Carl, Bert offered to point the officers to the other witnesses who were able to confirm that he was at his workplace all afternoon on the nineteenth. The police officers, having heard and recorded Mrs Riebold's statement that Bert was at work for the entire afternoon, saw no need of further confirmation.

As Barry Chambers, the officer who ran the Ambulance Control office at Warley, was later to remark that any unofficial absence of Bert Spencer from his place of work would have been noticed and duly reported. Indeed any such absence would have been a formula for potential chaos in the hospital reception and discharge area.

Bert Spencer was eliminated from the murder inquiry. His alibi had the merit of being simple and easily checked, and supported by an honest, genuinely disinterested witness, with many more standing in the wings prepared to add even more confirmation. The investigating officers were satisfied that it was cast iron. However, the unqualified civilian campaign group, long after the event at Yew Tree Farm, were unsatisfied with the police's conclusion, when all immediacy was long lost.

xii. The Missing Records

Three weeks after Bert Spencer's arrest, early in January, 1980, spurred by the apparent coincidences linking the farmhouse murders, police officers went to Corbett Hospital for the purpose of checking the past movement records in the ambulance liaison section. They found that most of the sheets relating to 1978, up to and beyond the date of Carl's murder, were missing. This equated to nearly 10 months of missing records from 12 January to late October '78. There were also nine days missing from 1977 and 13 days missing from 1979.

These records were handwritten notes made by Bert Spencer on a day-to-day basis. They were written on large A3 size loose sheets, detailing the movement of patients in and out of Corbett Hospital. Informally made out, they were purely a visual aid for the liaison officer – at the time, Bert himself. There was no requirement for the sheets to be filed, stored, or passed on to any other department – unless there had been some notable happening on a particular day, in which case the day's report sheet would be sent to Ambulance Control at Warley.

When Bert first took over the position of ambulance liaison officer he simply followed the existing custom and practice, and added each day's sheet to the piles kept on the shelves beneath the section counter.

There was, at that time, no security in that area of Corbett Hospital. Anyone could walk in off the street unchallenged at any time of day or night. They often did and thefts were common – even carpets and office equipment had gone missing from the reception and discharge area. It could be that the missing records had been quite innocently removed for use as scrap paper *or* their absence could be regarded as highly significant. The directional significance is, however, open to several interpretations. Viewpoints are conditioned by partiality and by the interested party's knowledge of the location and the systems employed within the section.

The campaigners said that Bert Spencer removed the vehicle/patient movement sheets in order to hide the fact that he was absent from his workplace that day – in which case the sheet would have been either incomplete or written partly in someone else's hand – owing to Bert Spencer's absence. Had he the need to disguise non-attendance on the day of Carl's murder, it would have been a simple matter for him to have ensured that an appropriately detail record sheet took its place on the shelving. Removal of the records could only work to Bert as a disadvantage – as it certainly did.

Of course, when the discovery that the paperwork was missing was made, Bert had been absent from the workplace for three weeks, held on remand in Winson Green prison – awaiting the trial for the murder of Hubert Wilkes.

More significantly, later in January, 1980, the senior officer at the ambulance control section, located at Warley, some 12 miles from Corbett Hospital, Barry Chambers, was interviewed by police. They were querying the method of recording the movements of ambulance service personnel, such as Bert Spencer. Officer Chambers explained that all such movements were logged in a diary at Ambulance Control at Warley when individual officers rang in with the relevant information. The diary was kept by the table, directly outside the window of Chamber's office. When a book was filled it was then filed away. To his amazement, when he was asked to produce the book covering the period of September 1978, he found that that too was missing!

The diary was used only to record official movements by officers between hospitals in their area – and basically to provide a check on claims for petrol expenses. While some officers used it to book personnel at other locations on and off duty, others did not bother to make such entries. Although it appears apparent that Bert was meticulous at filling in forms and records of all movements.

While access to the diary was freely available, the table on which it was kept was in open view of the ten staff in the crowded office. Anyone attempting to remove either the current book or one which had been filed and completed would have been observed and questioned. Nevertheless, the book and the loose sheets at Corbett Hospital were missing.

Unlike the disappearance of the record sheets at Corbett Hospital, there is no way in which the diary at Warley could have been removed by a zealous cleaner or in any other accidental way. Bert himself had not been to the Warley office, certainly in any official capacity, for many months. Taking a somewhat partisan view, had it been necessary, could Bert Spencer have found some more simple, sensible and less incriminatory way of covering his tracks? Otherwise we have to look at only two other possible explanations. Firstly, that someone removed the movement records out of sheer malice in order to place Bert Spencer in an unpleasant position – as was certainly the result. Having said this, it seems slightly implausible that the missing records were so varying in dates. Someone trying to place Spencer in the frame, one assumes, would be more selective and only highlight on a few days surrounding the paperboy's murder date. Or it could have been someone with a misguided sense of loyalty, who thought that it would be a helpful way of extracting Bert from an undeserved problematic situation. Again this is open to speculation, as one assumes any 'good Samaritan', however misguided, had to have some knowledge of what the sheets said about Spencer's movements. If the records showed that Bert was at his station on murder afternoon – then why take the sheets? I think this becomes even more doubtful when you look at the missing records at Warley – which required some inside knowledge and stealth.

Towards the end of my research about solving the mystery of the missing records I received a call from Bert stating, 'Before being seconded to Corbett hospital as liaison officer I had been a control officer at Warley ambulance station. The building was two tiered, downstairs was the station officer's location facing the street.'

The office overlooked the car parking area and was manned by the station officer and switchboard operator.

'It was not possible for any visitor,' Bert continued, 'to arrive without being noticed. There always used to be an "occurrence" book where almost everything was recorded. The chief ambulance officer would read that book daily and initial the last entry.

'On top of that station office was the main control room, manned by a bank of four female telephone operators, the duty control officer, a second controller planning the next day's workload, and the superintendent; Barry Chambers.'

Chambers' desk was in a glass-fronted office overlooking the control room and also overlooking a small side table containing a book in which daily events were recorded. Any control officer taking over could look in the book and see at a glance any occurrence before he arrived, any major accidents being dealt with, and by whom.

There certainly were no instructions to submit the book to any higher authority at any time. It was simply a useful tool in a very busy control room.

'It should be pointed out that it would have been impossible for anyone to enter that control room un-noticed,' added Spencer, concluding, 'My place of work was about 15 miles away from that control room and the record book did not go missing until after I was in custody.'

It would appear that the Warley office, in Smethwick, was pretty impregnable, certainly during working hours. Bert Spencer paints a quite vivid picture of a thriving office where unauthorised personnel would be scrutinised and questioned.

However, Bert does end by saying that '... the record book did not go missing until after I was in custody.'

Firstly, the Smethwick record book was only investigated AFTER Bert killed Hubert Wilkes, as the police suspected he may have been involved in the Yew Tree Farm murder – a few hundred yards from Wilkes' farm. It was discovered missing in late January 1980 – when Spencer was indeed in custody for the murder of the elderly farmer. But no one knows when it actually went missing as no one had looked for it. One has to assume that the complete record book was stolen sometime after 31 December 1978. As of 1 January 1979 a new book would have been started and the old '78 one filed away.

If you look at the chronology of events – the police did not charge the Bridgewater Four until 9 February 1979. So the important record book was available to steal from the Smethwick control room a good five weeks **before** the press announced the murder charges for the Bridgewater Four. During this time Bert would have still been a main suspect – especially if the police had not charged the four men.

Despite the shadowy mystery posed by the missing records, which was revealed by the police investigation, there were two sidelights helpful to Bert's case that emerged. Barry Chambers readily affirmed that had Bert Spencer left his workstation unofficially and without the proper notification having being made then he would have been missed and someone would have reported the fact. In the matter of his killing of Mr Wilkes, the hospital records could have been some small help at his trial when the subject of premeditation was under consideration. The records showed that Bert Spencer had pre-booked an extra week's holiday, to begin just days after the unforeseeable tragedy, in order that he might help Mr Wilkes during the busy pre-Christmas turkey preparation period. It was hardly the action of a man with murder on his mind, but the fact was not brought up in court.

xiii. The Identification Factor:

Even the police, during the early investigations, harboured a thought that the killer or killers were known to the victim. Otherwise, why would anyone murder a 13-year-old boy who certainly posed no physical threat to a burglar? If this was a cold-blooded shooting, and there was no panic or accidental discharge of the murder weapon, then unless a psychopath was behind the barrel – there had to be some link between the murderer and the paperboy.

In 1970 the Spencer household moved to 21, Ascot Gardens, in Wordsley. At 25, just three doors away, lived Brian and Janet Bridgewater, together with their three children. Carl was just five at the time. When the Spencers moved to Kingsley Road, Kingswinford, Carl Bridgewater was 10. At the time of his murder, Carl was 13. Perhaps Bert would have recognized the teenager, perhaps not. Having said that, it would be consistent to assume the paperboy would have certainly recognised Spencer – as his adult appearance would have changed little. The fact that his tear ducts were not working it was assumed, as covered in *Chapter 4 – Connections and Investigations*, by the campaigners, and in the early days the police, that Carl knew his killer. I think this is possibly a step beyond as any 13-year-old boy faced with a loaded shotgun, whether he knew the assailant or not, would be terrified.

The key factor here maybe the appearance of the murder weapon. Surely Spencer would have only visited the farm, if he intended to relieve the occupants of their money and antiques, when the property was empty. He was known to the old people so he would have been recognised immediately. Following this line of thought, if Spencer had carried out any robbery, knowing the place was unoccupied – why take a shotgun?

It is also a highly ruthless individual who, even in the process of committing a burglary, eliminates a witness and especially a child. The discovered crime at most would have secured a suspended sentence to a non-career criminal like Bert

Collusion

Reviewing the evidence and arguments there is little that stands up in the face of reasoned examination or the close scrutiny that such serious allegations merit. Very little disturbance on the surface picture is required in order to uncover the reality beneath the manufactured media-projected images. A reality which throws into confusion any argument which espouses the theory suggesting that Bert Spencer had any involvement in the heinous crime which was enacted at Yew Tree Farm on 19 September, 1978.

On the Monday, 6 December, 1993, the Home Secretary, Michael Howard, averred that he would, in future, be considering the weight of public opinion when determining a convicted man's release date. The problem inherent in such democratic thinking is that public opinion has little chance of being informed opinion, blinded, as it usually is, by the attractive dust of highly coloured sensationalism and hyperbolic inaccuracy.

A man in the unenviable situation of Bert Spencer, gagged and fettered, has little chance of persuading public opinion to lean in his direction. Those with access to the resources of media time and space, will, of course, enjoy every advantage in the mismatched contest. By their constant hounding of Bert Spencer, the pro-Bridgewater Four campaign group have squandered years of potentially productive time and effort. Perhaps unaware of the moral of an Aesop fable, they had lost the substance of their quest by grasping instead at the shadow. The time dissipated in misdirected effort could have been concentrated in making their main thrust an attempt to demonstrate that the Bridgewater Four had solidly supported alibis. Instead, the themes which have been produced are raggedly threadbare and lacking in the under-pinning necessary to evince an aura of credibility. Conversation and retraction, false witness and changed evidence, truth and falsehood, have been ground up in the same pestle and mortar to form an almost unfathomable solution.

In taking the tangible but convenient tack of attempting to foist guilt and suspicion onto a third party, the campaigners have taken a narrow and dead-ended track, following blindly in each other's footsteps. Had the wider view been taken, results more to their desired effect may possibly have been achieved. For anyone with a genuine belief in the innocence of the Bridgewater Four or who approaches the affair with an open and questioning mind, there were, as it had later proved at their successful appeal, obvious gaps in that part of the scripting of the tragic drama, which is in the public domain. There were salient points to address and vital players to be coaxed into view, not least the actions of The West Midlands Serious Crime Squad, disbanded in 1989 following an investigation into allegations against some of its officers of incompetence and abuses of power, and which included several officers who took part in the investigation of Carl Bridgewater's murder.

Instead, the campaigners locked their sights and their thinking solidly and exclusively onto Bert Spencer, with all the robotic intransigence of an Exocet missile. Oddly enough the furore surrounding Bert Spencer died down somewhat when the Bridgewater Four were released on appeal in 1997, when the convictions were overturned. Although, even today, any mention of the Bridgewater Four, including any anniversary of the horrific murder, there is always a mention, often with a picture, of Bert Spencer's connection with this terrible crime.

II.

The Fight for Freedom

∙∙

There is little doubt that the major contributing factor with the renewed interest in Bert Spencer was the news of his slaying of Hubert Wilkes, just half a mile from Yew Tree Farm. This was just over a year since the murder of the paperboy, and four weeks after the conviction of the Bridgewater Four. Two violent shotgun murders, in a sleepy Staffordshire town, in adjoining farms, within 13 months of each other – surely there must have been a connection?

Ann Whelan heard the news on the radio on the morning after the murder, in mid-December 1979, after rising early to go and visit her son who was in Liverpool prison. Spencer had never been far from her thoughts since Michael Hickey had been convicted of the murder of the 13-year-old paperboy less than a month earlier. Whelan's one-woman campaign had begun.

If the awful possibility that the Holloway House murder may in some way be connected to the one at Yew Tree Farm had not already crossed the mind of Chief Superintendent Stewart, Whelan fired off a letter to him that very afternoon stating in no uncertain terms that she believed there must be a link between both violent crimes.

The fight continued for the mother and, although it was slow and frustrating, her relentless letter writing was to be rewarded with a significant and influential confidant. In the February of 1980 Ann wrote a letter to Paul Foot at the *Daily Mirror*, who had just started writing a weekly column. At first Foot was naturally cautious. After all, the case had been concluded, in a blaze of publicity, three months previously with the jury reaching a relatively swift and unanimous verdict. Furthermore, there had been an unchallenged confession from one of the accused.

Then, on 12 June 1980, the lawyers of the Bridgewater Four were sent a bundle of case documents by the Director of Public Prosecutions. These valuable documents were copied and passed on to Ann Whelan. In October the same year Paul Foot met Ann and her husband Fred. In that same month Foot wrote the first of many articles about the case, and very few, if any, did not include a reference to Bert Spencer.

The conscription of Paul Foot brought obvious advantages as he took on board the chosen party line, keeping the murder in the public eye through his *Daily Mirror* column. At every sensitive period the campaign would produce, either directly or indirectly, some major obstacle to strew across Spencer's path to obtain a release date. The project had to be kept alive. So much would be implied if they were never to cease their efforts. Bert Spencer was in the unenviable situation of a pit-trapped tiger, with a platoon of lancers poised on the rim above, safe to inflict wounds as they pleased.

The campaign started to gather a lot of public interest, fuelled by Foot's total obsession surrounding the case, which was rapidly becoming a standing joke at the *Daily Mirror* offices. Added to this was Ann Whelan's unwavering and solid maternal fight to seek justice for her son, Michael. The crusade, as that is what it was becoming, could be divided roughly into two main areas of attack. Apart from the constant pillorying of Bert Spencer, the campaigners' sought to discredit the actions of the Staffordshire police, claiming that confessions had been both doctored and extracted by force. Their goal was to try and seek new evidence and question or destroy old evidence, and in doing so, force the Home Office to refer the case to the Court of Appeal.

There is somewhat of a misconception, to a few not familiar with the process, with regards the requirements or purpose of the Court of Appeal. We tend to be obsessed, often promoted by the media, in the guilt or innocence of the accused.

Lord Justice Roch, presiding over the successful 1997 appeal, stated, 'This Court is not concerned with the guilt or innocence of the appellants; but only with the safety of their convictions. This may, at first sight, appear an unsatisfactory state of affairs, until it is remembered that the integrity of the criminal process is the most important consideration for courts, which have to hear appeals against conviction. Both the innocent and the guilty are entitled to fair trials. If the trial process is not fair; if it is distorted by deceit or by material breaches of the rules of evidence or procedure, then the liberties of all are threatened.

'This Court is a court of review. The Court reviews the trial process to equip itself to answer the question, "Do we think that the conviction appealed is safe or do we think it unsafe?" The Court is not a court of trial or of re-trial. Persons accused of serious crimes are tried by juries in the Crown Court.'

The Court of Appeal's stance can conflict with our basic understanding of a presumption of innocence, sometimes referred to by the Latin expression; *Ei incumbit probatio qui dicit, non qui negat* (the burden of proof is on he who declares, not on he who denies), is the principle that a defendant is considered innocent until proven guilty. The burden of proof is thus on the prosecution.

This 'presumption of innocence' of course does not apply to the police – and neither should it. In fact the opposite is often true. I am not sure our detectives would get very far if they presumed every suspect in their custody innocent.

With the trial looming it had been hoped, if not expected, that Pat Molloy would do the right thing. The witness box is where he could shine and shed some light on the whole sorry affair. Little did his former best friend, Jimmy Robinson, and the Hickey cousins know that it was already agreed, months before, that Molloy would never give evidence at the trial. Argyles solicitors in Tamworth, as discussed in the 'brief to counsel', had already instructed barristers, John Gorman QC and Malcolm Lee, that their client would remain mute. It was a huge risk as it also meant Molloy could not underline his alibi notice, which was in his evidence, that he was at Carol Bradbury's flat, dozing by the fire, with Robinson and Carol upstairs in bed. The trial started on 8 October 1979 and would last over a month.

The devastating decision was disclosed on the seventeenth day of the trial, at 4.00 pm, just after the third accused in the case, Michael Hickey, had finished giving evidence.

Mr Gorman got to his feet to deliver the most important sentence in the whole trial, 'My Lord, we call no evidence on behalf of Molloy.'

To say it caused outrage to everyone in support of Robinson and the Hickeys would be an understatement. Up until that point the three defendants had given frank and honest accounts of themselves – as far as any Birmingham underworld criminal can. After all they were career criminals capable of vicious armed robbery, but they said they were not cold-blooded child killers. Vincent Hickey had also made a reasonable effort to explain his early verbal contradicting confession.

However, with Molloy refusing to challenge his verbal and written confession, from that moment on, the case went downhill rapidly. The defence lawyers up until then had been flamboyant and confident, now they appeared deflated and tired.

Molloy, the prosecution witness, with his damning signed confession, would be the deciding factor in getting his co-defendants unanimous guilty verdicts.

Regarding grounds for appeal against the conviction, the case was an unusual one in some respects. Right from the start of the trial there was a certain degree of optimism. This was based on a legal point of law, repeated time and again during the trial by the judge and barristers, surrounding the Molloy confession. The point was that the statement of one accomplice is not evidence against another – unless that accomplice goes into the witness box. So it appeared the law was on their side.

The jury had heard the full signed confession made by the Irishman on 10 December. They also had it in writing in front of them. The document implicated Robinson and the Hickeys in the murder of Carl Bridgewater. As we know, Molloy claimed that he had been upstairs when he heard the shot and had rushed downstairs to find his three co-defendants arguing over a smoking gun.

The statement *was not evidence against anyone except Pat Molloy*. So said British law. So said the judge and so said the lawyers. The jury were told over and over to put the statement, which they had heard and read, out of their minds except in so far as it implicated Molloy. They had to rule out all consideration that it incriminated the other three.

As is so often the case, in regards to legal theory, this was an admirable situation. In practice the jury had in front of them a confession that stated that all four were at Yew Tree Farm and that Robinson and the Hickeys were in the very room that the boy was murdered – together with a recently discharged shotgun. It is almost inconceivable that this did not influence them in the most dramatic way.

If this was the judicial application of the law then surely the Irishman should have been tried separately, with his confession kept from the ears and eyes of the jury, which tried the other three.

The other point, which was an early winning motion put forward by the defence lawyers for Robinson and the Hickeys, was to have no mention of the admitted Chapel Farm armed robbery. The judge's ruling was a big blow to the prosecution due to the fact that both jobs had been incredibly similar. Although there was a big downside with the fact that Vincent could not explain why he initially placed his three co-defendants at Yew Tree Farm – to cut a deal for immunity from prosecution or bail at the very least. So his initial confession looked extremely suspect and weak to the jury.

One would assume that if the Irishman had been at Yew Tree Farm when Carl Bridgewater was murdered, he would have been delighted with the manslaughter verdict and his twelve-year sentence. By skilfully steering Molloy clear of the witness box his lawyers had managed to persuade the jury that he had been unaware that a shotgun had been taken to the farm and that he had taken no part in the killing. The highly alarming sentences of twenty-five years handed down to Vincent Hickey and Robinson was a measure of the value of Molloy's lawyers' advice. Michael was seventeen and therefore detained at Her Majesty's pleasure until he reached the age of eighteen.

If the Irishman kept his head down and behaved himself he could expect to be back on the streets in eight years. Considering, also, his help given to the Staffordshire police, he must have been an ideal candidate for early parole. He could also rely on the prison authorities to keep him away from the other three, who were marked men after being convicted of child murder. The most vehemently abused and violently attacked was certainly Michael Hickey. On one occasion he found some razor blades in his cell with some written advice to 'do the decent thing'.

Now that the Bridgewater Four were in the prison system the man they accused of the crime they were serving time for was soon to be part of that same system. Bert Spencer, just seven months after their sentences were given out, was a convicted murderer and could be walking the landings of any prison in the country, although he was a Category A prisoner and watched constantly.

Although the prison authorities quickly became aware of the potential powder keg situation, Bert comments, 'They kept us separate at all times.'

Although Molloy had passed away in 1981 – the Hickeys, Robinson and Spencer would all remain in the system for nearly 15 years until Spencer's release in 1994.

Like the other three, Molloy was told immediately after the trial that there was not the slightest chance of a successful appeal against either the conviction or the sentence. The verdict by the jury was unanimous; the judge's summing up flawless in law and the severity of the sentences reflected the callousness of the crime. Basically his counsel, Mr Malcolm Lee, wrote to him sixteen days after the verdict and advised him to shut up and bite the bullet. Molloy did the exact opposite.

From his first day as a convicted man he started a campaign against the judgment which appeared to be in his favour. The Irishman demanded the forms he needed to seek leave to appeal under the Criminal Appeal Act.

On 11 December, just three days before Bert Spencer was to blast away his friend Hubert Wilkes, he wrote of his written confession (Exhibit 54);

'My statement is not a true account, and it is a revenge statement against the Hickeys and Robinson...

'To get the truth out of Vincent I made that statement and put Michael in it as well. At the time in question, I did not know the Hickeys to speak to, but I thought by what Vince was saying to the police he must have had first-hand knowledge of what happened at Yew Tree Farm, and was covering up for someone and was trying to involve me, Jim and John Burkett (Burkett carried out the Tesco armed robbery with Robinson).'

At this point there was no mention of police brutality, but that would follow. With the release of the documents by the Director of Public Prosecutions about Spencer, a new friendship sprung up with Fred and Ann Whelan. Ann had actually driven Carol Bradbury, Robinson's girlfriend, up to Liverpool to see Pat as early as January 1980. Ann was a good influence on the case and helped change Molloy's attitude towards the Hickeys. Ever since he heard that Vincent had named him as one of the murderers of the paperboy, the Irishman had been consumed with bitterness against the whole Hickey family.

Ann Whelan also engineered what seemed an impossibility – a reconciliation between Pat Molloy and his old pal, Jimmy Robinson. Robinson was finally persuaded to put aside his utter disgust for the Irishman for the common good of the appeal.

Unity between all four of them was essential he maintained, commenting repeatedly, 'We must have one Counsel for all of us!'

On June 9 1980 Whelan visited Malloy in Liverpool prison. Even before a word was spoken Pat took out the upper row of his false teeth and showed them to Ann. There was a crack from top to bottom in the centre, which had crudely been stuck together. Molloy went on to explain that the teeth had been broken during his interrogation at Wombourne. This was the first real hint of any violence taking place during police interrogation.

In a letter written to his lawyer in the October, incorporated in the official documents for his appeal, he stated, '... A bearded man who I think is called Perkins came into my cell, who did ask me about Carl and his death. He told me all about V. Hickey and Jim Robinson. Perkins showed me a statement signed by Vince, saying he was the driver and me and Jim and

John Burkett (Burkett had a cast iron alibi for the day of the murder) was at Yew Tree Farm with him ...

'I was questioned and insulted and called a thick Irish Mick. I was struck on the face several times which broke my teeth, that was by Perkins, while he repeatedly asked to sign a statement saying I was at the farm upstairs robbing it ...

'Before he left finally that night, he went out of the cell and half closed the door to. The bearded one rushed back in and struck me a severe blow to the stomach and said he would be back in the morning for my signature ...

'I signed Exhibit 54 out of revenge on the others and out of fear of more beatings and ill treatment.'

With the allegations which he had bottled up for so long finally out in the open Molloy set to work writing to organisations and individuals, including his family, the Whelans and Robinson. During the first five months of 1981 he wrote almost every day. In May he finally sacked Argyle's and Malcolm Lee, arguing that their behaviour at the trial was crucial to his appeal. The Irishman even agreed to take the truth drug, which Ann Whelan said she would pay for. The Hickey cousins had both previously taken the drug and had passed with flying colours. Having said that in a letter written by W. C. Canning, Consultant Psychiatrist, who had conducted the test, pointed out, 'It is true to say that a determined person even under the influence of any abreactive drug can suppress material'.

In another letter via the *Express & Star* (27/10/83), Tony Bishop wrote to Michael Hickey about Spencer's refusal to take the truth drug. Bishop concluded by saying it was disappointing that Jimmy Robinson had taken and failed, or the test was inconclusive, a previous polygraph test.

Pat Molloy was approached by Robinson's very capable solicitor, Tony Fryer, and a meeting was set up enabling the solicitor to represent him. On Friday 12 June 1981, the very day he was to meet Tony Fryer, Molloy collapsed and died whilst playing football in the exercise yard.

On the basis of witnesses' retractions and other 'new evidence', application for leave to appeal was granted. Shortly afterwards, on 2 December 1981, the Court of Appeal, presided over by Lord Chief Justice Lane, refused the application following a one-way hearing. The Lord Chief Justice concluded that there was nothing unsafe or unsatisfactory in the original convictions and the introduction of the Spencer Factor was nothing but a red herring. After the judgment Ann Whelan stood and voiced her protest, including the suggestion that DCS Stewart had helped to secure the convictions by lying.

Patrick Molloy had submitted applications for leave to appeal, the grounds being of his own composing, which did not come before the court owing to his untimely death in June.

Michael's lawyer had made it clear to Ann, as all the lawyers had done with their clients, that there would be no grounds for appeal as the case stood at trial, but that if any new evidence appeared then the chances of an appeal might improve. It had already been established, as Ann Whelan's New Year's Resolution, that she would seek out and confront all the main prosecution witnesses.

I think that both Paul Foot and Ann Whelan were very vigorous over the years with regards to hunting down the key witnesses in the developing drama. Many were persuaded to change their testimony. There were complaints that the prosecution witnesses had been threatened and harassed before and after the trial. In fact, by the end of 1980, at least four witnesses for the Crown claimed to have been so pressurised to change their statements. However, there is no suggestion that either Foot or Whelan were responsible in these cases.

It was not just those two who were active, Whelan especially with great success, but the remaining three convicted men also started their campaign of rooftop protests. Without doubt the most impressive was played out by Michael Hickey, who climbed up on the rooftop area of Gartree prison on 24 November 1983. The weather was extremely fierce and he was totally reliant on his fellow prisoners to feed him. These were the very prisoners who were often openly hostile and violent towards him. However, Michael's voice, and those of his co-defendants, screaming their innocence were beginning to be heard.

Hickey had taken several balls of string and homemade hooks up onto the roof which he fashioned into fishing lines, dangling them to the cells below. After several days rations started to materialise. The authorities became wise to this procedure and began dishing out punishments for prisoners caught feeding Michael. As time went on, with the weather becoming unbearably cold – reaching six degrees below zero, respect was being established and more and more inmates risked losing remission by using the fishing lines to send food and gifts. Hickey spent the festive period on the roof. In fact on Christmas Day he received a whole Christmas dinner sent up on the hooks from D Wing. The message attached stated, '… From your pals below. We wish you luck and hope something is done soon.'

Michael Hickey finally came down 89 days later on 21 February 1984. This was a world record for a prison rooftop protest, longer by far than any other carried out by a prisoner. His demonstration was perhaps one of the most remarkable acts of endurance in the whole history of protest.

Of course these rooftop remonstrations, which all three participated in, had an additional value. Under the spotlight of the world media, as various agencies on the ground and in the air, via helicopter, captured the men and their fight for justice, Bert Spencer could be labelled as the real murderer of the paperboy. They all daubed clear messages that Bert killed Carl Bridgewater. Some, like Robinson, used catchy phrases and Michael Hickey, while on the roof of Long Lartin prison, cleverly fashioned a large plastic carton, with the bottom cut off, using it as a makeshift loudhailer. He was able to communicate to campaigners and journalists below. Spencer was always a good topic of conversation.

With the incredible Gartree rooftop demonstration ringing in their ears, together with pressure from the campaigners and high profile media exposure, the Home Office did announce a new enquiry into the case on 30 July 1984. Less than four months later they coldly announced 'no action' as a result of the inquiry. In all, the Bridgewater affair received three independent police investigations into various aspects of the case, all producing the same negative result.

From the very start of the long road towards the Court of Appeal there was plenty of drama to regularly fuel the media fires. There were five hunger strikes by Vincent Hickey, continued rooftop protests, retractions and denials of retractions by key witnesses and, of course, the successful truth drug tests by the Hickey cousins. Amongst all this campaign activity there was always the soft option of hounding Bert Spencer in print and on television. It was a good story, which was milked to the full, not least by Ann Whelan, the sympathy-evoking mother figure, with Paul Foot ensuring that it did not stay long out of the public eye.

There is no doubt the publication of Paul Foot's best-selling book, *Murder at the Farm*, in 1986, significantly increased public awareness of the plight of the Bridgewater Four and the campaign to fight for their release. A year later Thames Television broadcast an hour-long documentary, *Murder at the Farm*, based on Foot's book. It was a huge success with very high viewing figures. The impact from the highly emotive and at times questionable documentary was obvious. Less than six months later on 15 October 1987, Home Secretary Douglas Hurd referred the case to the Court of Appeal.

For the convicted men and their supporters it had been a 10-year journey from the murder of Carl Bridgewater to their first full hearing in the Court of Appeal. This most significant appeal must have had every pro-Bridgewater supporter licking their lips with anticipation. The full Court of Appeal sat to reconsider the case of the Bridgewater Four. It was to take 41 days, even longer than the time taken over the original trial, becoming one of the longest appeal hearings in British criminal history. It was to set a further record of being the most expensive appeal hearing to date. The cost to the British taxpayer was in excess of £1,000,000. No doubt the campaigners' awaited the proceedings with high hopes and bated breath.

The hearing began on Monday 21 November 1988. For Michael Hickey's mother, Ann Whelan, it had been a particularly long and stressful road. However, Whelan, together with Paul Foot and the campaign group, would make sure Bert Spencer too was made to feel distress in full and frequent measure.

At an early stage Mr Ben Hytner QC, putting the case for the Hickey cousins and Jimmy Robinson, gave notice of the anti-Spencer tactics, which would be employed. He told the court that Bert Spencer's name would be featured prominently and made the suggestion that it could have been Spencer who had murdered the paperboy 10 years previously. On Wednesday 23 November, under the headline 'KILLER NAMED!', the *Daily Mirror* was even more specific, commenting, 'Former ambulance man Hubert Spencer was named yesterday as the killer of 13-year-old newspaper boy, Carl Bridgewater ...'

Hytner promised that fresh evidence would be produced against Bert Spencer. However, as the hearing progressed the 'fresh evidence' served only to demonstrate the yawning gap between clever presentation and reality. It was claimed that Bert was in a 'frenzy' when arrested, that he was a regular visitor to Yew Tree Farm and that his car contained a 'burglar's kit'. The QC also challenged two old chestnuts – Spencer's alibi and the infamous 'piece of card'. The alibi, so strongly supported by Mrs Barbara Riebold, would be the subject of brand new evidence and that proof would be demonstrated that Bert Spencer had both written and planted the piece of card.

This gross assault on Spencer was, however, to fail, as each point was clinically examined and dismissed. By the 12 January, several weeks into the hearing, Mr Jeremy Roberts, QC, leading for the Crown, was even in a mood to allow himself a brief moment of levity. Regarding the 'fresh evidence', he was moved to remark that it served only to strengthen the prosecution case.

'It's all jolly good stuff,' commented the distinguished QC, adding, 'and we would like to see more.'

It was not a happy time for the campaigners. On 15 December Paul Foot had been accused of misleading the public. On top of that one of the linchpins of their case, the retraction of the prosecution witness, Brian Sinton, had been badly buckled. At the original trial he had given evidence that Michael Hickey had confessed to the murder of Carl Bridgewater and to actually having pulled the trigger. The confession was made, so Sinton claimed, while he and Michael Hickey were taking a shower at Winson

Green prison. In the hope of obtaining a retraction, Ann Whelan and Paul
Foot scoured the north of England for him in the areas of Barnsley and
Scarborough. Eventually, Ann Whelan tracked him down after a long hunt,
made no easier by the fact that Sinton had changed his name to Barraclough
and that seven years had elapsed since Sinton had given his evidence. Ann
Whelan obtained the retraction she had hoped for and had secretly tape-re-
corded the conversation.

In the postscript to his book, Paul Foot wrote, 'We comforted ourselves
that Sinton had retracted his trial evidence to Ann, to me and to Jim Nichol
without any pressure and to no apparent advantage, while the pressure on
him to co-operate with the authorities when he was in prison was obvious...'

However, it was brought out in court that when Ann Whelan had finally
cornered Brian Sinton and persuaded him to change his evidence, she had
been accompanied by a 'powerfully built man with a record of violence'. Mrs
Whelan told the appeal judges that she had brought pressure to bear on no
one and that she was unaware of the man's criminal record.

The evidence of graphologist Derek Davis, was, so the campaigners'
believed, their unshakeable pièce de résistance. It was paraded for inspection
before the court and clinically demolished by Home Office experts. Mr Davis
was drawn to admit that the card could, indeed, have been written by anyone.

In considering the 'fresh evidence' which was offered in respect of
Bert Spencer's alibi, that he was at his workstation in Corbett Hospital on
the afternoon of the murder, Lord Justice Russell described witness, Mrs
Barbara Riebold, as 'transparently honest' and commented that he was
impressed with the testimony.

Regarding the claim that the killing of Hubert Wilkes was a 'copycat'
murder, Lord Justice Russell dismissed the suggestion, declaring that it was
nothing of the kind.

About the long running attempts to incriminate Bert Spencer in the
murder of young Carl he declared, 'We are satisfied without any doubt that
Spencer played no part in the events at Yew Tree Farm'.

Lord Justice Leonard stated that the court had heard nothing by the way of fresh evidence that could have influenced the view of the jury. The date for the delivery of the reserve judgment was set for 17 March 1988.

With probably one eye closed and unaware of some of the irregularities surrounding the case, the judgement was somewhat inevitable and often unforgiving. With the defendant's case in tatters, and with so much at stake, the scene was set for a dramatic day in court. With their unquenchable thirst for drama the media people were not to be disappointed.

The reserve judgment was delivered in a 238-page document, which took almost six hours to read. In it the three judges ruled that the summing up of the judge at the original trial, Mr Justice Drake, could not be faulted and that the convictions of the four men were safe and satisfactory. The judges further totally rejected claims that the murder might have been committed by Bert Spencer or that the burglary and murder at Yew Tree Farm could have been the work of one man alone. Of Robinson, Mr Justice Leonard said that the case against him was strong and convincing. Regarding Vincent Hickey, Mr Justice Potts said that he had demonstrated in a police interview that he had detailed knowledge of the raid on Yew Tree Farm to which only a participant could have been party. Vincent Hickey was, he said, a hardened criminal and his evidence had been dishonest and treacherous. The evidence against him, said Mr Justice Potts, was 'overwhelming'. Turning to the case against Michael Hickey, the judge attached no weight to Brian Sinton/Barraclough's allegation of having heard Michael Hickey confess to the murder. The prosecution had, he said, proved beyond reasonable doubt that he was at Yew Tree Farm on the afternoon of the murder. As the judges announced their rulings, Jimmy Robinson and Vincent Hickey erupted in fury.

First Robinson leapt to his feet, screaming, 'You fellas don't know your arses from your elbows.'

Vincent Hickey hurled a string of rosary beads at the judges, shouting, 'We are innocent. You'll be needing these!'

Both men were dragged from the court, leaving Michael Hickey sitting quietly as their families and supporters shouted abuse and applauded the demonstration. Some were ejected by court officials.

Later, Ann Whelan, close to tears, stood up to shout, 'Your judgment, sir, is outrageous. How can anyone believe the evidence?'

Distraught, the tears now flowing freely, she was led from the court to spend the closing hour watching the proceedings through the windows of the court doors, a sad and lonely figure.

With the campaigners' case now shattered and three men returned to prison to complete their long sentences it might have been expected that a long chapter was finally closed. However, Ann Whelan's fierce maternal instinct was far from crushed by this heavy blow. She vowed that the fight to prove the innocence of her son and his associates would go on. Paul Foot described the judgment of the Court of Appeal as, 'disgraceful'. He went further. In the Daily Mirror of 23 March, 1989, he expressed his rage and frustration under a banner headline branding the three judges as, 'MEN of STRAW'.

The Staffordshire police force were of a different opinion.

A spokesman said that the verdict of the appeal judges, '... exposes as a total sham the tissue of lies and half-truths which have been put forward over the years in an attempt to discredit the actions of the Staffordshire police,' adding solemnly, 'It is sincerely hoped that the long-suffering Bridgewater family will now be allowed to get on with their lives.'

However, the latter sentiment was to prove to be only a pipe dream. Seven weeks after the appeal judgment, lawyers acting for the Hickeys and Robinson were busy seeking leave to appeal to the House of Lords. The date for the High Court hearing was set for 17 May, 1989. Later, on 13 July, three Law Lords ruled against allowing the Bridgewater three further leave to appeal.

In many ways the Home Office and the police authorities had underestimated the growing public interest in the case. Concern was saved for the Bridgewater Four and support was never going to evaporate.

Undismayed by the public demolition of his claims against Bert Spencer, Paul Foot was again writing to him in prison, just two months after the judgment of the Court of Appeal. The tone of the letter struck a strange note, written, as it was, to a man whom Paul Foot had been publicly persecuting for almost a decade. The letter was dated 23 May, 1989, and carried a reference, My/103. After mild comment on the fact that Bert Spencer had called him a liar in letters of protest to various media sources, Mr Foot continued in a vein, which gave the impression of a man seeking sympathy. He wrote;

> '... I am very despondent about the judges' decision in the Bridge-water case. I think their judgment is wrong from start to finish. I remain utterly convinced that the three men are quite innocent of this crime. The dreadful thing about the judgment is the dashing of the hopes of the three men and their families. I hear that Jimmy Robinson, a grown man, and a strong one, wept for a whole week after the verdict. Vincent is very ill and Michael Hickey has slumped into his former silence and half madness, repeatedly saying to everyone around him; "Please get me out of here, I didn't do it."'

There was, however, the expected sting in the tale albeit, by Mr Foot's standards, a small one. The letter continued;

> 'I stick by what I wrote about you in the book, and said on television ...'

To emphasize his points, Mr Foot enclosed a copy of Murder at the Farm, a flyleaf suitably signed and dedicated...

PENGUIN TRUE CRIME
MURDER AT THE FARM

Writer and journalist Paul Foot wrote for the *Socialist Worker* and was editor of the paper during 1974 and 1975 before joining the *Daily Mirror* in 1979. He was named Journalist of the Year (Granada's *What the Papers Say* Awards) for 1972 and Campaign-

ing Journalist of the Year (British Press Awards) in 1980. He has written two other books about suspected injustice: *Who Killed Hanratty?* (1971), which challenges the verdict of the jury in the case of the A6 murder, for which James Hanratty was found guilty and hanged, and *The Helen Smith Story*, which investigates the mysterious death of a British nurse in Jeddah. His other books include *Immigration and Race in British Politics* (1965), *The Politics of Harold Wilson* (1968), *The Rise of Enoch Powell* (1969), *Why You Should Be a Socialist* (1977) and *Red Shelley* (1981).

To Hubert Spencer

May, 1989.

It was clear to Bert Spencer that the campaign of hounding had in no way run its course. He wondered if there were yet more variations to be played on the theme that had tormented him for so long. At rare times when there was a lull in the campaign against Spencer, the occasional newspaper article would appear with a picture of Bert, with the above banner 'IS THIS THE REAL KILLER OF CARL?' There would always be heightened media attention when his paintings were exhibited or when he won a prize for horticulture. During the final leg of his prison sentence there was certainly a concentrated effort to push Spencer forward, as the killer of the paperboy, as suspect number one. This intensified when Bert was transferred to an open prison, North Sea Camp, in Lincolnshire. Perhaps the pro-Bridgewater Four faction were disturbed that their target could now set his sights on the road to release. Once Bert Spencer was a free man he would no longer be a helpless scapegoat. He would have normal access to legal redress. No more would it be possible to libel him with impunity.

At the start of 1991 firm evidence was being accumulated regarding the validity of Exhibit 54 – Molloy's signed confession. It was Michael Hickey's solicitor, Jim Nichol, who had now not only taken up the baton for the three living men, but also representing the family of the deceased Irishman.

So far most efforts were directed at the evidence against the Hickeys and Robinson. During the 1988 appeal the dead Pat Molloy had not been represented and the argument about him was confined almost exclusively to whether or not the judge misdirected the jury about his claims not to have been at Yew Tree Farm. Any suggestion that his confession could be shown to be unsafe was new and crucial evidence.

It started off when Foot's book landed in the hands of The Rev Andrew Morton. Mr Morton had developed his own technique for studying language patterns. The procedure had been accepted into criminal trials. Morton contacted the journalist and was able to conduct an experiment using Exhibit 54 and comparing them to letters Molloy had sent from prison.

Almost immediately Mr Morton concluded, 'The confession is not Molloy's. It was made up by more than one person.'

This was of course incredible news. DC Perkins, who took down the Irishman's confession at Wombourne police station (11 December 1978), had always insisted that Molloy had dictated every single word, and had been scrupulously written down by the officer. There were three other reports from leading experts, two commissioned by the *Daily Mirror*, which concurred with Mr Morton's findings. One of these was Dr John Harris, a lecturer in linguistics at the University of London and an expert in Irish dialects. The various reports cast serious doubt on the authenticity of Molloy's confession.

In June 1991 Jim Nichol sent the language experts' findings to the Home Office as part of a new petition to refer the case to the Court of Appeal. Nichol also included a growing dossier on DC Perkins, whose conduct as a detective in the West Midlands Serious Crime Squad was getting worse by the day. His appalling disciplinarily record would show that Perkins was involved in 17 of the 97 cases investigated by the Police Complaints Authority (PCA).

Four months after the petition was submitted the then Home Secretary, Kenneth Clarke, announced yet another police enquiry, this time to be conducted by the Merseyside Chief Constable Jim Sharples. Hope was raised and the men in prison, their families, the campaigners and supporters, now had both this enquiry and the outcome of the petition to appeal to bolster that hope.

Added to this wave of confidence the BBC's *Rough Justice* programme broadcast their own documentary, *Who Killed Carl Bridgewater?* Viewing figures were high and so was morale. Later that year a repeat showing of Thames Television's documentary, *Murder at the Farm*, yet again controversially highlighted the Bridgewater Four's innocence and Bert Spencer's guilt.

Any optimism was crushed on 3 February 1993. A courier delivered the decision to Jim Nichol's office. The letter announced, 'The Home Secretary has concluded that there are insufficient grounds for his intervening further in this case.'

This time it was Jimmy Robinson who made the rooftop protest. On 23 February, three weeks after the ruling, he climbed onto the roof of Gartree prison in Market Harborough, Leicestershire, where he stayed for a remarkable 82 days. Newspaper and television coverage of the event included the message painted in large white letters on the roof, 'You don't have to be in MENSA to realise it was Spencer.' Bert Spencer was at the time awaiting the decision of the Local Review Committee regarding his release.

A fellow lifer at North Sea Camp said to Spencer, 'It's just not on, Bert. Every time your release date is on the line, the bastards come up with something else. The Home Secretary must have a stack of good reports on one side of his desk and on the other a pile of shit even higher.'

Certainly, the pressure was being put on Bert Spencer and those charged with the task of assessing his suitability for release. Just two days after Jimmy Robinson came down from the roof of Gartree prison, leaving behind his defamatory and campaigning message on the tiles, yet another lifeline was thrown to the campaigners. On Monday 17 and Wednesday 19 May 1993, BBC2 broadcast the two-part powerful movie, *Bad Company*. The three-hour TV film surrounded the murders at Yew Tree and Holloway House Farms.

'Two years previously I had been contacted by a script-writer from Derby called Don Shaw,' explains Foot. 'He intended, he said, to write a TV screenplay about the Carl Bridgewater case and its aftermath. I was enthusiastic, and so was Ann, especially when Mr Shaw made it plain that he believed the men were innocent.'

Bad Company was commissioned by the BBC at Birmingham's Pebble Mill, and directed by David Drury who was responsible for *Prime Suspect 3*, for which he won a BAFTA. The drama made great television, as long as your name was not Bert Spencer.

The casting was good and the acting brilliant, However, it was a dramatised production – but delivered as fact. It starred Angus Deayton as journalist Paul Foot and a young Johnny Lee Miller, playing Michael Hickey. Miller would later take Hollywood by storm and was to marry and divorce Angelina Jolie.

The reviewers delighted in embracing the programme's primary agendas – the swaying of public opinion surrounding the guilt of the Bridgewater Four and implicating Bert Spencer in the murder of the paperboy.

In itself it was a good story of a mother's faith, determination and courage sustained through years of trauma and heartbreak. Alas, Don Shaw turned it into yet another trial by television. Anyone familiar with another of Shaw's creations, his book 'The Golden Key', which was designed as an intellectual treasure hunt with a cash prize of £50,000, will have been prepared for what was, at best, the free use of dramatic licence. 'The Golden Key' was originally published on 4 November 1982 by William Maclellan Ltd.

The Golden Key treasure hunt finally evaporated in a mist of unanswered questions despite investigations by the *News of the World*, the radio programme *Punters* and even Esther Rantzen's 'That's Life!'. Perhaps a yardstick of the anti-Spencer content of *Bad Company* can be extracted from the history and mystery of the treasure hunt.

Briefly, Don Shaw declared the hunt closed after about five years, sold the then useless copyright of the book, stated that the object of the hunt, a wooden key painted gold, had been removed from its hiding place and then refused to divulge its original burial site.

'At least one claimant had provided the publishers with photographic evidence of the dig and was prepared to provide the reasoning behind his deductions,' explains Bert Spencer. 'He still is and would relish the opportunity to discuss the matter with the elusive Mr Shaw.'

Witness to the burial was that noted and respected Falklands warrior, Major General Sir John Jeremy Moore, KCB, OBE, MC & Bar.

'Unfortunately, he too is reluctant to divulge details,' adds Spencer.

Given such a background some aspects of *Bad Company* will raise no eyebrows. In Don Shaw's dramatised movie the headquarters pub of Joe Hickey, the Dog and Partridge in Selly Oak, Birmingham, became The Regent. Although these discrepancies, together with some others regarding locations, are commonplace, other inaccuracies were not. It was suggested that an empty Eley 5 shotgun cartridge case – the same type of ammunition that was later used to kill Hubert Wilkes – had been found immediately after the murder of Carl, just outside Yew Tree Farm. In fact the empty case was found some days later, almost a mile away in Doctors Lane at Gorse Corner, an unofficial traveller campsite. *Bad Company* moved Yew Tree Farm even closer to Holloway House; that half a mile had been reduced to less than 300 yards.

'There were other important discrepancies,' remarks Spencer, adding, 'The large glass display case of stuffed foxes became a set of china figures. The discredited evidence of handwriting expert, Derek Davis, was dragged out yet again as though it had never been successfully challenged. Even Paul Foot was moved to remark that the drama had sequential faults.'

Don Shaw excused such inaccuracies on the grounds that they were necessary to provide, 'dramatic focus and shape'. With such a huge wave of public interest there followed a televised studio discussion, which was fair and objective, unlike the comments of the newspaper and television reviewers, who seemed to be blind to the point of reduced perception.

In that same discussion it was suggested to the writer, Don Shaw, that a drama such as *Bad Company* could only be justified on the basis of it presenting new evidence, and that there was no such evidence to be found.

Don Shaw dissembled as he answered, 'What is new evidence?'

Paul Foot assured the viewers by stating, 'There is plenty of new evidence coming in on this case.'

He was correct, but the nature of the revelations to come could hardly have been pleasing to him or the other campaigners. Another member of the panel, Peter Hill, of television's *Rough Justice*, rightly said that the story of the Bridgewater Four and Ann Whelan's fight against the odds would go down in the folklore of the nation. If the documentary, *Murder at the Farm*, had been the 'Court of last resort' then *Bad Company* was certainly, 'beyond the last shot'.

The campaigners disagreed. Three weeks later solicitor, Jim Nichol, was presenting a dossier to the Home Office. Included in the new evidence was a letter again discrediting a prosecution witness; information purporting to defame DC Perkins –who had died in October 1993. The officer had been a member of the now disbanded and a somewhat disgraced West Midlands Serious Crime Squad. He was chiefly responsible, as we have read, in writing up the confession of Patrick Molloy who had placed himself, Robinson and the Hickeys at Yew Tree Farm. Bert Spencer was not to escape mention in the dossier. It was stated that Nichol had in his possession a sworn statement, previously mentioned, from a dealer in antiques that he had sold a double-barrelled shotgun to Bert about 10 weeks before Carl was murdered. It was further claimed that this information was given to the police at the time of the original murder investigation. Spencer denies this allegation and claims it was not a subject raised during his lengthy interviews with the police.

Bad Company had unleashed a cascade of new support for the

Bridgewater Four, together with even more speculation that the ambulance liaison officer was responsible for the murder of young Carl. Ann
Whelan's cottage was inundated each day with hundreds of anguished letters from people wanting to join the campaign. Bundle after bundle was
forwarded from BBC's Pebble Mill. Paul Foot, following a dispute at the
Daily Mirror, was also receiving mail at his new place of work at *Private
Eye*. However, one letter was to significantly stand out amongst the rest. It
was written by Tim O'Malley, the foreman of the jury at the Carl Bridgewater trial in 1979. O'Malley went on to explain he had already written
to the Home Secretary, with the letter concluding, '... The TV drama I
saw this week, *Bad Company*, moved me very profoundly and was the
motivation for me to write to you. I want to do all I can to help the cause
...' Foot took no time in telephoning O'Malley, at the time an accountant
and prominent Labour councillor in Stafford. The journalist begged him
to make his conversion public. He agreed at once and ITN's Jennifer Nadel
interviewed O'Malley at his home. The interview got top billing on ITN's
news bulletin on 2 June 1993.

The Home Secretary, Michael Howard, promised to 'look very carefully'
at the comments of Mr Tim O'Malley, the foreman of the jury which had
found the Bridgewater Four guilty in a unanimous decision in 1979. After
14 years, Mr O'Malley had changed his mind and now felt that the four men
were innocent and that there had been, '...a terrible miscarriage of justice
...' It is important to add that O'Malley had reached this conclusion mainly
after viewing the heavily dramatised TV film, *Bad Company*. On 8 June,
with support at an all-time high, Jim Nichol presented the Home Office with
a new petition.

However, before the month of June was out, the scales were to be
tipped heavily in the other direction. The revelations were published in the
News of the World on the 20 and 27 of June. Mr John Blackburn, MP for
Dudley West, revealed that he was in possession of a letter from a married
woman* who was 13 years of age in 1978. Incredibly, she claimed that on
the afternoon of the murder, 19 September, 1978, she was passing Yew Tree

Farm and saw a car she recognised and standing by it was Jimmy Robinson, who she knew. The car was parked in the road, outside Yew Tree Farm.

Mr Blackburn also described as, 'pure 24 carat gold', a sworn affidavit by an ex-village policeman, Mick Palmer* – also in June. Mr Blackburn went on to say that it should be passed immediately to the Home Secretary, Michael Howard. The essence of Mr Palmer's statement was that he claimed he spent hours with Robinson in a police station cell at Bromsgrove divisional headquarters. They played cards to pass the time. Mr Palmer had strict instructions *not* to discuss the case with Robinson, but he said, Robinson seemed full of remorse and readily offered an account of the tragedy. Mr Palmer could not pass on the information he had gleaned for fear of being disciplined for disobeying his rather difficult instructions. Robinson had talked compulsively, said the ex-policeman from Romsley Village; the arrested man had claimed that Michael Hickey had been left downstairs at Yew Tree Farm to detain Carl while the others ransacked the upstairs rooms. They heard the gun go off and ran downstairs to find a weeping Michael Hickey standing over Carl and holding the shotgun. Mr Palmer quoted Robinson and describing Michael Hickey as, '... a head-banger and a case ... Crazy, just crazy.' Robinson made no such admission to the officers who interviewed him – either at the time or later.

At the time, Mr Palmer allegedly went further. In his opinion, if the three surviving members of the Bridgewater Four were to be set free it would have been making nonsense of the whole British legal system. He had left it so long before revealing what he knew because, he said, it seemed that justice had been done. Now, he felt the slanted nature of the frequent media attention could lead the public to believe in their innocence.

'They are wrong,' he said, 'they're guilty as hell.'

The ex-policeman was ready and willing to repeat his new evidence in court, should he be required to do so. He emphasized the fact that he was belatedly speaking out because he feared that a great injustice was about to be done.

'I don't think people realise how evil the people in this gang are – ruthless professional villains with records as long as your arm,' said Palmer, adding, 'Enough is enough. Everybody is treating the men as innocent, but James Robinson told me in his cell how Michael Hickey killed Carl. I'm appalled that an appeal might be allowed now that we have a new Home Secretary.'

Police involved in obtaining Pat Molloy's confession have been the subject of much criticism. Mick Palmer, however, left the West Mercia Police force with discharge papers describing his record in the force as, 'exemplary'.

After these, what seem to be outrageous, disclosures appeared in the *News of the World*, another followed in the next issue. This time the information came from a former prison officer, now a publican, Barry Shorthose*. He offered to appear before any enquiry there may be in the future to give his evidence. Shorthose claimed that he had a conversation in a police van as he was escorting Pat Molloy to the trial in 1979. The former prison officer claimed that Molloy had told him that he had come downstairs at Yew Tree Farm to see Jimmy Robinson hold a cushion to Carl's head before pulling the trigger. Molloy confirmed that the Hickeys too were present at the incident.

Although two unconnected witnesses, at the time a policeman and a prison officer, had claimed to have heard voluntary statements made by two of the accused men in which they both admitted being present at Yew Tree Farm at the time young Carl was so savagely and unnecessarily murdered – the alleged confessions were wildly opposing. The information and allegations mentioned in the last couple of paragraphs were highlighted during Mark Roman's original research. I could find no mention of these during my subsequent research.

While there appeared to be a lull after the publication of this alleged new evidence against the four men, the activity of the campaigners had taken another tack and it was all simmering beneath the surface.

On 22 October, 1993, it was ruled in High Court that the Home Secretary, Michael Howard, had acted unlawfully in denying that Michael Hickey – and others like him who were serving their sentence in a hospital situation – access to the normal parole review system. It was ruled by Lord Justice Kennedy that prisoners continue to serve their jail sentence even if they were, like Michael Hickey, in a mental hospital. The campaigners were hopeful that this would bring about Michael's early release. However, on 15 November, Michael Hickey himself seemed determined to burn that particular bridge.

In a taped interview on Central Television News, Michael Hickey, confirmed, 'If they say you are going out on condition that you are showing signs of remorse and you are showing guilt and you realise that you have done your time, then I'll tell them to stick it.'

'So, are you going to refuse to go before the parole board?' asked the interviewer.

Hickey's response was immediate, 'Of course I'm going to refuse.'

Michael Hickey's contention made sense. His dilemma was appalling. Expression of a demonstrably sincere remorse is a prerequisite of a favourable report from the assessing body, the Local Review Committee. Obviously, before an expression of remorse can be made guilt has to be admitted, and that, Michael Hickey, has steadfastly denied since the day of his arrest.

Just a couple of days after Michael's powerful statement, television channels devoted lengthy news time to the untiring solicitor, Jim Nichol. He was again presenting a dossier of fresh evidence to the Home Office. After an investigation in late May, instigated by ITN television, Dr Eric Shepard, Home Office forensic psychologist, had revealed considerable discrepancies regarding the already suspect confession statement of Patrick Molloy. He had found that the record of police notes and the Detention Record were incompatible. The Home Office were said to be looking carefully at this fresh evidence and Staffordshire police had requested that the Merseyside force reinvestigate some aspects of the case, although it was said that this was not a new investigation.

At the trial in 1979, the jury were instructed to disregard Molloy's confession as evidence against the other three. This was a difficult instruction to comply with as the jury had already read Molloy's statement. To be told that it could only be regarded as evidence against himself, was a legal nicety which the twelve good people of the jury must have found hard to comprehend. Does new evidence then that the confession was a concoction of the police – if proven to be true – affect in any way the validity of the prosecution case against the other three? The answer, of course, was yes.

To cap a day which had seen yet another dossier on the Carl Bridgewater case presented to the Home Office – in the hope that the matter would once more be referred back to the Court of Appeal – Ann Whelan and a group of her supporters held a candle-lit vigil outside the Home Office building. This time there was no mention of Bert Spencer on the banners that were displayed.

The next move in the Bridgewater Four campaign was the publication of an A4 sized advertisement in the Observer on Sunday 21 November, 1993. Under the heading, 'JUSTICE FOR THE BRIDGEWATER FOUR', it called upon the Home Secretary to refer the case yet again to the Court of Appeal, on the basis that fresh evidence had emerged which threw serious doubts upon the men's convictions. The end piece of the document was a polite call for donations to be sent to the Bridgewater Four Support Group. Funds, it said, were urgently needed to help publicise the campaign. Support was pledged by several hundred people, called from the serried ranks of household names in several theatres of life. Included in the group it was no surprise to read the names of the Birmingham Six and the Guilford Four, all who had been freed by the Court of Appeal.

During 1994 the inexhaustible Jim Nichol fired off two more petitions to Home Secretary, Michael Howard. One was with regards yet more information about the authenticity of Molloy's confession and the other to do with unidentified fingerprints found on the paperboy's yellow bike mentioned early. This latter evidence emerged from documents finally provided by the prosecution, that fingerprints were found on the bicycle, which did not belong to the four sentenced men. We know the bike was picked up and thrown by the killer or killers into a pigsty at Yew Tree Farm. It was Nichol's opinion that the fingerprints belonged to the murderer.

On 7 December 1995 the Bridgewater men and their campaigners received a crushing blow, as Michael Howard announced he was 'minded to refuse' to send the case to the Court of Appeal. The Jack Russell mentality of Jim Nichol resulted in him petitioning The Home Secretary again less than ten weeks after Howard's refusal, once more on the grounds of Molloy's confession. This was followed up by his final petition, on the very familiar same subject, on 8 May 1996. Following this barrage of attacks the tenacious solicitor was rewarded with some good news. On 12 June that year, Judicial review proceedings started against the Home Secretary. The review was asking for a court order instructing Michael Howard to send the case to the appeal court. On 17 July 1996, following a lot of pressure from all corners, the Home Secretary finally referred the case to the Court of Appeal.

The crusade had come a long way, with twists and turns of infinite variety. Little did they know, this established solid group of faithful campaigners and supporters, that freedom for Michael Hickey, Vincent Hickey and Jimmy Robison was just around the corner.

NOTE: *The allegations made by 'married woman', Mick Palmer and Barry Shorthose was supplied by notes prepared by Mark Roman – allegedly supplied by The News of the World. I made extensive searches and found no information to support the sighting or the confessions. However, since the collapse of The News of the World in 2011, archive searches have proved difficult.

12.

The Last Appeal!

....

The prosecution finally admitted they could no longer sustain the case against The Bridgewater Four and on Friday, 21 February 1997, the three remaining members of the original trial were released on unconditional bail. The three men were Jimmy Robinson, 63, Vincent Hickey, 44, and his cousin Michael Hickey, 35. The time was 2.00 pm and the men, still dressed in rough prison clothes, walked out of the large ornate gates of the High Court in London's Strand. This was their first moment of freedom since their arrest, in December 1978, over eighteen years previously. This historic event had been leaked to the media the previous evening and the Court of Appeal was packed with journalists. The news dominated every newspaper front page, radio bulletin and television broadcast.

The Hickey cousins and Robinson were greeted with tumultuous applause and cheering from their many supporters. As they left the court buildings, they hugged their families and Michael Hickey bent down to kiss the ground. Once the immediate euphoria had died down, like most mis-carriages of justice of this magnitude, when people had spent many years shouting their innocence, they denounced the criminal justice system. First in line was the Staffordshire Police force.

Robinson said, 'It was not a case of one rotten apple in the barrel, they were all rotten. You had to be rotten to get into the barrel. It wasn't about overzealous policemen thinking they had the right guys, it was a concerted conspiracy.'

Vincent Hickey stated, 'Not only have the police been devious and deceitful by keeping innocent men in prison. Far worse, after having a child killed, they have deceived Mr and Mrs Bridgewater.'

He went on to pay tribute to his own mother and of course, Michael

Hickey's, for the way they had campaigned for their release. Robinson said that Anne Skeet and Ann Whelan should be rewarded in the New Year's Honours List.

Robinson, added, 'The problem for the Staffordshire Police force was that they happened to fit-up Ann Whelan's son. They got a tiger by the tail. That woman and our solicitor have told people who didn't want to know. They were long lonely years, we have cried with despair and people have looked at us with contempt in their eyes for killing a kid. I am not bitter but I am angry it has taken so long. This is not new evidence; it is stuff that has been there from day one.'

Nick Molloy, the son of Pat Molloy, said, 'I feel very sad. It's great to see these men today. I salute the heroes these men are. They have courage, true courage.'

Mrs Whelan was glad that the battle was over, but she remained angry that the men had suffered years of abuse.

'I was very much on my own for years,' she said. 'But I just fought and fought and fought. The worst time was when people refused to listen. The authorities knew they were innocent, but they didn't want to hear. There is still a lot of fighting to be done, but Michael just needs time to think now.'

Spencer had a feeling about what was coming, although he knew he would probably have a bit of a respite during the actual appeal proceedings, which lay ahead. Once again, the spotlight of guilt was about to focus on Paul Foot's own personal prime suspect – Hubert Spencer.

After many unsuccessful appeals over the years, on Wednesday 30 July 1997, at the Royal Courts of Justice in the Strand, London, the Bridgewater Four Appeal Court Judgment started. This case is perhaps one of the most shocking and infamous of the recent miscarriages of justice, following in the footsteps of The Birmingham Six and The Guilford Four. It was also a momentous step regarding Jimmy Robinson, Michael and Vincent Hickey, and of course, the family and memory of the late Pat Molloy.

In the Court of Appeal Criminal Division Lord Justice Roch, Mr Justice Hidden and Mr Justice Mitchell, started the appeal in the case of Regina versus Michael Hickey, Vincent Hickey, James Robinson and the deceased Patrick Molloy.

Mr Fitzgerald QC and Mr Blaxland appeared on behalf of the appellant Michael Hickey. Mr Jones QC and Miss Ellis appeared on behalf of the appellant Vincent Hickey. Mr O'Connor QC and Mr Turner appeared on behalf of the appellant James Robinson. Mr Mansfield QC and Mr Wood appeared on behalf of the appellant Patrick Molloy. Mr Roberts QC, Mr Coker QC and Mr Clement stood on behalf of the Crown. The stage was set and all the actors were in their places, with more waiting in the wings to be called. There was, following so many years of bitter disappointment and misery, with so many false starts, so much hope only to be replaced with doom, an air of relief and positivity. It was not only a time for Justice to be done, but also to be seen to be done, although as the curtain went up the opening address was somewhat of an anti-climax. Although it may sound somewhat clinical, or even cold, the Appeal judges were only interested in whether the four appellants had received a fair trial back in 1979.

With somewhat of a dour opening, underlining this fact, Lord Justice Roch began, 'This Court is not concerned with the guilt or innocence of the appellants; but only with the safety of their convictions. This may, at first sight, appear an unsatisfactory state of affairs, until it is remembered that the integrity of the criminal process is the most important consideration for courts, which have to hear appeals against conviction. Both the innocent and the guilty are entitled to fair trials. If the trial process is not fair; if it is distorted by deceit or by material breaches of the rules of evidence or procedure, then the liberties of all are threatened.

'This Court is a court of review. The Court reviews the trial process to equip itself to answer the question, "Do we think that the conviction appealed is safe or do we think it unsafe?" The Court is not a court of trial or of re-trial. Persons accused of serious crimes are tried by juries in the Crown Court. Some of the appellants Counsel have come close to asking this Court to pronounce on the guilt or innocence of an appellant or the truthfulness of an appellant's alibi.'

In any appeal of this enormity, the transcript ran to over 120,000 words, there were many references to various aspects of the case that the defence was not happy with in regard the original trial. As we have read in *Chapter 11 – The Fight For Freedom*, which highlights the unsuccessful 1989 appeal, certain areas were visited once again.

The difference with the new appeal, and sitting alongside other points of law picked up by the Bridgewater Four's solicitor, Jim Nichol, was new evidence surrounding Exhibit 54 – Molloy's signed statement. In fact it was the sleuth-like solicitor who uncovered this new and striking evidence that threw serious doubts on the fairness of the trial of the four men in 1979. There were many factors pertaining to the Irishman's signed statement.

Exhibit 54

Following a brief outline of the case, Lord Justice Roch moved straight on to the conviction and sentencing following the 1979 trial. He then outlined the appeal process. The central hub and driving force that had got the case referred again back to the Court of Appeal was Molloy's signed confession.

Roch began, 'We now turn to the appeal of Patrick Molloy. The submission that is made is that these confessions were inadmissible because they were obtained by oppression.'

The eminent and eloquent barrister Michael Mansfield, QC, was representing the late Pat Molloy and family. Mansfield – republican, vegetarian, socialist, and self-described 'radical lawyer', has always participated in prominent and controversial court cases and inquests. The QC started with how the police dealt with the Irishman while in custody.

It appears to be true that the Molloy was subjected to various inhumane police tactics to try and extract more and more information. This included keeping Molloy locked up for many days without access to legal representation. Pat Molloy was arrested on 8 December and did not see a solicitor until 18 December. Mansfield complained, '... that it was part of the police strategy to see that Patrick Molloy was kept isolated from the outside world and in particular from legal advice. These, it is suggested, were deliberate breaches of the Judges' Rules and Section 62 of the 1977 Criminal Law Act.'

He had been deprived of sleep, with various officers banging on the cell walls when the Irishman tried to sleep. It is alleged he had also been deprived of liquids and the dehydrated Molloy had to hand scoop water from the toilet basin.

The complaint of physical ill-treatment and threats of violence were not made by Molloy to his solicitor at the first opportunity. It was actually after service of the committal papers upon him that Patrick Molloy complained to his solicitor that the police had subjected him to violence. He claimed DC Perkins had hit him and in doing so had broken his denture.

This piece of evidence regarding physical violence towards the Irishman was dealt with some scepticism by Lord Roch, explaining, 'Clearly if that had occurred prior to the making of Exhibit 54, that would have amounted to oppression and his confessions would have been inadmissible. Those allegations were not made at the trial. Indeed Patrick Molloy instructed his lawyers that he did not want them to "particularly attack the police". Our attention has been drawn to two letters written by Patrick Molloy after his conviction, which would be surprising letters indeed had he been subjected to physical violence whilst in police custody. So far as this court is aware, there never was any evidence of physical injury to Mr Molloy at that time and no independent evidence of any damage to his denture. Following the making of Exhibit 54, Patrick Molloy was never in contact again with DC Perkins, DC Leeke or DS Robbins. He was seen during the evening of the 10 December by DCS Stewart, DCI Watson and DC Lycett. He made no complaint, although he was given the chance to make such a complaint when DCS Stewart asked him whether he was all right, and, a little later, whether there was anything else he wanted to say.'

Roch now introduced the most shocking and alarming piece of evidence, he stated, '... the resort by the police to a trick, namely the production of a document which purported to be a written statement by Vincent

Hickey implicating Patrick Molloy, (Michael Hickey) and James Robinson in the offences committed at Yew Tree Farm.'

The crucial piece of evidence, now being discussed, that would lead to the release of the Bridgewater Three, lay undiscovered in their files for years until their solicitor, Jim Nichol, found it in the late '80s. There was always much doubt about the contents of Molloy's confession – which the detectives claim the Irishman dictated to them verbatim. This mainly concerned the phraseology of the suspect, which was not only inconsistent with earlier comments but was also at odds with his education and Irish roots. Added to this was the timescale involved inasmuch as some of the notes written up by officers, given the time restrictions between the start and end of the interview, meant that Molloy would have had to rattle off words at an impossible pace. This research was into the speed at which notes and statements are written. The speed of writing is expressed in characters per minute (cpm). Research into notes that are accepted as genuine notes taken by police officers showed that speeds varied between 44 cpm and 155 cpm. In some cases notes would have had to be have taken down by DS Robbins at over 200 cpm, a speed which Dr Hardcastle described as impossible.

It was Jim Nichol's doggedness that exposed another vital clue with regard to the veracity of Molloy's confession. Whilst routinely going over it for the umpteenth time he noticed impressions below the exhibit label on page 1 of Exhibit 54. This was to prove to be a major factor.

Lord Justice Roch explained, 'These impressions had been made before page 1 of Exhibit 54 had been written. They were from a *caution* in another statement purporting to have been made by and signed by Vincent Hickey. That statement had almost certainly been written on witness statement paper used by the Staffordshire police force in 1978. Such paper would have been at Wombourne Police Station but not at Redditch Police Station where Vincent Hickey was being held and questioned.'

The signed confession statement by Patrick Molloy taken in Wombourne police station in December 1978, which proved vital to the conviction of all the men, was subjected to Electrostatic Document Analysis (ESDA), in 1990. ESDA, a technique not available when the men were sentenced, can show if documents have been altered and reveal impressions left by other sheets of paper.

So basically ESDA had revealed two areas of concern. One was a written caution in which Vincent Hickey allegedly made a full statement incriminating, together with others, Patrick Molloy. It was true, in his early interviews; Vincent had placed Molloy at Yew Tree Farm, but he had not made an official caution statement in this form. The second point was that this statement had been signed, allegedly by Vincent. Even the police agreed that Hickey had never signed such a document.

Early experts to examine the document using the ESDA process were unimpressed. Forensic scientists Robert Radley and Dr Anthony Hardcastle found no sign that the statement had been tampered with. And the only imprints they could detect were consistent with those that they would have expected on a document taken from a stack of witness statements.

Jeremy Roberts, QC, for the Crown, confidently told the Court of Appeal, 'They found impressions of a familiar caption which one finds at the beginning of every statement under caution.' The QC added, 'There was nothing in the least surprising about finding that there. It is exactly what one would expect to find there.'

What they did not realise, was that the name Vincent Hickey could, in fact, be seen in two places in that caption. Molloy always claimed that he had been tricked into making his admission by being shown a confession by Hickey. However, the police said no such statement existed. That was disproved by the discovery of Hickey's name and *signature* among the few words protected by the exhibit label on the front page of Molloy's statement. Most of the other imprints had disappeared with handling over the years. What Radley and Hardcastle did not know was that Hickey was interviewed in Redditch police station, 25 miles away from Molloy, and any statement he made could not have been written on the same pad.

When Nichol discovered the signature on the Hickey 'statement' he immediately had it examined, and his suspicions appeared to have been borne out. Molloy's interview was carried out by Detective Constable John Perkins and Detective Constable Graham Leeke, with Detective Sergeant John Robbins sitting outside taking notes. On behalf of the Crown, Mr Roberts QC, had to admit that Vincent Hickey's statement was clearly a forgery. It was stated that impressions in the body of the caption are in handwriting that certainly appeared very similar to DC Leeke's and the impressions in the signature of Vincent Hickey, which is certainly not a genuine Vincent Hickey signature, are very like the handwriting of DC Perkins. In fact samples of the handwriting of 12 police officers were obtained and examined by Dr Hardcastle and Mr Radley, two of the expert witnesses called to give evidence during the appeal. These 12 officers were all the officers who might have had contact with Patrick Molloy or with Vincent Hickey. They included DC Perkins, DC Leeke and DS Robbins. The impressions forming part of the 'caution' contained details, which were *similar* to DC Leeke's known writing. There were significant differences between those details and the handwriting samples from the other 11 police officers. Dr Hardcastle sounded this note of concern, that because not all the fine detail can been seen from an ESDA trace it is not practical to make a fully effective comparison.

The signature 'Vincent Hickey' provided a more restricted comparison because it was simpler and contained fewer characters than the impressions from the caution. The handwriting specimen from DC Perkins was closest to the writing, which made the impressions of the purported 'Vincent Hickey' signature. Although there were some features that were not well matched, such as the capital 'V' in the signature and the capital 'V' in the sample, Dr Hardcastle could accept that DC Perkins could have written the purported signature.

Of this signature, the other expert, Mr Radley, said in giving evidence, 'There is a broad correlation of most detail with the writing of DC Perkins, although there are some points of difference. Of the samples I have examined DC Perkins' writing matches most closely the writing of 'Vincent Hickey' and he is the most likely author of the 'Vincent Hickey' entry.'

Mr Roberts further told the appeal judges, 'The Crown accepted that there was no other sensible explanation that we can properly put forward other than Molloy's claim that his confession was improperly obtained.'

Mr Perkins, who has since died, was disgraced in 1989 after he was caught falsifying a statement, which failed in a court. In 1992, Merseyside police interviewed Mr Leeke and Mr Robbins, but they strenuously denied Molloy's allegations. One called them 'absolute rubbish', the other 'utter drivel'.

Pat Molloy's claim that he had been shown this forgery was never believed in the many reviews of the case since 1978. Great credit should go to Jim Nichol, solicitor to the men, who decided to go back over all the evidence in preparation for their latest appeal. Mr Molloy's confession was always central to the case against all three men.

The top defence QC, Michael Mansfield, put it rather succinctly, when he said that the fake confession was 'only a small part of serious, substantial and widespread police malpractice involving a number of very high-ranking officers down to the lowest, who must have been involved in what was going on'. Again he underlined that the particular ground of Molloy's confession meant that all the convictions were unsafe, and Lord Justice Roth agreed that without it, the Crown would have had no case.

Michael Mansfield, who has forged a formidable reputation as the 'poor man's advocate' for he specialises in cases of suspected miscarriages of justice, often when many others, including the lawyers, have thrown away the key. He never gave up on this one, having been convinced at an early stage that, together with solicitor Nichol, Malloy was telling the truth. In the Bridgewater case, as in many other notable ones, he was one man against the system and, not for the first time, he eventually won.

Simon Regan, editor of *Scallywag*, commented, 'At the time, in 1997, John Perkins was safe from any legal reproductions for his handling of the Bridgewater Four, as he died four years previously. Probably from high blood pressure brought about by trying to live with his guilt.' Regan continued, 'At the time his sidekick, Graham Leake, was still very much alive and, immediately after the release of the surviving three, his solicitors, Russell Jones and Walker made a defensive statement on his behalf protesting his innocence and insisting that over the past 18 years he had been cleared of any offences by countless different inquiries. He was cleared, however, before ESDA was able to prove beyond doubt that he was a fellow conspirator and participant in a most heinous piece of police malpractice.'

The judge in the original murder trial, Sir Maurice Drake, told BBC's *Newsnight*, 'It is deplorable that justice has been perverted on bent police evidence.

'No-one has ever alleged that the original trial was conducted unfairly or that the summing up was in any way inaccurate. Irrespective of how strong the other evidence may have been it has been found that the police misbehaved.'

When the official proceedings were concluded and the convictions had been quashed by the Court of Appeal, Ann Whelan had the last word, 'It's all been worth it. They haven't got justice. They've got their freedom but not justice.'

*   *   *

The night of the men's release was, understandably, one of euphoria mixed with some serious reality checks. None of the men slept well in comfortable beds and unlocked rooms. Their adjustment would take time. It had been nearly 19 years since the three had enjoyed civilian life and it was a total contrast to the trauma and stress of prison life. The everyday things that most of us take for granted seemed like ultimate luxury after their imprisonment. However, you have little choice of becoming somewhat institutionalised and they obviously had no halfway house or weekend releases to let them adapt to the outside world. It was always going to be the mind that needed to adjust and this takes time. Sadly, at that time, the authorities offered little in the form of any psychological therapy.

BBC Scriptwriter, Seth Linder, in a 1997 *The New Statesmen* article, titled Freedom – living with it …, said, 'The fight for freedom is over, but the hard part is just beginning for the Bridgewater men.'

Ann Whelan explained to Seth, 'He's very up and down, sometimes very angry, sometimes hyper. He has broken down and cried, especially when he's talked to prisoners still inside. He's had terrible stomach cramps because the food is so rich after a prison diet. He hasn't slept in a bed yet, in fact he's hardly slept at all and he's asked me to remove the light in his room – he slept with a light on in his cell for ten years. He wouldn't travel in a train carriage because it would be too claustrophobic after the cell and he says he gets lost in the house because there are so many rooms.' That is how Ann Whelan, the mother of Michael Hickey, described her son three days after his release as one of the wrongfully convicted killers of the newspaper boy Carl Bridgewater.

Jill Morrell, who co-authored, with her then boyfriend John McCarthy, the bestseller, *Some Other Rainbow: Their Own Story*, was a leading campaigner for the Bridgewater Four. British journalist McCarthy had been a hostage in Beirut for over five years during the Lebanon crisis, being one of the longest held hostages there. Morrell believes the Bridgewater men's need for counselling is in some ways greater than that of the Beirut hostages.

'It's coming to terms with the wasted years that are hardest, explains the author, 'Michael, for instance, has spent half his life in prison – he's lost those years and can never get them back.' Jill Morrell wrote the campaign booklet, *The Wrong Men* (published by the Bridgewater Four Support Group).

I remember Gerry Conlon telling me personally about being released as one of the Guilford Four, wrongly convicted for the IRA bombings in London. He said how shocked he was to see people on mobile phones and thought that they were Secret Service operatives talking about him. Sadly Gerry passed away on 21 June, 2014 and I miss his inspiration, intelligence and fearlessness. Gerry was a campaigner for the Bridgewater Four. In some ways there were similarities to what Molloy had alleged happened during his time in custody, although the 20-year-old Belfast lad had it far tougher as a suspected IRA terrorist. Conlon, along with fellow Irishmen, Paul Hill, Paddy

Armstrong and an English woman, Carole Richardson, became the so-called Guildford Four. They were convicted in 1975 of planting two bombs a year earlier in the Surrey city of Guildford, which killed five people and injured dozens more. The four were sentenced to life in prison.

At their trial the judge told the defendants, 'If hanging were still an option you would have been executed.'

Conlon continued to protest his innocence insisting that police had tortured him into making a false confession. In October 1989 his position was vindicated, when the Guildford Four were freed after the Court of Appeal in London ruled that police had fabricated the hand-written interrogation notes used in the conviction. Also crucial evidence proving Conlon could not have carried out the bombings had not been presented at the original trial.

Gerry wrote the powerful bestseller about his horrific ordeal, *Proved Innocent* (Hamish Hamilton Ltd 1990 and Penguin Books Ltd 1994) and a very powerful and moving film followed; *In the Name of the Father* which was released in 1994. Daniel Day-Lewis, playing Gerry Conlon, delivered an Oscar nominated performance.

The West Midlands Serious Crime Squad, who had dealt with the Bridgewater case, had been disbanded in 1989 in a blaze of publicity, which never really went away, of corruption and abuse of power. The most recent figures, from October 2014, reveal that a total of 33 appellants have had their convictions quashed in cases involving the squad.

The police and judicial authority had never had Bert Spencer in their sights for the murder of the paperboy. It is true that they had certainly considered Spencer a serious suspect, together with quite a few others, but slowly the list was whittled down and interest in Spencer waned. The same could not be said of the Bridgewater men, Ann Whelan, Paul Foot and the growing body of campaigners and some armchair supports. It would appear that now was the perfect time to strike home their advantage. The Bridgewater Four were cleared and free, and Hubert Spencer was once again prime suspect – public enemy number one!

So, whether the Bridgewater men felt like having a large celebratory party, in full public view, was another matter. The campaigners and supporters expected it and wanted to revel in their eventual victory, after all, their faith had been vindicated.

A few days after their case was quashed by the Court of Appeal the three surviving members of the Bridgewater Four; Vincent Hickey, Michael Hickey and Jimmy Robinson – celebrated with their families and campaigners at the London Irish Centre in Camden Town. Simultaneously the scene was set for a lively television studio debate taking place on *Weekend Television Live*, back in 1997, who were cutting back to the on-going party for various comments, including from the original foreman of the jury at the trial, in 1979, Tim O'Malley.

In the studio, which was obviously a brave move, was Bert Spencer and his second wife, Christine. The other guests included, coincidently, my old pal, Gerry Conlon, Sir Ivan Lawrence MP, Councillor John Mellor and Anthony Scrivener QC. The interviewer was the former Central News presenter, Mike Morley.

Following up on the expected reassurances of Sir Ivan that things had changed in the police set up, Gerry was quick to jump in, commenting, 'The police have become professional witnesses and in some cases professional liars. And when you have terrible miscarriages of justice happen, and my father died in prison like Pat Molloy, and then you get one police force investigating another, it's like asking the Mafia to investigate organised crime.'

Councillor Mellor, talking on behalf of the Staffordshire Police Authority, was quick to criticise Conlon's words. He came across as somewhat pompous and I am not sure he did himself or the police any good. Scrivener QC was also critical of the police and the judicial system.

It was quite clear that we had come a long way since 1979 and at the time of broadcast 18 years later, tape recorded interviews and other technology had been put in place, including DNA profiling.

In the audience was Martin Burton, former Superintendent of the West Midlands Police, who had been speaking to former colleagues involved in the Bridgewater case that very day. He spoke passionately about their total incredulity at what had happened in the last couple of days. It was obvious that most, if not all, of the police who had been involved in the case did not agree in anyway with the decision of the Court of Appeal. He went on further to criticise the ESDA process with regard to the caution statement and Vincent Hickey's alleged forged signature – the backbone of the successful appeal. He explained that the most important failure of ESDA was that it could not determine when those indentations were made. Burton questioned whether this was actually, as some legal representatives of the men had described it, in fact 'radical new evidence'. His inference was obvious – the indentations picked up by ESDA had been made after Molloy claimed he had been shown the Hickey signed confession. Surprisingly there was no expert produced to respond to the refuted analysis of the ESDA test.

Via a television link at Central's Oxford studio, next up was Forensic Psychiatrist, Dr Eric Shepherd, who was commissioned by the Home Office. He confirmed his findings regarding the uncertainty surrounding Exhibit 54, Molloy's signed confession. He left little doubt, both in the minds of the audience in the studio and the viewers at home, that the written statement was not that of Pat Molloy and the alleged time given for the Irishman to dictate the confession was totally inconsistent.

It was time for former Chief Superintendent, Barry Mason, to speak, but again there was little concern about the findings during the Bridgewater appeal and his words were mainly confined to improving police procedures to stop these types of allegations.

It was now Bert Spencer's time in the hot seat. Hemmed in between the two former high-ranking Superintendent police officers, the presenter, Mike Morley, asked why Spencer had been interviewed 20 times by the Staffordshire Police about the Carl Bridgewater murder?

A smart suited Bert, looking stern but composed, stated, 'Because people over the years, various people, have made various allegations. Alleging, for example, that I had confessed to them in prison. Well each time that happened there had to be a full investigation, and there was.'

Presenter Morley challenged Spencer with some of the evidence against
him in the Carl Bridgewater case and Bert was quick to respond.

'Paul Foot and Co dismiss circumstantial evidence in their case,' points
out Spencer astutely, adding, 'but he takes up that circumstantial evidence
in my case.'

The presenter was quick to respond, 'I'm not really interested in Paul
Foot. I mean a lot of people point their finger at yourself and it must affect
your life?'

'It does, they've pointed the finger at me for about 17 years' replied
Spencer. 'The Bridgewater Four started it, Ann Whelan and Paul Foot and
Co have carried it on.'

After some toing and froing Morley asked the all-important question,
'What can you say that convinces people that they are so wrong to point the
finger at yourself?'

Bert answered, 'I did not do it. I was nowhere near the place on that
day. I had no involvement in that crime.'

The last words were given to Conlon when asked about the mental
state of the surviving Bridgewater men. After a brief argument between Conlon and Christine Spencer, after she had clearly claimed that the Bridgewater Four were responsible for the murder of the paperboy, he addressed the
problems the men faced.

'How they can get their lives back together is RAF Lyneham should
be opened up, the same way it was for Terry Waite, for John McCarthy,
for Jackie Mann, for Brian Keenan. They should be given the same psychological help they were given, the same physiatrists. We were prisoners of circumstances hostages of injustice. We should always be treated
the same.'

During this provocative and powerful speech the director kept cutting
back to a somewhat stony-faced Spencer. Bert had in fact conducted himself
with dignity and put his point across with controlled authority. His next
television challenge would be up against the might of Ann Whelan in head-
to-head battle.

Under the shadow of the blaze of publicity and euphoria, The Staffordshire Police were keeping their heads down and displayed what some would
say a dignified silence. Following the successful appeal, in the eyes of the
law there was at least one empty cell and a major unsolved child murder to
clear up. However, they did not refocus their enquiries and made no official
public statement. It was no real secret that most of the police involved in
the case believed the original verdicts were correct and the Bridgewater
Four had simply slipped through the net via some of their colleagues' over-
zealousness. As some would comment about the 'good old days' – maybe a
few corners were cut, but they got their man.

In what was to be the final showdown, as far as a face to face televised interview was concerned, took place during a special extended Central News edition. It was shortly after the successful appeal hearing for The
Bridgewater Four in 1997. The two heavyweights were Ann Whelan and
Bert Spencer, together with his second wife, Christine. The referee was the
respected presenter Bob Warman.

Before what was obviously going to be a volatile and abusive exchange
could commence, there were some emotional segments of the men trying
to adjust to civilian life. It was an extremely emotive scene when Michael
Hickey was shown the tiny windowless office room that his mother, Ann
Whelan, had fought her campaign from. Inside the claustrophobic headquarters of the Bridgewater Four, the nerve centre spearheading the operation, the walls were festooned with letters and pictures – not a slither
of wallpaper could be seen. Large boxes of files filling the space between
the carpet and ceiling made the room even smaller. Paul Foot had used
the place for months whilst writing his book, *Murder at the Farm*. Before
Michael could even utter a word, his face crumpled and tears followed. The
next shot saw Michael sitting on the settee, holding his mother's hand, like
a small child would. The pain and torment was very plain to see in his face,
as he reflected on the time he had spent locked up behind bars. After all he
was just three year's older than the paperboy he was charged and convicted
of murdering back in 1979. Michael had three serious mental breakdowns

whilst protesting his innocence in various regimes. Although it did come across he had a sense of humour, sharing the odd joke and winking at the camera.

Quite pointedly the interviewer suddenly asked Michael, 'What would you like to see happen now over the next few months to do with your case?'

'I don't want to contemplate that because that can make my head very unbalanced,' he responded straight to camera. 'I just want to enjoy life, go round and speak. I don't want to talk about injustice and bent coppers – let the judges sort that out, I don't want to fight that ...'

Vincent Hickey was seen confidently driving to his old house and he did appear more robust. Vincent ended his segment at his mother's home, Ann Skett, who had also helped greatly in support of the campaign. Jimmy Robinson was notably absent from any clips.

It was then back to the studio with Bob Warman. The gloves were off as the presenter sat between Bert Spencer, and his then wife Christine, and the tireless Bridgewater campaigner, Ann Whelan. Whelan had been responsible, together with Foot, for highlighting Bert's association with the Bridgewater murder. A lot of mud had been slung over the past 18 years and much of it had stuck to the former Ambulance Liaison Officer.

The interview started with a few words from Whelan about the successful appeal decision to let the men out on unconditional bail. She went on to firmly point out that there was an empty cell her son had just vacated, with the emphasise now to find the real perpetrator of the murder of the paperboy, who, she added, is walking the streets a free man.

Warman's first question to Whelan, 'So do you now feel the need to join the search to find that man?'

'... I won't rest, let's put it like this, until the perpetrator of that child, the killer of that child, is behind bars. And let's remember this family as well, the police have an onus to go out, and they haven't got to search too far, and arrest the perpetrator of it.'

Warman repeated her words about the police not having to look too far, adding, '...you know who Carl's killer is?'

'Yes,' shot back the mother, 'and it did not just start from my own personal detective work, by the way, it was material that was handed over to me.'

Throughout Whelan's speech the camera often conveniently cut back to the solemn face of Bert Spencer. His face reflected a brooding silence, as of yet he had not been called upon to respond.

When it was officially established, during the interview, that Ann Whelan was accusing, once again, Mr Spencer, it was an aggressive stance from the normally gentle presenter.

'Did it start in any way,' still directing his questions to Whelan, 'with the headline in the *Daily Mirror* this morning, I killed Carl.'

At which the presenter held up the front page to camera. To the right of a huge capital letter headline, 'I KILLED CARL', was a picture of Spencer. It was yet another prison confession, which we have dealt with earlier in this book.

Eventually, after some more accusations from Ann Whelan, Warman turned his to attention to Bert.

'... Now after reading that this morning a lot of people are going to draw the conclusion that you killed Carl Bridgewater.'

Bert took the *Daily Mirror* newspaper off the presenter, stating sombrely to camera, 'Maybe that people are. But firstly can I say, from my wife and I. Brian and Janet (Carl Bridgewater's parents) we have no choice but to defend ourselves and to keep this alive in front of you, we must.'

'Well, let me ask you this, do you share a sense of relief that a great wrong has been righted?' asked Warman.

'I don't believe a great wrong has been righted,' replied Spencer, adding, 'I think a lot of other people don't, according to their views.'

'Is that because it was rather convenient for you that the Bridgewater three were locked up, for a long, long time?' responded the presenter.

Spencer went on to explain it had the opposite affect, in terms of the spotlight being on him. As he pointed out, allegations of so-called confessions had dogged him for 18 years. The members of The Bridgewater

Four had also purportedly made scores of confessions according to fellow inmates, prison staff, police officers and even civilians.

What was promised or at least the aim, oddly enough not from the constabulary, but the Bridgewater men, and most of their family headed by Ann Whelan, Paul Foot, and one assumes the legal team who had fought so hard for the freedom of the men – was to find the murderer of the paperboy. However, things did not turn out as expected. The huge chase that was a natural progression of nearly two decades trying to clear the names of the Hickeys, Robinson and the late Molloy, was to turn their attention to hunt down the real killer, in their eyes, Bert Spencer.

Certainly the police seemed to have lost interest in the case, which was now officially an unsolved violent child murder. Over the following years the very people who had investigated the crime, The Staffordshire Police force, never carried out even a cold case file investigation on who killed Carl. During my research for this book very few senior officers, although now all retired, would speak to me on or off the record. The unofficial view appeared to be that the Bridgewater Four had escaped justice in a successful appeal in one of the highest court of laws in the land – the Court of Appeal. I know with some officers it was a matter of loyalty and others genuinely felt the original conviction was correct.

At the time I did feel a need, as a relatively early campaigner for the Bridgewater Four, for a conclusion to the murder mystery.

Everyone connected with the campaign needed the support, energy and media influence of the likes of Ann Whelan and Paul Foot. It appeared they had suddenly lost interest in their favourite quarry – Bert Spencer. Certainly the newspapers, radio and television media kept Spencer's name alive as a suspect, whenever there was an anniversary or news story about the Bridgewater case.

Maybe the monumental battle, fought so hard and for so long, meant that they had no stomach left to see the job through to the end. Even before the winter of 1997 any interest from the campaigners had dribbled to the odd article in obscure local newspapers. We know that Whelan and Foot were fighters, and even the remaining Bridgewater men realised there would be no closure until the real murderer was exposed. Doubt would forever be their demons. Their inactivity and silence could only do them harm over the years.

In real terms the Court of Appeal's decision only rested on the original convictions that they deemed were unsafe at the 1979 trial. That was the job of the appeal judges. It was not their position to decide on the innocence or guilt of the four men.

After all I had learnt about the case, I wanted a final look at the evidence. Somehow I felt all the pieces of the jigsaw were contained within the pages of this book. In the last chapter, *Final Thoughts*, I wanted to sum up my feelings as freely as possible. I wanted to try and take a retrospective, and as objective as possible, look at all the events surrounding *both* farm murders, together with other areas of the case. This included not only Foot's book and mine, newspaper, radio and TV coverage but also the 1989 and the 1997 appeals, the latter which ran to 120,000 words. I also took into account the dramatised Don Shaw movie, *Bad Company*, as well as the two documentaries; BBC's *Rough Justice* offering – Who Killed Carl Bridgewater? and the Thames Television documentary, *Murder at the Farm*, the latter based on Foot's book.

An enlightened examination might shed some light on the shadows that clouded parts of this riveting and tragic mystery. I came up with some intriguing conclusions. Yes it was pure conjecture, and what I hoped to be intelligent speculation, but some of the hypotheses were quite alarming.

I often used the basis of a famous quote by Sherlock Holmes, 'It is an old maxim of mine that when you have excluded the impossible, whatever remains, however improbable, must be the truth.'

13.

Final Thoughts

••

When I first came into contact with Bert Spencer I carried with me a lot of pro-Bridgewater campaigner baggage. This was obviously fuelled by press and media coverage – headed by Paul Foot and Ann Whelan. I had read the book and watched the documentaries; *Who Killed Carl Bridgewater?* and *Murder at the Farm*, together with the dramatised film, *Bad Company*. I had a general feeling and an attitude from the community around the area, where I lived, where both murders had been committed. It was a general consensus that the murderer of Carl Bridgewater and the killer of Hubert Wilkes, was the same man, and that was the Ambulance Liaison Officer. As far as the slaying of the paperboy, Bert Spencer, it was suggested, had literally got away with murder.

Over the years following the paperboy's murder I heard nothing to contradict the thought that Bert Spencer was involved in Carl's death. I don't think I actually ever heard a word in his defence.

I was mostly ignorant of the fact that up until 1994 he was incarcerated in one of Her Majesty's prisons, so he was basically bound and gagged. The freedom of prisoner speech was heavily restricted in those days. Even as a fiction novelist trying to access various prisons for research, during the '90s while writing *Framed in Guilt*, I was regarded with great suspicion by the Home Office. I was questioned as to exactly what I wished to write about and what areas I was going to cover in the novel. I had to sign many forms to guarantee that the prisons I was cleared to visit would not feature in the book. There were obviously important security reasons, especially as my main character in the book was a successful escapee. However, I knew there was far more to it than that. They were highly suspicious of me, as a novelist, and were concerned at how the general prison regime would be portrayed.

It was made quite clear from the start that any information gleaned from inmates or prison warders I spoke to should not be used if it was detrimental to the prison service in general. During the early days of my research as I travelled the country visiting such establishments as Strangeways prison in Manchester, the notorious HMP Wakefield in Yorkshire and the experimental institution, HMP Grendon, situated in Buckinghamshire, although I was always greeted with respect, my every movement was monitored. All my questions were delivered straight out of the Home Office Prison Service Instructions (PSIs) and Prison Service Orders (PSOs) booklets.

My main 'home' for research, and where I spent several days, was the lifers D wing at Wormwood Scrubs, the same wing where Bert Spencer, who'd recently been released from North Sea Camp, had spent quite a proportion of his prison term. Things did become far more relaxed the more time I spent at the establishment and I was allowed a certain amount of freedom. It always sent my nerves tingling as I arrived at the infamous and most filmed prison entrance in the world; Gate 5, Wormwood Scrubs.

I thought I had it tough as a civilian trying to get information out of the Home Office, but for an inmate it was more or less impossible. All of Spencer's correspondence, incoming and outgoing, would be scrutinised and censored with Victorian sternness.

So, again, without any allowed feedback from Bert Spencer during his prison years I was swept along with the press and media euphoria as the Bridgewater Four campaign reached a positive crescendo, resulting in their sensational release of the remaining three, on unconditional bail, at the Court of Appeal on 21 February 1997.

I did assume, wrongly as it turned out, that the campaign, headed by Ann Whelan and Paul Foot, would go on and that they and the large number of supporters they had attracted would pursue Spencer in the manner of hounds hunting a fox and direct every effort towards him being convicted of the murder of the paperboy. After all this was an unsolved murder case and their prime suspect, they believed, was walking free in the shape of public enemy number one; Hubert Spencer. Alas, it did all die down very quickly.

Interest, that had been so tireless and unrelenting, pointing accusing fingers at Spencer, had waned somewhat.

Of course any article relating to an anniversary connected to the case, or anything to do with the three surviving members of the Bridgewater Four, always included a snide remark or strong reference to Spencer and his connection with the murder of Carl Bridgewater. Most pieces would include a recent photograph of Spencer and text covering the usual question marks pointing at his guilt surrounding the paperboy, together with an outline of the murder of his friend, Hubert Wilkes.

I suppose the question on my mind and part of the emphasis of the book surrounds Paul Foot. How far can an investigative journalist go when he believes he is in the right? I have no doubt that Foot genuinely believed that Bert Spencer killed 13-year-old Carl Bridgewater in cold blood. However, is he allowed to persecute a particular civilian who was eliminated from the murder enquiry of the paperboy? I have no problem with his fight for justice of the Bridgewater Four via his column in the *Daily Mirror*, through documentary footage and in dramatised film. Although the latter is a dangerous area to exploit as it was delivered as fact. Also, in what is I feel an unprecedented case, the Bridgewater campaigners, whipped up by Foot's media barrage, not only tried to clear the names of four men they felt were innocent of the crime, but also to point a finger at a man who had been eliminated as a suspect by the police with subsequent judicial statements and appeals stating that Hubert Spencer was in no way connected to the murder of Carl Bridgewater.

Paul Foot certainly ran with the baton that Spencer was the real killer, but it was handed to him by Ann Whelan. Again I have no question regarding her belief in the innocence of her son. I also have no doubt she believed that Spencer was ultimately responsible. For Whelan to feel angry and bitter was natural and I do not think we can blame her for believing in her son's innocence from the start. Whelan was prepared to do almost anything to see Michael set free and found innocent of this terrible crime. As Ann made it very clear to presenter Bob Warman in her verbal attack on Spenser during a 1997 Central News segment, it was not her who started it. She picked up the gauntlet to wave at Spencer only after she had received all the documentation surrounding the case from the Director of Public Prosecutions.

My other reason for writing the book was to examine all the evidence surrounding not only the murder at Yew Tree Farm but also the one at Holloway House Farm. There was certainly a lot of information about the cases out there. After all the Bridgewater Four campaign had raged on for nearly two decades, keeping the story in the media spotlight. Also, more importantly, there were Spencer's many official letters he penned and received, copious notes he had made and press clippings he had saved. There was a skeleton of a manuscript he worked on with Mark Roman whilst both were incarcerated in North Sea Camp. Most of written notes forming an early raw draft of the manuscript contained new evidence or challenged some of Paul Foot or the campaigners' findings. It also gave a voice to Bert Spencer to put his side across and shed new light where there was darkness, especially surrounding the slaying of Hubert Wilkes. Of course one has to take into account that Spencer had well over a decade to put many of these points across – most of which were not disclosed during his trial.

So who did kill Carl Bridgewater?

I have tried, as far as is humanly possible, to be as objective as I can when taking an overall look at all aspects of the case. Some of my conclusions are just possibilities that could have happened given the evidence accumulated over the years. I have also included some arbitrary thoughts, especially when there appeared no other obvious rationale for certain events.

An early question for the police, media and public was what exactly were the robber or robbers looking for? It was known that Robinson and the Hickeys showed an interest in cash, although one assumes they could find a suitable fence to pass on jewellery or the odd antique. We know Spencer was interested in antiques and at one time a serious dealer with a shop outlet. Whoever burgled Yew Tree Farm were definitely after antiques, as not only were there missing ornaments, but several pieces were found placed around the outbuildings. When you look at the total disarray that was caused throughout the large roomed farmhouse – money must have been a priority and jewellery maybe a secondary consideration. We are not looking at huge sums worth of stolen antiques; around £400 was the value of the goods eventually taken from the farm. Even in 1978 it was a relatively low figure – especially if the spoils were expected to be shared between a gang of men. The antiques that were found in the outbuildings, including the cameo brooch, may have doubled the take, if that. At the time 60% of armed robberies took place in the boroughs of London, with a further 20% of armed raids outside the capital committed by Londoners. In nearly all of the cases where a weapon was used the financial gain was apt to be quite high – after all if caught the punishment could be eight to 12 years minimum. The targets were usually banks, building societies, security vans, cash depots or large stores and businesses, the latter two usually wage snatches. Remote and dilapidated farmhouses were not an obvious objective.

There have been millions of words in the media, which continues to this day, dedicated to the Carl Bridgewater case. One obvious line of enquiry was the motive for the killing of a defenceless child who would pose little or no physical threat to an adult. Head of Staffordshire CID, DCS Stewart, and his colleagues all agreed that Carl had almost certainly walked in on a crime in progress. It looked as if he had been marched inside, ordered to sit on the settee and shot in cold blood.

As the reporter from *Real-Life Crime* magazine (#94 – 2004) stated, 'Stewart and the rest of his team were shocked and baffled by what seemed to be an inexplicable killing. They knew that even the most ruthless of criminals would never normally harm a child – it just wasn't done. In Stewart's experience people who victimised children were reviled by other criminals to the extent that even when they were jailed they had to be segregated for their own safety.'

Surely there were only a few possibilities.

DCS Stewart, stated, 'The paperboy's killer was either a psychopath, maybe fired up on drugs or Carl had stumbled across someone he knew – and had to be silenced.'

One also could not rule out the possibility that the shotgun, while threatening the boy, had gone off accidentally – although in some ballistic reports it stated that it could take as much as 9lb (4kg) of pressure to release the trigger.

I think some valuable lines of enquiry were lost and many directions of investigation dismissed as most interested parties, as time passed, dominated their focus on two main protagonists. After the trial and conviction for the murder of the paperboy, followed by the murder and conviction of farmer Wilkes – it was always the Bridgewater Four v Bert Spencer. The public, via either the police or the media, were encouraged to pick either one or the other. Paul Foot, with his bestselling book, documentaries and a dramatised film, placed Spencer as public enemy number one. The former Ambulance Liaison Officer's preferred silence did not help his case. Even during his trial he remained somewhat reticent, which he carried on through his prison years, although he was somewhat gagged and bound by the Home Office.

Conversely, if either were ultimately responsible, there was one obvious and striking contradiction. If the Bridgewater Four were responsible one has to assume they expected Yew Tree Farm to be occupied, in the same manner Chapel Farm was (although we know for certain Molloy was not part of the Chapel raid). One assumes it is much easier and quicker to get results by threatening the occupants in order to get them to hand over money and valuables. Otherwise why take a shotgun unless you intend to intimidate the residents – such a soft target was unlikely to pose any physical threat? These men could be violent, apart from Molloy, if the need should arise. Your average bugler targets empty houses or will visit premises at night when it is hoped the occupants are asleep.

If Bert Spencer was responsible then it had to be assumed he knew the place was empty, as the elderly couple living there knew him and could simply identify him to the police afterwards. Of course he could have been disguised, but this really held unnecessary risks, as an armed robbery would have brought much police interest. Certainly locals were quite familiar that the residents did occasionally take trips away from the farm. This also asks the question, if Spencer was responsible and he knew the farm was empty – why take a weapon in the first place? The only suggestion that Spencer was lying when he said he did not own a shotgun during the time of the murder was from the evidence, previously mentioned, of the Worcester antique dealer couple, who claimed that Spencer purchased a gun off them in the July of 1978. Together with Mrs Fitzpatrick's statement that Bert had shown her a shotgun, he said he owned, in the boot of a previous employer's car. Bert had told her, she alleged, he carried it for protection against the possibility of being mugged and he used to make everyone aware of the fact – but he claimed this was back in 1975 – three years before the murder. However, as mentioned before, there appears to be some discrepancy here with crucial dates. Foot's book, together with notes made from the unsuccessful Court of Appeal hearing in 1988, claims Mrs Fitzpatrick told the police she had seen the gun in Spencer's *own* car boot in1978, the important murder year, and had worked with Spencer several times during that year.

I eventually narrowed my main question – who possibly killed Carl Bridgewater? –down to three possible scenarios, one of which has to be correct. The basic headings were;

1). The Bridgewater Four
2). Bert Spencer
3). Unknown Suspect(s).

This was a time to reflect in an exploratory fashion on some of the outstanding factors that surrounded the case and laws of chance and probability. It includes some positive and negative speculation, as well as proven good or damning evidence. It is total conjecture and many people will have different versions and other ideas of what happened on that bright, Tuesday afternoon on 19 September 1978.

1). The Bridgewater Four

Firstly, you cannot just take, in total fairness, the four men as a whole. Under this category it may have been one or more of the Bridgewater Four – and you have to consider another suspect or suspects who simply slipped through the police net.

Paul Foot was very good at quoting coincidences in his assumption that Spencer was guilty of murdering the paperboy. Foot was an experienced and award winning journalist, greatly praised by his colleagues and readers of his column and book. There is no doubt that a lot of his speculations were grounded and worthy of his investigative background. There was always going to be an enormous amount of speculation as there was little or no forensic evidence. Although there was a certain quantity, if not quality, in most of the witness statements – they were often vague and contradictory.

As far as three of the Bridgewater Four – Robinson and the Hickeys – their biggest coincidental hurdle was the armed robbery at Chapel Farm. It has been well documented in this book that it was a fairly remote farm, with elderly residents, and the weapon of choice was a shotgun. This is an undisputed fact and accepted by the three men, the police, Whelan, Foot and the campaigners. Their object, at Chapel Farm, was cash and they achieved their goal with a shotgun, threats and actual violence.

At the 1997 successful Court of Appeal hearing Lord Roch, stated, 'Before considering the four appeals and the safety of the convictions of the four appellants on Counts one and two in the indictment, it is desirable that we make some general observations.

'Inevitably suspicion will remain that these men, or some of them, were the perpetrators of these offences; the admissions made by two of them contain details which, if not fed to them by the police, were details that only persons involved in the offences, or who were confidants of such persons, could have known; the reasons advanced by both for making these admissions which they later claimed were false are reasons which many people would find difficult to understand and accept; the similarities between the offences at Chapel Farm and Yew Tree Farm recognised by Patrick Molloy himself as creating suspicion that both had been committed by the same people; the inability of some appellants to remember where they were at the vital time, the initial false alibis advanced; the later emergence of the alibis relied on at trial and the absence from the witness box of those witnesses who might have been expected to support those alibis.'

What is important here is the phrase; '... the admissions made by two of them (Vincent Hickey and Pat Molloy) contain details which, if not fed to them by the police, were details that only persons involved in the offences, or who were confidants of such persons, could have known ...'

Sadly huge doubt has to be laid at the feet of the West Midlands Serious Crime Squad in the handling of the case. There appears little doubt that some officers were less than truthful in their efforts to secure the men's convictions.

Regarding the 1983 Brinks-Mat £26 gold bullion robbery, in Will Pearson's excellent book, *Death Warrant*, he explains, 'In those days, stupidly, interviews were not generally tape recorded or documented other than in written form by a police note taker, and they certainly were not video-taped. This left the prosecution vulnerable to the frequently used defence ploy of claiming that the written account had been altered or even wholly invented by the police. Unfortunately this sometimes happened for real, as corrupt or misguided police officers became frustrated with what they took to be the inadequate machinery of the law – or simply decided it was time a villain who 'had it coming' went to jail. The practice had come to be known colloquially as 'verballing'. In the bad days of the 1970's, it became harder and harder to persuade British juries that verballing had not taken place – with the result that some police officers became convinced that they might as well verbal the accused – the defence would assume they had anyway. The whole thing became a ludicrous – and very counter-pro-ductive – vicious circle. It took the introduction of audio taping and video cameras to correct it.'

I have been told by various senior police officers that you never admit to certain crimes like child murder, unless there is overwhelming evidence against you. However, I can see this being an initial front at convicted child murderers entering the prison system, but time tends to wear down the culprit and they usually choose the segregation order of Rule 43. Also such denials from a convicted prisoner rules out any chance of parole or early release. You have to show remorse before you can even be considered – and defiant inmate protesting his innocent is guaranteed to serve his full tariff if not a little more.

Following Vincent Hickey's initial verbal confession, which he continually stated was purely to secure a favourable deal with the police, all three men categorically denied ever being at Yew Tree Farm. Molloy, following a fairly lenient manslaughter conviction of 12 years, protested his innocence within days of leaving the trial behind him. His death in 1981 ended his energetic denials of guilt. The remaining three men demonstrated with amazing levels of endurance with many months of roof top protests that lasted until their successful appeal in 1997.

The other big plus was also the Hickeys agreeing to take and pass the truth drug test. Something Pat Molloy also agreed to do before his death. The prison community, both inmates and prison officers, are naturally sceptical about inmates pontificating their innocence – but after just two years of incarceration, the three remaining men, had won the respect of many of the staff and convicts.

By the time bestselling author, Jill Morrell, former boyfriend of Beirut hostage, John McCarthy, had launched her book, *The Wrong Men*, published by the Bridgewater Four Campaign Group in 1995, support was overwhelming. Politicians, barristers and solicitors, human rights activists, media personal, celebrities, writers, organisations and the public were growing in numbers by the day. Their main aim was to get the Home Secretary to refer the case to the Court of Appeal.

2). Bert Spencer

This is quite straight forward, although if Spencer was the killer of Carl it is possible he may have had at least one accomplice.

We must remember Bert Spencer never stood trial for the murder of the paperboy and the police, and more importantly the judiciary, were never convinced that he was guilty, certainly following the conviction of the Bridgewater Four. We know that police interest in the former Ambulance Liaison Officer did intensify when he shot his close friend and employer, Hubert Wilkes. Over the years Spencer was interviewed over twenty times – mainly due to the alleged confessions that haunted Spencer's 14 years in prison.

As with the Bridgewater Four much of the speculation and coincidences have already been covered in this book. Although Spencer's alibi was only confirmed by one person, his former colleague Mrs Barbara Riebold, she was interviewed on a number of occasions. Although some of these early statements were quite short, during a Home Office investigation Mrs Riebold made a 19-page statement and never wavered from her insistence that Bert was at Corbett Hospital all afternoon on the day of the murder of Carl Bridgewater.

One of Spencer's biggest hurdles was the missing records, which would have documented any movement on Tuesday 19 September 1978. There were two forms of documentation. The first were handwritten notes made by Bert Spencer on a day-to-day basis. These were kept at Corbett Hospital with little or no security. The second book of reports was far more significant. These were sent to the senior officer at the ambulance control section, Barry Chambers, located at Warley, some 12 miles from Corbett Hospital. When the police interviewed Chambers in 1980 they were missing. Now these documented notes took some procedure knowledge, cunning and ingenuity to steal.

Bert himself can only give two explanations. The first was it was the work of a do-gooder, owing to some misguided loyalty. On the face of it this does appear unlikely. One assumes that a friend or colleague going to such lengths would simply check the date in question and if this was to prove that Spencer was at his station on the murder afternoon – such a theft could only risk dire consequences. The other alternative offered was that it was some mischief-maker trying to cause Bert problems. One assumes that such a devious move would involve the perpetrator stealing only the records connected with the day in question, and perhaps those a few days either side of the important date, 19 September 1978. In reality the police found that records were missing for most of 1978, up to and beyond the date of Carl's murder. This equated to nearly 10 months of missing records from January 12 to late October 1978. There were also nine days missing from 1977 and 13 days missing from 1979. This actually might work in Spencer's favour as it would appear that the movement documentation sheets were not looked after properly and the system was haphazard – which was not the case. Spencer himself agreed, as others pointed out, he was meticulous when it came to keeping a log of staff movement, including himself, and the Warley office was equally proficient at maintaining accurate records.

3). Unknown Suspect

Although under this heading it mainly deals with un-named suspects, certain people have been put forward or names suggested. Once the Bridgewater Four were tried and convicted the police were obviously not looking for other suspects and neither should they. As previously documented, it appears that the authorities are always reluctant to admit that mistakes will happen and have happened. However, there were other suspects considered at the time of the murder. It has been alleged that at least 30 serious suspects were initially considered during the early days of the murder and most, if not all, eliminated as the enquiry progressed. Once Vincent Hickey had turned up at the police station, with his solicitor, to answer charges relating to the Chapel Farm armed robbery, the police focused their attention on him, and him alone. His early verbal confession only convinced the police they had the right man, and they were convinced some firm interrogation would reap the whole gang connected with the Yew Tree Farm murder. Shortly after they had the names of Jimmy Robinson, Michael Hickey and Patrick Molloy.

Following Molloy's alleged voluntary verbal and signed confession was secured, as far as the Staffordshire Police force were concerned the case was solved. Interest in any other suspects outside the Bridgewater Four ceased. However there were other lines of enquiry, admittedly some evidence the police were unaware of, and some serious digging could have taken the investigation in a totally different direction.

What the police were aware of at the time of the murder were unidentified fingerprints found on the paperboy's yellow bike. Added to this was another unidentified fingerprint found on the farm window, facing the road, which someone had obviously used as one means of access or exit during the robbery. The main route into the farm appears to have been the rear door, although officially this is the front of the property, facing farm land – this the police knew as there was a spade with red paint on it that had been used to force open the door.

With regard to the window fingerprint, after the police had eliminated people who had regular, and legitimate, access to the property (i.e. the owners, cleaners, window cleaners, friends and of course police officers connected with the case) they ran checks using the Automatic Fingerprint Recognition (AFR) database and came up with a blank. They then appeared to lose interest in this piece of evidence; after all it could have been made at any time and quite innocently.

The second set of fingerprints, which were discovered by the police quite early on during the enquiry, appeared on Carl's bicycle. These set of unidentified prints were listed as D and F. The forensic evidence obtained by the police at that time indicated that these fingerprints were unlikely to have been those of an adult male and 'were most likely to have come from a young person who had yet to achieve full growth'. The defence did not challenge this during the 1979 trial and it was not until 1994 that the location of these prints on the bicycle frame, which it had now been suggested were indeed made by an adult, were of vital importance. The position of prints

D and F was consistent with it being picked up and thrown into the pigsty where it was found. This was another strong reason to take the case back to the Court of Appeal on grounds of non-disclosure by the prosecution.

So were these unidentified fingerprints found on the paperboy's bicycle important? We know that the intruder or intruders at Yew Tree Farm were all wearing gloves, so it would mean if these were made by one of them they would have had to remove them before handling the bike. It would also mean that this person had no criminal record following yet another negative result after a second finger print test.

I think after what must have been total panic and shock following the murder of the paperboy, anything could have happened. Once anyone had exited via the farm doorway it is quite possible gloves were removed. It was a sunny September afternoon and anyone walking around wearing gloves may have drawn some suspicion – especially if there were a group of men. There was also damage to the front wheel spokes of the bicycle, which was consistent with a foot being placed on it, one assumes by accident. Had someone fallen over the bike and in temper the person had picked up the machine and violently threw it into the pigsty – not realising they were not wearing gloves? If such a person had, it was certainly not either Spencer or the Bridgewater Four.

The only other piece of evidence came to me by accident while I was writing the book and articles appeared, following my progress, in various newspapers. One night I was in the Kings Head restaurant in Bridgnorth, my home town, when I was approached by a middle-aged man in his early 50s, who introduced himself as Robert Davies*. He asked me if I was writing the book about the Carl Bridgewater murder – which I confirmed. He had read articles in the *Sunday Mercury* and *Birmingham Post*, by journalist Mike Lockley, in which I had given several interviews, together with Bert Spencer. He appeared quite nervous and asked if he could have a quick chat with me after I had finished my meal. In the adjoining Stable Bar we sat down and he told me what seemed like an incredible tale and one that I had never heard before.

It appears that back in the late 1970s his mother worked at various local hospitals as a cleaner and general help. She would often travel, together with nurses and other staff, on the hospital transport bus. There were two men in the front, a driver and a passenger, which seems odd and somewhat unnecessary unless the vehicle was also used to transport patients and it required two staff to get wheelchair bound individuals on and off the bus. Mr Davies, who was about 15-years-old at the time, said his mother was always very worried and concerned about sharing the information she heard the driver and his mate, who she thought were either brothers or possibly related, discussing on several journeys. Robert had in fact tried to urge his mother to speak to the police, but she was too frightened and genuinely feared these men.

It appears the men would often openly talk about a sawn-off shotgun they possessed and how they could make some easy money by robbing people. He was not sure but he thought the driver was a local man to the area of Yew Tree Farm, possibly Prestwood. In fact he thought the service may have been known as the Prestwood Hospital Transport bus – and the men often referred to as the 'break' drivers.

Mr Davies was not sure but he thought these conversations may have taken place shortly before the murder of the paperboy, where guns, plans and money, were chatted about openly, with not only his mother, but other hospital staff, mainly nurses, within earshot.

Mrs Davies left the hospital service in the mid '80s and became a dinner lady and heard no more about it. She had died in 2012 but it had always been on Robert's mind. It was quite rare his mother would even discuss it, even in later years.

Were these men just a couple of wags, with a somewhat warped sense of humour, spouting off to try and impress the almost exclusive female passengers? Or was there any truth in what the men were talking about?

Bert Spencer had his own thoughts on this mysterious story, 'I have spoken about a laundry van driver and I wonder now if my assumption that he was a laundry driver may have been incorrect and this van with two brothers mentioned may well have been the one seen often passing Yew Tree Farm?

'It was Janet Cotter who also talked about two brothers (Rushton) and said the van driver carried uniforms, I think with hindsight that this is where information may have become mixed-up.

'It could now with hindsight and with Robert Davies' recall be that the two brothers we all assumed were innocent got mixed into this mess via that piece of card with the van registration number on it.'

Spencer went further, 'Couple this with the fact that one of the brothers, named as the van driver, was a boyfriend of the notorious Janet Cotter, who in turn was associated with the dangerous Keith Littlejohn, former armed robber and prison escapee.'

I think as far as Littlejohn was concerned, and he was definitely a convicted violent armed robber, one would assume the insignificant financial gain from a place like Yew Tree Farm, would have held little interest to him.

The actual function and mode of transport is of interest, as Spencer adds, 'The van could have carried cleaners, nurses, laundry, uniforms, parcels etc. between Wordsley hospital and Prestwood chest hospital. But all along it has been painted by Paul Foot and Janet Cotter as simply a laundry van, with its driver having been wrongly implicated by whoever instigated the infamous 'piece of card'. It is all supposition of course at this stage.'

It does appear strange that no one ever mentioned this piece of vital information or anything, not even anonymously, was told to the police or leaked to the press. Maybe it was just another red herring and another blind alley that seems to surround this most extraordinary case.

Summing Up

It took over two years to research and write this book, *Scapegoat for Murder*, and when people found out, usually via the media, I was nearly always asked the same question – who did I think murdered the paperboy? I may not have been the world's leading authority on the case, and what inevitably surrounded it, but I must have been in the top five. I can say that during my journey putting the true crime book together my views changed several times. Some days I was convinced I knew who the real murderer was, only to see my strong convictions disappear as I discovered fresh evidence or old remembered evidence clouded my mind and I was back to square one.

It is a very complex case, as there are many aspects to it. I think if you look at the accumulation of events as a whole it becomes highly intricate and almost unfathomable. I think you have to examine decisive and key areas, but the central hub is the Yew Tree Farm murder. The biggest failing here and quite surprising is the total lack of forensic evidence. Even if DNA was not then a tool for the forensic investigators, the lack of any physical or trace evidence meant it would have had little positive results in this case.

I think few would argue this was a simple robbery that went tragically wrong. The crux of the matter being the use of a shotgun, which might have been taken into the farmhouse in order to intimidate any residents who may have been there or the perpetrator(s) may have routinely carried a weapon in their vehicle. It may even be considered that the weapon was taken as part of an alibi, as people did shoot on Holloway House and Yew Tree land.

I have some of the crime scene photos and it appears that the farmhouse was in some disarray. The house was quite large with many living rooms and bedrooms. There appears to be a mixture of techniques with regards searching areas like cupboards and bedroom furniture etc. Some of these, exposed via various reports, appeared haphazard with little structure. Other parts were more methodical and showed a certain amount of care – like the stacking of the draws in one of the bedrooms and the careful placement of the antiques in the outbuildings. However, there appears to be many items and cash that were missed and an untouched safe – was this due to incompetence or due to the disturbance by the paperboy?

There is no doubt in the initial police press releases that they were looking for a criminal gang. This was a theme the judiciary also kept returning to. In examining the crime scene photos, which indicate the chaos caused, one would think that more than one person had been involved. However, I cannot offer with any great certainty that this was the case. Yes there were aspects of both disorganised and organised elements associated with the break-in – although these may even have been deliberate. You would need an accurate time frame of how long the person or persons were at the farm to make a judgment on the number of people involved, on the basis that the more there were, then the quicker the ransacking could be achieved. Again a detailed examination of the crime scene photographs of each room searched would be needed. Unless, of course, you had previous MO (Modus operandi) documentation of individuals which would show a pattern of search techniques.

I appreciate there was some unchallenged confessional evidence in this case put forward by Vincent Hickey and Pat Molloy, but the way in which many of the interviews were documented makes it almost impossible to differentiate between the truth and police's interpretation of the truth. At the time the whole system was most unsatisfactory and totally open to abuse, not only by the suspects but also by the officers in charge of the case.

One aspect of the two areas of entry to Yew Tree Farm is interesting and potentially an area of conflict. It is not easy to fully appreciate how much of a risk breaking in through the widow was, especially as it faced the driveway and the main road – the only advantage being the ability to watch out for anyone approaching the property. It appears a more subtle entry point as opposed to the more aggressive, possibly noisy and bold entry via the farm door, away from the main road, with a spade.

Bert Spencer speculated that this could be a separate burglary and one that ties in the carefully placed antiques found in the outbuildings. At first this assumption appears somewhat incredible and unlikely. A more open and reflective look reveals that this scenario does answer a few questions about the crime scene. It is alleged that both Vincent Hickey and Pat Molloy referenced the window as a means of access. Hickey claimed in his verbal statement to the police that this was the original entry but he was 'too fat to get through' the window. This does seem unlikely as if you see the pictures of all the Bridgewater Four, a few months later, Vincent did not appear unduly overweight. He was 25 years of age at the time and one assumes quite nimble. Molloy claimed in his written statement that as they approached the farm, Robinson immediately broke-in through the window and let the rest in via the farm door – which we know to be untrue, as it was forced open from the outside. Could this have been the police 'verballing' the two men in an attempt to get the evidence at the crime scene to fit the confessions of the accused?

Bert Spencer has put on record that on the odd occasion the elderly couple had a day away from Yew Tree Farm, it was quite obvious to any locals. Unless the weather was extremely severe, the door facing the main road would be wide open and the elderly Fred Jones would be leaning against the gate watching the world go by. This was the equivalent of the Royal Standard flag flying at Buckingham Palace, showing that the Queen was in residence.

This closed farm door could act like a flashing beacon to any opportunist burglar passing by Yew Tree Farm. One could assume if this indeed did occur, where there were two separate unconnected burglaries; that the first was via the window. It would then be sensible to follow a certain pattern of events that are revealed by the crime scene evidence. We know that a selection of antiques was found placed in the outbuildings, behind the farmhouse and away from the road. These could have been accessed via the farm fields or picked up in a second return pick-up by a car. We also know that some bulky antique items were stolen from the farm, together with a heavy bag. If this was the scenario, it would have taken place after 11.30 am (when the elderly couple left for their trip out) and probably no later than 4.00pm. It is obvious it was before the killing, which happened shortly after 4.20 pm, as no opportunist burglar had time to rob the place afterwards and the sight of a murder scene would have had them fleeing for their life. Again, and this is only speculation, that this first intruder was looking for antiques and probably antiques only. In most houses their wealth is displayed on sideboards, walls and tables. It may even have been common knowledge the couple owned a safe – so there was little chance of money or jewellery of any worth lying around.

Maybe, as Spencer suggests, that this earlier thief had a boat and escaped across the fields and away from the main road. Or their vehicle was parked near the canal in Stourton, in the opposite direction of the busy Lawnswood Road.

Studying the witness statements we can see, after 3.00 pm onwards, that most vehicles appear to be mainly blue estates, plus a few varied cars and vans. Robert and Janet Light noticed a blue estate car reversing from the drive at around 12.30 pm and, at 2.40 pm Mrs Catherine Moyle spotted a blue Ford Cortina estate parked on the A449 some 100 yards or more from the farm.

Paul Foot and the Bridgewater campaigners' favourite vehicle was spotted at 1.30pm by Alfred Bishop and, at 2.50 pm in great detail, by Roger Edwards. This was the same car Bert Spencer drove – a pale blue Vauxhall Viva. In the early weeks following the murder this statement from Mr Edwards was certainly the one that got the police most excited. It was also the reason Spencer became a serious suspect. In the statement the witness claimed he saw 'a reasonably new pale blue Vauxhall Viva, turning into the driveway. The driver, male, about 55 years of age, dark, wavy, greying hair, wearing dark blue uniform tunic with one shoulder pip.' Edwards saw no passenger.

Spencer was quick to put the record straight and pointed out that his vehicle was not new. He also mentioned that he had straight hair and his dark blue uniform had two pips not one. Bert also added that at the first sight of any sunshine he never wore his navy tunic whilst driving.

In a reconstruction for a documentary surrounding Foot's book, *Murder at the Farm*, he claimed to have solved the one pip/two pip discrepancy. As previously mentioned, Foot points out that from Edwards' point of view, with the driver turning into the Yew Tree Farm driveway, the arm, and therefore the shoulder, is raised in turning the wheel and a shoulder pip on the driver's arm disappears. Although Spencer attacks this theory, stating that he always feathers the wheel, as any experienced driver should, so his shoulders remain the same – and both pips would be visible.

It was only natural that after Edwards' statement that a huge, wide-ranging search was made of anyone who drove a blue Vauxhall Viva, who also wore a navy uniform and also owned a shotgun licence. Bert Spencer was the only name that showed up on the search, so it was not surprising they interviewed him a few times and again double-checked his alibi with Mrs Riebold. Once again she confirmed that Bert had not left the hospital on the afternoon of the murder.

If there was this second burglary – what were they after? Although it may have been the other way around, it appears this was possibly a more random burglary where the intruder or intruders trashed the place and concentrated on the contents of draws, cabinets – containers of any kind. They would likely be on the lookout for hidden money and possibly jewellery or the odd personal small priceless heirloom. It was a large rambling farmhouse with many rooms and hiding places. The search appeared mainly disorganised with, as expected, some speed and urgency, with little regard for any personal items that held sentimental value. And, most importantly, the robber or robbers, turned up armed with a shotgun. So the farm was expected to be occupied.

The more I have looked at similar robberies it is quite rare indeed to find such a soft objective, with almost certainly no huge cash reward, being targeted with a firearm. It is a weapon of choice for criminals who wish to intimidate or for possible protection. Although even the most desperate armed robber knows the end must justify the means – this was not such a case.

It is quite clear that if Robinson and the Hickey's had not robbed Chapel Farm, two months after the Yew Tree Farm murder, they would not have been serious suspects in the Carl Bridgewater case. Conversely, it is quite likely that if Spencer had not blasted his friend Hubert Wilkes, just a few hundred yards from Holloway House, he too would not have been the target and labelled suspect number one for the murder of the paperboy.

However, both incidents did happen and have not been challenged by the people who perpetrated them. Without the large shadow hanging over the West Midlands Serious Crime Squad being a law unto itself events may have been clearer. The whole police force appeared to be riddled with officers going it alone and owning their own rulebook – all helping to muddy the water. Ann Whelan and Paul Foot launched a huge public campaign, which quite rightly threw huge doubt on the Bridgewater Four convictions, but it also placed Bert Spencer as prime suspect in the killing of Carl Bridgewater. Even though he had never seriously been a major suspect, for any length of time, in both the eyes of the police and the judiciary with regards the slaughter of the paperboy. A very sad point is that for some years now the authorities have not re-opened the case or even opened up a cold case file on this unsolved child murder.

My last words on this terrible tragedy have to go to the main victims, Carl's mother and father, Janet and Brian Bridgewater, and their family. Yes there are many victims in this central case, but their hope ended on 19 September 1978. The Bridgewater family have kept a dignified silence, speaking publicly only twice after many years since the murder of their cherished son.

The last time was in 2008 on the 30th anniversary of their son's murder when Brian recalled, 'Carl was a lovely lad. He was really cheerful and quite helpful. He was in the Scouts and really enjoyed it. He loved to go fishing and was a normal, good boy. He would try to help anyone he could. There was one friend who attended Scouts with him and he had trouble cleaning his shoes. So Carl would always help him. That's the sort of boy he was.'

The couple, who still live in the home they shared with Carl, in Stourbridge, West Midlands, often share stories about the 13-year-old after laying flowers at his grave which lies in the nearby Holy Trinity churchyard.

'We do wonder what he would have been like today,' said Janet. 'What he would have looked like? How many children he would have had and what he would have done for a living? There's a lot of 'if only's' when we talk about him.'

Carl's dad, Brian, a retired pipe fitter, stated, 'We know in our minds who the killers really are.

'However, I think if the case were reopened it would be too traumatic for the entire family. I don't think people realise what we have gone through'

I doubt if we will ever be certain of who killed the paperboy on that September afternoon in 1978. The person who pulled the trigger might still be walking the streets today a free man. After nearly 40 years the violent culprit might be dead and taken this terrible secret to the grave. Everyone will have their own view about who was ultimately responsible. So who really did kill Carl Bridgewater?

14.

The New Documentary

••

I was always quite confident, following the huge media interest in my book, that following its publication – that a production company may approach me regarding a documentary.

Although I had interest from two major companies I was both very excited and flattered to have the extremely prestigious ITN Productions as an early front-runner. They had been established for over 50 years in the business. Added to this, a very large cherry was placed on the cake, as Channel 4 would broadcast the programme. In the early stages it was either going to be a 90-minute one off special or even three one-hour episodes.

It was beyond my wildest dreams when I received a call, quite early on in the process, by the eminent criminologist and television presenter; Professor David Wilson. David (I can call him that now) was a huge hero of mine and I had seen him on television on all the major criminal cases, together with presenting programmes of his own and reading his books.

David Wilson is Professor of Criminology and founding Director of the Centre for Applied Criminology at Birmingham City University.

Born in Sauchie, Clackmannanshire, Scotland, his early life began on a dairy farm, possibly an unlikely beginning for a path that would bring him face to face with some of the world's most violent men.

In 1975, three years before the horrific murder at Yew Tree Farm, the young Wilson studied at the University of Glasgow until 1979. An award followed at the St Andrew's Scholarship of New York. His career course was somewhat set in stone for a profession surrounded by some of the most dangerous criminals that darker society had to offer – both interviewing and also hunting them.

By 1983 he had completed his PhD at Selwyn College Cambridge, and immediately joined HM Prison Service as Assistant Governor at HMP Worm-wood Scrubs.

While at Finnamore Wood, at just 29, he became the youngest govern-ing Governor in the country. David was always destined to be an all-rounder – between October 1983 and April 1997 he worked tirelessly as a Prison Governor.

It was in 1997 his work was rewarded and he secured his academic appointment in September 1997, he was Senior Policy Advisor to the Prison Reform Trust.

Through my research as a fictional novelist I was extremely lucky to visit many criminal institutions nationwide, granted excess by the Home Office, but without doubt one extraordinary revolutionary institution changed my whole view of prison reform. It came one summer evening in the late '90s when I visited Grendon in Buckinghamshire. Grendon was opened in 1962 as an experimental psychiatric prison to provide treatment for prisoners with antisocial personality disorders, under the direction of a medical superintendent. The place grew into one of the most successful prisons, with a tremendous record for prisoner reform.

It was at this ground-braking establishment, Professor Wilson ran the sex offender treatment programme. At present David is the Chair of the Grendon Friends Trust, which supports the unique and pioneering thera-peutic work of HMP Grendon – the only prison in Europe that wholly oper-ates as a therapeutic community.

Professor Wilson currently advises on many high-profile cases for var-ious police forces and has provided training to new Senior Investigating Officers who will take charge of murder inquiries.

His current research interests range from the phenomenon of British serial murder, family annihilation, professional hit men and lethal violence within organised crime, to all aspects of prison history and penal reform.

David Wilson is a very generous, warm and kind man. He donates his time and effort working with a number of charities and voluntary organisa-tions, all connected with prisons and penal reform.

Reform courses through the professor's veins and it is obvious his work, and that of his colleagues, that this is the only positive way to engage recidivists and reduce the current growing criminal population.

The initial calls I received regarding a future documentary were from experienced filmmakers – producer Rik Hall and director David Howard. It was an added bonus to find out that David had read and enjoyed an earlier book I had written about Ken Loach's Northern classic movie *Kes* – called *Life After Kes* (published in hardback by Get Publishing and later in paperback and on Kindle by Apex Publishing Ltd.). I knew immediately following several conversations that these were people I wanted to work with. From the beginning they appreciated the sensitive nature of what we were all trying to do. Bert Spencer had already appeared in two highly controversial documentaries. These included a BBC programme series *Rough Justice*. The episode was called; Who Killed Carl Bridgewater? A more aggressive documentary – *Murder at the Farm* followed. This latter offering was based on Paul Foot's bestselling book of the same name.

Our first meeting took place at one of my favourite restaurants in my hometown of Bridgnorth – The George Hotel, over-looking the beautiful Severn Valley Railway. I was picked up at another favourite haunt of mine, The Falcon Hotel in Low Town. I climbed in the back seat, next to the director, David, with Rik driving and Professor Wilson in the front.

When we arrived at the George, David and Rik went to the bar and Professor Wilson and I sat at our table. I must admit I was quite nervous to meet this modern day Sherlock Holmes. I need not have been concerned as the conversation flowed with ease – just the normal chat of two people meeting for the first time face to face. David and Rik joined us and we all bonded immediately and I felt straight away these men, of high intelligence, humour, had a genuine feeling that we were starting on a journey to make an honest and true piece of film that would try to set the record straight. It was obvious we were going to approach the production, like I had the book, to hopefully find the truth surrounding this double tragedy. A tragedy that left two of societies most vulnerable members dead. The murder of a 13-year-old boy, Carl Bridgewater and the shooting of an old farmer, Hubert Wilkes.

I had previously been a part of a BBC documentary surrounding my book, *Life After Kes*, plus other productions. I knew the route to broadcast was rare. Previously I had experienced a mixed journey when I was trying to get *Life After Kes* made into a documentary with my writing partner and close friend, TV presenter Melanie Sykes. Mel and I had sat through many meetings with all types of production companies of all sizes. We had also written a comedy drama, *Bern and Glo*, and had received high-level collaboration with established companies – even gaining funding from mainstream television. You have to develop a very thick skin with such powerful negotiations.

In the mid '90s I was under contract with established USA production company, Son's of Thunder Productions, which was headed by the high profile actor and producer, Stan Foster. I had a few projects secured by Stan, a man I trusted and is still a very good friend today. One contract with them was for a screenplay I had penned for the world bestselling book, *Killing Time*. Noel Fellowes had originally written the book and I had updated it, with a foreword by the highly respected Sir Ludovic Kennedy. Kennedy, who sadly passed away in October 2009, was a British journalist, broadcaster, humanist and author best known for re-examining cases such as the Lindbergh kidnapping, the murder convictions of Timothy Evans and Derek Bentley, and for his role in the abolition of the death penalty in the United Kingdom.

Noel Fellowes' story was all about his miscarriage of justice for murder and his subsequent complete vindication – the second only during the 20th century. I had written a screenplay and it shows the level of power Foster had in the film industry as it was under consideration of director and screenwriter, Oliver Stone. Alas the screenplay was not taken up by Mr Stone as the script had a flaw – most of Noel's violent time spent in various prisons, due to the fact he was an ex-police officer – refusing to take Rule 43, enabling him to be segregated from the main prison population – was spent alone. He was ostracised by all inmates.

*   *   *

My biggest thrill during the meeting at the George Hotel was that both the director, David Howard and Professor Wilson had both read *Scapegoat for Murder* and enthused about it. Rik had not managed to read it but knew all about it.

We ordered our food, with David Howard showing more enthusiasm for the menu – I think I gained 10lb just listening to him order. Congruously Professor Wilson's order would have kept a stick insect nourished for a few hours only. Rik and I, who is probably half my weight, consumed something somewhere in the middle.

The meeting was very open and entertaining – the hours passing in what felt like the blink of an eye. We all knew afterwards that we were all on the same page and were kindred spirits bonded by a common cause – to offer Bert Spencer a platform to put his story across. It was going to be powerful, compelling and brutally honest television.

From that first meeting it was obvious Bert Spencer was always going to be the focal point of the whole process. I was the go-between and researcher, and also appearing in the programme to discuss my book.

After many conversations it was decided that ITN's team of David Howard and Rik Hall should meet up with Bert Spencer on his home turf of Spalding in Boston, Lincolnshire. It was always decided that Professor Wilson should not meet Spencer until we had scheduled the first day of filming. It was still very early days and the documentary was far from being commissioned by Channel 4.

The venue was The Supreme Inn. I picked up Bert, together with his partner Christine, at around 7pm and took him to the hotel. Quite rightly after all the terrible media coverage Bert had received over the past 35 years linking him to the Carl Bridgewater murder, with over 14 years behind bars and unable to defend himself, another documentary was going to be a harrowing experience. The many, many experiences on screen and in print had left Bert untrusting and nervous of how he would be portrayed. It is true that award-winning journalist, Mike Lockley, representing the *Birmingham Mail* and *Sunday Mercury*, was the only journalist to give Spencer a fair hearing in the press. I had had many conversations with Bert assuring him that this was his chance, in conjunction with my book, to get his story across. It was clear from the outset that he was at least prepared to meet the ITN team and listen to what they had to say and take it from there.

I need not have been concerned as the meeting flowed freely, together with his partner, Christine and myself. Both Rik Hall and David Howard conducted themselves with great understanding and professionalism and immediately put Bert at ease. By the end of the dinner everyone at the table was happy to exchange and sign preliminary contracts.

After signing contracts to take the project forward to the next phase it was now part of the deal to delay the book launch to tie in with any future Channel 4 broadcast. I contacted my publisher, Steve Caron, managing director of DB Publishing and JMD Media, and we discussed the proposed delay. Steve recognised the huge implications of having a Channel 4 documentary 90-minute broadcast, or possibly a series, would have an enormous impact and raise the profile of the book.

I knew from the first day of filming, surrounded by a fantastic ITN Productions crew that they were about to make something special. The journey for all concerned, especially Bert, was going to be powerful, exhausting and very emotional. I am still not sure where the documentary journey will end, who can tell, but I am very honoured to be a part of it.

THE END

Epilogue

....

I originally joined Amnesty International in the early '80s and wrote letters and attended the odd demonstration. I am not sure what exactly happened but I became interested in the Birmingham Six, who were shouting very loudly, protesting their innocence. By 1991 they were free men and my attention turned towards fighting miscarriages of justice. I always took each campaign very seriously and judged it on its own merit. I tried to weigh up the evidence for and against the appellant or appellants. I was personally involved, mainly as a freelance journalist, in the Guildford Four and Maguire Seven, quite rightly all had their cases against them quashed also by 1991. As previously mentioned I also became involved and followed the progress for the Bridgewater Four.

Currently I am heavily involved with the Jeremy Bamber campaign, which has been raging on for 30 years plus. I believe Bamber, then 25, was wrongly convicted in 1985 of murdering his adoptive father, mother, sister and her six-year-old twin sons in his parents' home at White House Farm. There is overwhelming evidence in favour of Jeremy's innocence; he took a polygraph test in 2007 and emphatically passed. I believe new evidence has piled up in this case proving Bamber's innocence, but still he remains in prison. He was told by the Home Secretary in 1994 that he would never be released. He is the only whole-life prisoner in the UK who is known to protest his innocence. If you wish to find out more about the case and the on-going campaign please visit www.jeremy-bamber.co.uk.

In all of the above cases the defendants were proved innocent and in most cases the real killers being found and brought to justice or in the case of Jeremy Bamber, it could only be one person responsible, if not Jeremy, then his sister, Sheila. She had twice spent time in a psychiatric hospital being treated for schizophrenia just months before the murders.

In the case of The Bridgewater Four there appears to be no closure for anyone who was either directly or indirectly connected with the tragedy. It is an unsolved murder. The police have given up some years' ago it would appear. However, they do say that if *new* evidence were to come forward then they would re-open the case.

If you feel that you have any information, however insignificant it maybe, that may help in the Carl Bridgewater murder case, then please do not hesitate to contact the author via email **sgolding@btopenworld.com**.

Acknowledgements

···

The Guardian, The Guardian Unlimited, The Express & Star, The Daily Mirror, The Birmingham Post, The Birmingham Mail, The Sunday Mercury, The Times, The Independent, The New Statesmen, Scallywag Magazine, The Herald, The Sunday Herald, The Bridgnorth Journal, The Sun, The News of the World, Shropshire Star, Real-Life Crimes edition 81 (published by Midsummer Books Ltd 1994), Real-Life Crimes edition 94 (published by Eaglemoss Publications Ltd 2004), ITN Productions, Channel 4, Sky television, Trinity Mirror Publishing Ltd, Sky Pick channel, Sky News, The Miscarriages of Justice Organisation, Thames Television, BBC1, BBC2, www.innocent.org.uk, Wikipedia, www.imdb.com, Bedfordshire University, www.heraldscotland.com, ITV, BBC, Central Television, BBC Radio, Channel 5, www.jeremy-bamber.co.uk, Helen Thomas (Sales Ledger Team Leader – Trinity Mirror Publishing Ltd), Charlotte Paxton (Syndication Executive – Editorial BPM Media), Steve Caron (JMD Media Ltd), *Reader's Digest, Murder at the Farm* by Paul Foot (published by Sidgwick and Jackson 1986, Penguin Books 1988 & 1993, review edition 1997), *Mountjoy: The Story of a Prison* by Tim Carey (published by The Collins Press 2000), *Unsafe and Unsatisfactory* by Tim Kaye (published by the Civil Liberties Trust in association with Birmingham University 1991), *The Wrong Men* by Jill Morrell (published by the Bridgewater Four Support Group 1995), *Death Warrant* by Will Pearson (published The Orion Publishing Group Ltd 2006), *How To Rob A Train* by Gordon Goody with Maurice O'Connor (published by Milo Books 2014), Rik Hall (Producer – ITN Productions), David Howard (Writer/director – ITN Productions), Chris Shaw (Editorial Director – ITN Productions), Bella Barr (ITN Productions), Professor David Wilson, Dave Blackhurst (Proofreader), Paul Dalling (Independent Proofreader), Eileen Ballantyne, Vincent Hickey, Bob Warman, Nicky Campbell, Ben Smithyman, Alan Smithyman, Dave Watkins, Hugh Lawrence, Mike Lockley,

James Fisher, Karl Aston, Mick Kelly, Sean Bean, Mick Kelly, Roger Morris, Anthony Wainwright, Gerry Conlon, Paddy Hill, John McManus, Dennis Turner, Smith Bernal (Computer Aided Transcription), Frank Roden, Richard Ford, Stephen Farrell, Carol Midgley, Helen Carter, Seth Linder, Simon Regan, QC Michael Mansfield, Mark Roman*, Professor David Canter (www.davidcanter.com), Kendra Meyer, Gary Manders, James McKillop, Professor David Wilson (www.professorwilson.com), Robert Davies*, Bradley Walsh, Jim Nichol, Anuji Varma, Jillian Edelstein, Tom Browne (Deputy Production Editor – *Reader's Digest*), Simon Hemelryk (Features Editor – *Reader's Digest*), Antoni Olmos (freelance photographer – www.antonioolmos.com),

* Donates a pseudonym on their request or for legal reasons.

17074774R00183

Printed in Great Britain
by Amazon